GOING ALL THE WAY

Also by Sharon Thompson

Powers of Desire:

The Politics of Sexuality (co-editor)

GOING ALL THE WAY

Teenage Girls' Tales of Sex, Romance, and Pregnancy

Sharon Thompson

HILL AND WANG
A division of Farrar, Straus and Giroux
NEW YORK

Copyright © 1995 by Sharon Thompson
All rights reserved
Published in Canada by HarperCollins*CanadaLtd*
Printed in the United States of America
Designed by Mina Greenstein
First published in 1995 by Hill and Wang
First paperback edition, 1996

Library of Congress Cataloging-in-Publication Data
Thompson, Sharon.
Going all the way : teenage girls' tales of sex, romance, and
pregnancy / by Sharon Thompson.
    p.   cm.
1. Teenage girls—United States—Sexual behavior.   2. Teenage
girls—United States—Attitudes.   I. Title.
HQ27.5.T48   1995   306.7'0835'2—dc20   95-8011   CIP

Previous versions of some material in this book appeared in Carole
S. Vance, ed., *Pleasure and Danger: Exploring Female Sexuality*; *Village
Voice*; *Journal of Sex Research*; Faye Ginsburg and Anna Lowenhaupt
Tsing, eds., *Uncertain Terms: Negotiating Gender in American Culture*;
and Alice S. Rossi, ed., *Sexuality Across the Life Course*.

For Sasha, Amy, Ashley, and all the girls to come

The truth is that the rich brew of our experience contains elements of pleasure and oppression, happiness and humiliation. Rather than regard this ambiguity as confusion or false consciousness, we should use it as a source-book to examine how women experience sexual desire, fantasy, and action.

—Carole S. Vance, *Pleasure and Danger*

CONTENTS

GOING ALL THE WAY

Introduction

═══════════

Well over ten years ago, I set out to interview pubescents about puberty. If there are more reluctant interview subjects, I have never come across them, and I soon started asking for teenagers' recollections instead. Teenage boys didn't have much more to say than pubescents, but when I asked teenage girls about puberty, they rushed into four- and five-hour narratives about sexual and romantic life: how I looked when he first saw me; how he stuck to me like glue; what we did that first night; how when she kissed me I felt like in a Harlequin novel; how he told me that he loved me but how could I be sure; how he stayed with me after the baby and that was how I knew he really cared; how I told her off before I hit her; what I said, felt, wanted, what he meant, what she answered, what I felt when she said he felt because she said she felt, because I had . . .

From the first interview that veered away from puberty toward sex and romance, I was hooked on girltalk—and not only because girls' stories struck me as the kind of news that makes social history. Those first interviews recalled the passionate talk of my own adolescence when the delicious intimacy of friendship assuaged the pain of a family romance gone to sour mash. Leaning against a pink flounced spread under an Iron Maiden poster, slurping Cokes in Burger King, clucking over photographs of summers at the shore—the true love cavorting with a watermelon, the life of a party, the best friend who became a true love—it all felt so familiar. Yet my friends had never told stories like these. Some I could barely believe. I quit asking about puberty altogether to concentrate on sex, love, romance, and pregnancy, the subjects of this book.

Gathering girls' tales became a vocation. Wherever I went—out for pizza, across the country—I took a tape recorder, but there was never enough tape. It was as if girls were hanging around shopping malls, roller rinks, and fast-food joints, under highway trestles and in the parks across from public schools just waiting to report on their experiences. Their accounts sometimes had a polished quality that made them seem rehearsed, and in a way they were. These were the stories that teenage girls spend hundreds of hours telling each other, going over and over detail and possibility, reporting, strategizing, problem solving, constructing sexual and existential meaning for themselves. Often bits from other conversations were worked in: snippets from lovers' discourses, arias of affection and fury, bitter recitatives. Speakers often broke into what folklorists call performance speech—acting out how another girl minced and threw herself at him, how the speaker turned on her heels and left her rival in the dust. Or they tried out Scheherazade performances, hypnotic and impassioned presentations designed to socialize loved wild boys. Sometimes objectives changed between clauses. Erratically, culture was on the party line, and so were the id and superego.[1] Girls mixed voices as skillfully as recording engineers, yet some of what I heard they had never told anyone, they said, lowering their voices, looking around to make sure no one else was listening, making me swear I wouldn't tell their friends.

Accounts typically began with teases, flirtations, and great amorous expectations. Romance was the first subject, the mysterious chemistry of attraction and the ensuing chain reaction: I wanted him, he wanted me, we, he, then I cared, then she came back, her and me, him and her, me and him, then he, now I need, or don't need, or fear, love. Parents came up mainly as interruptions or cautionary examples. Love was the challenge—the hardest thing to get or avoid, depending. Boys were love's stubborn mediums, often less important in themselves than for the affirmation they could confer. Sex was the final test, the apotheosis of romance, its transubstantiation into the body, and a rite of passage. Pregnancy was also a rite of passage and it was another test of love: something that might be good, that might be bad, but that probably wouldn't happen. Most of the girls who raced to talk so voluminously had had or were on the verge of having sex, and they considered their experiences of exceptional importance because they thought they were the first sexually active teenage girls in history. No girls had ever lived through what they had, they believed.

Adolescents traditionally see themselves as the first of a radically more sexual generation, a view that adults often support by casting the past, and our own youths, as good—pure, nonsexual—examples. My own memories fit this model to a degree. While I can't claim to have been good, I wasn't precocious either. The sexual histories of the girls I talked with were light-years ahead of mine. But although I don't know what I'd have done if anyone had actually tried to have sex with me between the ages of thirteen and seventeen (probably gone into rigor mortis), I recall years of unrequited desire when I did what I could to put myself in the way of sexual opportunity. Humid August afternoons, I wriggled into my taboo midnight-blue—almost black—shirred bathing suit with boned cups, tucked the straps under my arms, and lay out in the front yard imagining I was Kim Novak in *Picnic* while the seventeen-year-old boy who lived across the street played Rachmaninoff arpeggios and jazz riffs at a piano that I knew looked out through a picture window on my willing torso. Stretching toasted calves in the air so seductively that I moved myself, I dreamed as many versions of him sauntering over for a closer gaze and a profound conversation about Freud, St. Augustine, Hegel, and my eyes as he thought up variations on "Blue Moon." Rainy days, the girl next door and I practiced slow dancing and making out to "Unchained Melody" in the same recreation room in which we had recently doctored toads. One summer I dated a college boy who denounced my frigidity when nibbling my ear didn't melt my inhibitions as quickly his frat brothers, who charged him for the technique, had promised. I had melted, but that only made me more resistant. For all my daydreams, I knew the rule—repress or reproduce—and I made it through adolescence without getting pregnant. Many girls in my cohort weren't that lucky. Almost one in ten between fifteen and nineteen gave birth in 1957, one of many strong indications that teenage coitus has a history of long standing.[2]

The girls I talked with initially were mistaken. They were not the first teenage girls in U.S. history to go all the way, but they were right to feel that no girls had ever lived through what they had. Before the late twentieth century, most single girls who had intercourse voluntarily were willing to risk pregnancy because they expected to marry their first lovers, and most single girls who became pregnant married before they had their babies, in effect leaving adolescence behind. From the late seventeenth to the early nineteenth century, pregnancy may have actually increased the odds of betrothal, since children's labor was an important asset, especially in rural areas. Pregnancy rates did decline as mid-nineteenth-century urbanization made it difficult to bind suitors to precoital promises, but they rose again after World War I and continued upward until the late twentieth century. A significant percentage of young women did manage to forestall maternity with makeshift contraception or abortion, but for the majority biology was destiny, and as late as the 1960s teenage marriages prompted by pregnancy were common.[3]

From the late 1960s to the end of the 1970s, the legal situation changed dramatically. The competing interests of family planning, juvenile justice, and feminism rewrote the rules of female adolescence with a series of laws and constitutional initiatives gradually establishing girls' rights to due process, equal treatment, and, finally, somewhat by extension, contraception and abortion. As a result, teenage girls of the late 1970s had the ability to separate biology from destiny without breaking the law. In addition, they had the prerogative to stay in school if they were pregnant or had given birth as well as legal protection against the charge of delinquency—a term that had traditionally meant "sexually active" when applied to girls.[4]

These gains decreased the penalties for teenage sexual activity in general, and girls could no longer be punished for doing something that boys did with impunity. But the right to have sex was in no sense guaranteed, and the law still did not treat girls and boys altogether equally with regard to consent. In fact, in the early 1980s, the U.S. Supreme Court affirmed a law against sexual intercourse "with a female" under eighteen who was "not the wife of the perpetrator."[5] But by then those few teenagers who knew there was an age of consent assumed it applied only to sex with adults. Besides school, the body and the zeitgeist are the authorities girls know best: At the crest of the sexual revolution, with the gleaming new desires that feminism and the lesbian and gay movements had proclaimed and with most of the legal means to realize them, to try sex made more sense to most teenage girls than ever before. Though no studies exist on the incidence of same-sex experimentation during the period, there are many on intercourse. Just over a quarter of U.S. girls who turned eighteen between 1967 and 1969 had gone all the way. Over 50 percent of those who turned eighteen between 1979 and 1981 had.[6]

The tectonic shift in the rules of teenage romance generated an enormous amount of talk about sex itself, about love, and about the complexities of being a sexually active adolescent as well as many pressing questions about the changes in teenage romance. What was bad if sex was good? What should love mean if it didn't mean forever? What was the proper relationship between sex and love given that sex now so seldom led to marriage? What risks should one take for love? What did adolescent loneliness bode for adulthood? What did sexual uncertainty say about sexual identity?

For teenage girls, questions about sex and love are anything but rhetorical, and although romance is not finally under an individual's control, the answers they decide to live by profoundly affect their experience: whether they find pleasure or disappointment; become wiser or more stupefied, give up on education altogether or become adepts at balancing work, love, friendship, and family.

Talking romance is a female adolescent tradition; talking sex is not. In the 1940s, sociologist August Hollingshead observed that a "conspiracy of silence" surrounded teenage sex; Kinsey noted the "covert culture" in the 1950s. As recently as the 1960s, young college women reported that they didn't even tell friends about having sex unless they could represent it as a sign of progress in love. Even then they told far fewer friends than boys did —an average of two to boys' five. Girls who got pregnant were equally bound to the rule of silence. Most homes for unwed mothers strongly pressed white clients to give babies up for adoption and close the door on the past: never to speak with anyone about having had intercourse or having been pregnant. Not even with each other.[7]

African-American girls may have talked more openly about sex. They had never been able to hide its results the way white girls had since there were fewer institutions for unwed black mothers, fewer possibilities for confidential adoption. African-American girls also had a different sexual history, one marked on the one hand by the sexual coercion that so often occurred under slavery and on the other by a sense that sex was one of the few of life's pleasures that were available to them. Flashes of this talk appear in contemporary African-American fiction and in studies like Joyce Ladner's *Tomorrow's Tomorrow.*[8]

Other breaks in the silence included sexual rumors offering clues that some girls had done "it" (or something) and the game of Truth or Dare, in which players confront each other with the choice of answering an intimate question or performing a dare. Sexual rumors hardly represented progress. They simply upheld the status quo by dividing girls into good and bad. Truth or Dare, however, offered an opportunity to probe sexual experience, via the old baseball diamond model—as in, have you ever let a boy get to third base? By the late 1970s Truth or Dare questions commonly extended to intercourse and girls increasingly said— to each other and to many other interlocutors—that yes, they had done it.

As demographers made the most of girls' radical new willingness to say they had intercourse, the increasing percentages of girls who not only responded to questions about sex but did so in the affirmative stunned the nation. Sexual and generational anxiety compounded demographic concerns, panic set in. Fundamentalists railed against teenage promiscuity and abortion; family planning institutions made dire demographic predictions; and the press turned the fecundity and sexuality of teenage girls into banner headlines, four-color magazine covers, and prime-time specials. There was, we heard over and over again, an "epidemic" of teenage pregnancy. The figure 11,000,000 kept appearing in front of the word "pregnancy" even though it actually estimated the number of U.S. teenagers who had sex, not who got pregnant.

The rise in teenage coitus could have caused a disruptive population increase had the children of the postwar boom been as fecund as previous generations. But they were not. Integrating contraception and abortion into teenage sexual life would require years and that process is still taking place but teenagers managed well enough to avert a population explosion. In fact, the pregnancy rate of sexually active teenage girls declined so substantially from the 1970s on that the overall teenage pregnancy rate stabilized despite the rise in sexual activity, and the rate of childbearing among teenagers—African-American and white—declined to 51 per thousand in 1984 from its 1957 high of 97.3.[9]

This great teenage success story should have persuaded legislators and voters that the rights of confidential contraception and abortion served U.S. teenagers and the rest of the country well and should be protected. Instead, spurred by the antiabortion movement, as social scientist Rosalind Petchesky has observed, teenage girls' sexuality took on a "different meaning" in the context of lawful abortion, and the panic gained even more political momentum. Unwed pregnant teenage dropouts represented the dangers of sex; "one-half million unmarried teenagers a year getting legal abortions" advertised "the possibilities." In addition, the news that more and more *white* teenagers were becoming sexually active, with more getting pregnant and more carrying to term without marrying (almost 75 percent of white teenage girls between fifteen and seventeen who gave birth in 1970 got married; just over 50 percent did in 1981), shook longstanding prejudices about racial differences and maternity. Over a hundred thousand white teenage girls deciding to be single mothers said something about family values that the country did not want to hear. The result was a successful attack on the very rights that teenagers had clearly needed so badly.[10]

Meanwhile, demographers became fixated on locating the "causes" of "the problem." An enormous amount of work and money went into studies to isolate who was "at risk" and to assess the differences between those who consistently used contraception and those who did not. Studies often contradicted each other, with one finding self-esteem made all the difference, for example, another that pregnant teenagers had plenty of self-esteem. As the results came in and in and in (the literature on teenage pregnancy weighs a ton), they were so inconclusive that ultimately even Zelnik, Kantner, and Ford (the great triumvirate of empirical research on adolescence and pregnancy) conceded: "For the most part we have not been very successful in explaining the various aspects of behavior we have subjected to analysis."[11]

In the early 1980s, Laurie Schwab Zabin and her associates headed straight for the contradictions that had plagued other researchers and revealed the extent to which subjects' opinions belied their own practices. One Zabin study, for example, found that 25 percent of teenagers who said they wouldn't have sex without contraception also said they didn't use contraception the last time they had sex.[12] Zabin's finding was generally taken to support the broadly held assumption that adolescence left teenage girls perpetually "at risk" of being "swept away" by "unanticipated, unintentional passion" until, at last, researchers added coercion to the list of questions about pregnancy. Even read very cautiously, keeping in mind the wave of publicity about child abuse and sexual coercion in the 1980s and the extent to which a claim of rape can protect a young girl against parental ire, the results made it obvious that someone should have asked "whose passion" a lot earlier. In one study, almost 7 percent of respondents reported intercourse they hadn't agreed to, while 29 percent of a small sample of teenage mothers said they had had sexual intercourse as a result of "physical force."[13] Clearly, if some girls didn't use contraception because their passion swept them away, others were raped.

Teenage sexuality can no more be wholly explained in terms of girls' victimization than in terms of their desire, however. Many contradictions remain, and the more that is known about teenage sexual practice, the more new questions arise. Why do many girls say they chose to have sex they didn't desire? How can girls who make a million plans for first sex overlook contraception? What explains the fact that girls who clearly understand the danger of AIDS and other sexually transmitted infections so often have voluntary unprotected sex?

There's no getting beyond complications like these by simply analyzing the statistical data. To really understand what motivates the actions of girls, we have to consider sex and romance from their perspective by beginning with the issues that absorb girls themselves rather than with adult preoccupations. This book contributes to that effort by telling girls' own sides of the story of the brief but amazing period in the history of sex, gender, and adolescence when they knew of almost no reasons *not* to have sex.

The relevance of social history and developmental psychology to this kind of investigation is obvious. Narrative analysis, which plays an equally important role here, probably requires a defense. There's always a fictional element to a report, a distance, however small, between what actually happened and what is said to have happened. It doesn't matter how large or well balanced or of what age a sample is. It doesn't even make all that much difference how cleverly a survey is designed or whether blood samples or hormonal assays are taken at the very moment the questions are asked. Answers are still just that. Answers. Representations.

A study like this one in which respondents *describe* their experiences rather than just answer "yes" and "no" may be somewhat less likely to generate totally false reports than a survey. It's easier, after all, just to check off a "yes" instead of a "no" than it is to fabricate a credible story of sexual initiation, which requires a level of detail that's almost impossible to come by without firsthand knowledge. Other problems arise with long accounts, however: There's a notable tendency to present the self as a coherent or recognizable character—a good girl or a villainess, for example—or to tell a particular kind of story, a happy-ending comedy or a gripping melodrama. In this sense, although experience creates stories, talking back to and changing genres, stories without histories are stories we can't tell, and there's no fully understanding stories without taking their narrative history into account.[14]

Most qualitative studies, especially those that turn on close readings of long open-ended interviews carried out by one researcher, involve small samples. This one is unusually large and varied. From 1978 to 1986, I interviewed 400 girls, sometimes in pairs, occasionally in groups, but mainly one-to-one. Three-quarters of all the narrators had had sexual intercourse, about a quarter were teenage mothers. Ten percent identified themselves as lesbian; a few more had had sexual experiences with girls but did not identify themselves as lesbian. The interviews took place in the Northeast, the Midwest, and the Southwest, mainly in large and midsize cities, but I also interviewed in a small agricultural center and two suburbs as well in the course of two cross-country interviewing trips. About equal proportions of poor, working-class, and middle-class teenagers are represented, about 15 percent African-American, another 15 percent Puerto Rican, Cuban, or Chicana. Some girls talked with me just once, others several times.

Throughout, I relied on a snowball technique. Beginning with narrators met through friends, family, teachers, and counselors or by introducing myself in teenage hangouts (shopping malls, roller rinks, and pizza parlors, as well as school and social service settings), I went on to interview as many of their friends as possible. Often girls invited me to their homes to meet other friends or to talk at length. At first I was surprised at how few parents even questioned my presence. Later I was surprised when anyone objected.[15]

The longer I interviewed, the less I said. At the beginning of each interview, I typically explained the project and spelled out this agreement: We'd talk. I'd tape. Afterward the narrator could decide whether or not to let me include what she had said in the study and she could call me later and change her mind. I wouldn't tell what she said to anyone she knew, and I'd change all the names. Often girls broke in as soon as I mentioned "sex, romance, and pregnancy" and I wasn't able to explain the project until they'd told their tales. Occasionally, I filled in with a few questions: how old are you? what kind of family have you lived in? what's the first thing you remember about sex or romance? At the end of each interview, I asked a few yes-or-no questions about subjects that hadn't come up: oral sex? orgasms? same-sex experience? abuse? Often, also, I went back to ask about a contradiction or a break in chronology. Finally, I asked each narrator to think about whether she wanted to release what she'd said. One teenager changed her mind so often about what she would release that I eliminated her interview to stay on the safe side. Everyone else said yes, many observing they'd been moved to participate by the promise that I was going to pass their stories on for them. Even the most antifeminist felt obligated to give other girls the advantage of their experiences. They wished they had had that advantage themselves. Neither the literature of the past nor contemporary novels and reports had given them a sense of what was going to happen to them, many said—how they would feel, what they would want, what would worry them, what the odds for or against their dreams coming true were— and they didn't think that was right. Some of the *feelings* they had were in music but they had needed more than that.

I didn't ask every girl every question or always ask the same question the same way. I didn't ask about abuse or same-sex experience, for example, unless the interview or context raised the question. What I wanted to do was let girls say their piece. After every interview, I asked girls to refer other girls. By and large, they enthusiastically referred a *few* of their friends. "You have to talk to her!" was a common refrain. Significantly, girls rarely referred those they perceived as "different." Quiet teenagers sometimes brought along garrulous, extroverted friends, but few crossed clique, class, sexual status, or racial lines, and no one who was pregnant referred a pregnant teenager or teenage mother. The racial gap in the referral chain was passed over in silence; clique and class gaps could be heard in the talk about "other girls." A disapproving passage or refrain about such a girl is an almost involuntary reflex in girltalk. Two friends interviewed together often attacked a third (frequently cloaking the attack in the guise of concern). But while many narrators clearly had close acquaintanceships with the other girls who figured prominently in their narratives, they never gave an "other" girl a chance to air her opposing view, and I had to start a lot of snowballs to obtain a range of opinions and experiences. Occasionally, I resorted to institutional settings. Finding "enough" lesbian teenagers and teenage mothers, for example, required contacting groups and social agencies organized specifically to reach out to these girls.[16]

The more stories I found, the more important variation seemed, and the more persistent I became in actively seeking out stories that represented racial, ethnic, and sexual minorities as well as uncommon sexual and romantic points of view. If the result isn't a "representative sample" in the scientific sense of the term, this study is representative in its range and in the weight given to minority experiences and views.

Adolescence is usually treated as one, or at most two, stories (boys and girls or blacks and whites). Small ethnographic or psychological studies—even individual case histories—are often generalized to apply to "all girls" or "all teens"; a trend—a rise in sexual activity or pregnancy—is taken to mean that in no time *all* girls or *all* teens will experience exactly the same development. Yet two groups are unlikely to have the same perspective on an act that represents a dramatic change for one, a tradition for another. Moreover, different perspectives—different social and economic expectations and different views about the proper relationship between sex, love, and reproduction—lead to different constructions of, or stories about, teenage romance.[17]

While almost all the teenage girls who narrated this book probably once dreamed of a true first love that would last forever (Walt Disney productions alone ensure the survival of this idea), by the time I met them they had very different views of what love is and what it means: how long it is supposed to last; what it has to do with reproduction and where reproduction belongs in the life course; what the relationship between love and friendship is; whom you can love. In effect, they posited a variety of relationships between puberty and reproduction, sex and love, gender and sexuality, love and monogamy, and age and desire, and these relationships generated different formulas for teenage romance. Such variations structure this book. It begins with the accounts of girls who strove desperately to fuse sex and love at a moment when it was almost impossible to do so and goes on to explore how girls with very different desires, convictions, and expectations fared under the new conditions of their time: girls who preferred playing the field to pursuing steady love, for example; girls who chose, given expanding possibilities for women, to value work over love; girls who declined the right to separate sex and reproduction.

My notion of this project has changed many times in the course of the almost decade and a half in which I gathered and worked over this material. It began as journalism, but the more

I tried to do justice to what girls told me, the wider my search for explanations and comparisons became. Any decent piece of work, I came to believe, is grounded in history and social science and must fairly reflect the complexity, ambiguity, and range of the evidence. To work this way is to sift through and assess an enormous amount of evidence—historical as well as contemporary—and position a piece of work within the traditions of several disciplines. The extent to which this book rests on scholarship will be apparent from the citations, but in social science, method is as important as tradition, and these debts are less obvious. The approach here was inspired, largely, by the work and theories of feminist scholars. In addition, I've been provoked to work more rigorously and address more ticklish and subtle questions by many anthropologists, psychologists, and literary critics as well as a long line of commentators on girls and adolescence.[18]

I've been at this a long time. I've started and stopped; thought over what I've heard; started again; added and subtracted questions; reordered; reconsidered; rewritten. When I began, this material was current. Now it's history. But working slowly has its advantages and I'm glad of the perspective that the passage of time both forced and made possible. Because I interviewed for so long, I captured girls' startled responses to the new rules of sex and romance *and* the adjustments they made as they came to terms with change. These adjustments varied widely. Some girls jerry-built approaches to being sexually active out of long-standing traditions like true love, popularity, alienation, and best-friendship. Others devised fresh strategies and objectives, moving well beyond the magnetic field of nineteenth- and earlier-twentieth-century taboo to fairly sever the connection between sex and reproduction, bring love and work into alignment, and meet boys on level ground. Some of these approaches served girls well; others brought pain and loss. But both those that intimate tragedy and those that suggest how much reason there is for hope were well worth waiting for in their own right and for the insights they offer into the dynamics of teenage romance.

As teenage girls learned to manage relative equality and freedom, the country moved backward toward increasing repression and censorship, partly in response to AIDS. But even as AIDS has increased sexual terror, it has made it essential to come to realistic terms with sexual practice and thought. If ever adults

needed to know how teenage girls approach sex and romance—
what keeps them from using contraceptives or recognizing the
signs of pregnancy or sexually transmitted infection, what they
are thinking about, what they can hear, what might make it possible for them to hear—if ever teenage girls needed to know
their own prospects, it's now. And so this book keeps the promise
that I made to the girls who talked it into being: the promise to
pass on their words. I've analyzed and pooled girls' accounts and
placed them in perspective, but, finally, these are their stories
about what happened as more and more and more and more
girls went all the way.

1

Victims of Love

═══════════

Romantic Expectation and Sexual Consent

As soon as their children are old enough to understand sex, they send them to the *ghotul,* a dormitory
for adolescents. . . . Sleeping partners are rotated so
no one will be "ruined by love."

—Verrier Elwin, *The Kingdom of the Young*

Tracy started talking about Don the minute we got together.
She didn't stop to take off her purple satin jacket. She sat
down in the middle of a sentence:

It all started when my girlfriend Shelly began going with this guy.
He's seventeen years old. He's working. She really got attached to
him. . . . She wanted me to go out with one of his friends, but I
didn't like any of his friends. So one day Don passed by in his truck
when I was in a car with Shelly. He pulled up to my side and I'm
sitting there like, Oh my god, and he's looking at me and saying,
"Who's that blonde? Who's that blonde? I've got to meet that girl.
I love that girl."

Shelly told her to forget him, he had another girl. Tracy talked
it over with other friends, who also said:

"Don't get involved with him. He's the wrong guy to get involved
with because he dates too many girls."

ROMANTIC LOVE SCALE*

	Agree	Disagree
1. True love leads to almost perfect happiness.	☐	☐
2. When one is in love, the person whom he loves becomes the only goal in life. One lives almost solely for the other.	☐	☐
3. True love will last forever.	☐	☐
4. There is only one real love . . .	☐	☐

* Agree/Disagree:　(1) Strong　(2) Medium　(3) Slight

Scale taken from Ira Reiss, *The Social Context of Premarital Sexual Permissiveness*, 1967.

Shelly's boyfriend stopped at Don's house one afternoon when they were all on the way to the mall.

Next thing I knew Don had hopped in the car.

Tracy was thrilled. Recently she had bleached her hair and started sleeping in makeup on the expectation that just this kind of romantic encounter might happen at any moment.

That night Don took her out and treated her "like gold." They started to see each other. "Right away" he pressured her to sleep with him. This didn't surprise Tracy. As she reviewed the progress of love in her time:

> When I was little, like in seventh and eighth grades, the big things were just little things—like if he wanted to put his hand up your shirt or something. You know. My god, should I let him? That was the big thing, you know. Then as you got older, you figured out, hell, it's nothing. Then as you got into ninth and tenth grades, it was like, I want to get down. They'd come right out and say it. I'd go, "You know, I can't believe you're saying that." And they'd go, "Come on now, what's the matter with it?" and you'd get into this

big long discussion. See, the reason they can't really understand why a girl says no is because so many girls say yes.

Half the girls in her mideastern suburb had had sex, she said. The assessment sounded a little high but not by much. In 1979 half of fifteen- to nineteen-year-olds living in metropolitan areas reported having had intercourse. Sixteen was the average age for girls' "first time," and Tracy, who grew up in a working-class neighborhood that bordered a major city, had just turned sixteen.[1]

Tracy hung out mostly with girls who said they had not yet had sex. Those friends evaluated each other's sexual and romantic chances and experiences continuously, exchanging cautionary tales, working out sexual and romantic strategies, coming up with rules of thumb and battle plans, based on each other's experiences. A great deal of time went into the pros and cons of intercourse.

Part counseling, part sex ed, Pro and Con debates—a regular feature of girltalk—are founded on the relatively new assumption that teenage girls have the right to consent to intercourse. In comparison with age-of-consent legislation's underlying idea—that no sane, competent girl would ever voluntarily agree to going all the way—the concept of a right to consent is a clear advance, but it still implies a model in which boys desire and initiate, girls wait, waver, barter, and think rather than desire. Should I or shouldn't I? Why? Why not? If I do, will he . . . ?

Although they believed they had and would exercise the right to consent, and did not in any way think that merely having sex turned girls into sluts, Tracy and her friends were also the heirs of generations of girls for whom the consequences of going all the way made "yes" one of the most dangerous words in the English language. As a result, they still had an arsenal of reasons to fear sex. Three fears predominated—the fear of pain, the fear of abandonment, and the fear of pregnancy. Pain was so much a part of the Grand Guignol lore of teenage sexuality when they came of age that many girls almost seemed to be scaring each other off.

Everybody said, "Oh, it's going to really hurt and there's going to be a pool of blood."

Another heard:

Oh, it killed, it killed.

But while some girls imagined that in time intercourse would become pleasurable, or indicated that first intercourse would be worth whatever it took because of the knowledge it would bring, Tracy and her friends neither foresaw pleasure nor set great store by sexual knowledge. On the matter of pleasure, they were silent. On the matter of knowledge, they had a familiar theory: Innocence equaled desirability. The more you knew, the more sexual experience you had, the less your worth and the more likely you were to be abandoned—a dread fate they talked about over and over again.

It was the fear of pregnancy, however, that came up most often. On the face of it, Tracy and her friends had almost no reason to be scared about pregnancy. It was 1978 when Tracy and I first talked. Girls could obtain contraception easily; if something went wrong and they *did* get pregnant, they could afford first- or second-trimester abortions with the money they made from babysitting and working part-time. (Their state hadn't yet passed a parental consent or notification law.) But as more and more girls went all the way, pregnancy became a risk and an experience more and more girls faced and talked over with each other—a risk, in that sense, that seemed more imminent and frightening than ever. Antiabortion propaganda increased the atmosphere of fear by promoting the idea that abortion caused dire physical and emotional trauma.

At first Tracy didn't take Don's sexual pressure seriously. If his opening position was, Why not? hers was, Why? She had just turned sixteen, and she took pride in having reached this advanced age a virgin, an achievement she thought was rapidly becoming a rarity in her generation. She wasn't going to cede this advantage lightly:

I had only dated him a couple of times. I figured, why should I rush into anything like that, because, first of all, I never went to bed with anyone before, and I was scared, and I was unsure of myself, and I figured, why should it be with him? Like I have to get to know him better first and see how I get along with him and not go rushing into it because I felt like, you know, I'm not going to just give it up to anyone.

She knew he was still seeing another girl, too—Julie. Finally, he broke up with Julie.

And then we started seeing a lot of each other.

Now she had to take him seriously. He had given someone up for her and he had begun to talk about caring and commitment. This language moved her.

He told me he really cared a lot about me and he wouldn't just leave me and then he said, "What do you want? A lifetime guarantee?" He was thinking that I thought that if I was to go to bed with him, he had to stay with me the rest of my life.

First intercourse hadn't carried a lifetime guarantee since the turn of the century, when it was a token of betrothal in some communities. Even then a girl who consented to sex before marriage took a risk. In a big country, there was plenty of room for a man to get lost, and more and more did as cities multiplied. Through the 1950s, teenage marriages remained a very common, if less and less viable, resolution for teenage pregnancy, nevertheless. By the time Tracy came of age, however, they were rare, both because they were all but impossible to sustain financially and because girls who got "caught" had the new alternative of abortion.[2]

Tracy didn't know the history or the statistics, but she agreed with Don's presumption that a lifetime guarantee was out of the question.

I said, "That's not what I think."

She just thought she deserved some consideration:

I just want the person to care enough and not to say, "I got what I wanted," and then just run out on me, because that would hurt me a lot.

But how could she know in advance that he wouldn't. She worried about how she would take a loss she had seen a younger girl endure:

> I know a girl—fifteen years old. She's a cousin of a girlfriend of mine, and she was seeing this guy for about six or seven months. She thought he was just seeing her and nobody else because they were supposedly going steady. But he was seeing all these girls behind her back, and she didn't even know it. She got pregnant and he left her. Fifteen years old. That's bad. . . . She's going to be hurt for a long time because she really fell in love with this guy. He was eighteen years old, and out of school, and he was telling her stuff like, "Well, if anything would ever happen I'd take full responsibility, and I wouldn't run out on you, and I would help you see it through. I'd be by your side the whole way." As soon as she got pregnant, he was gone. I guess that's what I'm afraid of.

Seduced and abandoned. One of the oldest fears in the annals of female experience. But Tracy was not rehashing as old a story as it seems. She did not imply, for example, that seduction, pregnancy, and abandonment had ended her acquaintance's chances in life altogether. She didn't even think that the two should have gotten married. Rather, the fifteen-year-old "was going to be hurt for a long time" because "she really fell in love with this guy." She had been ruined, that is, not by sex or pregnancy but by love. The damage wasn't to her hymen, her health, or her marital chances; her ruin was psychological. She'd been old enough for sex but too young to go through the emotional distress of believing a love was true, having intercourse, and getting dumped.

TRACY WANTED proof that Don wouldn't make her feel bad about herself and her future if they had sex. She wanted, if not a lifetime guarantee, then just some token of his good faith; some auspicious sign. He had taken her out. He had treated her like gold. He had given up Julie, sat through endless Pros and Cons. What else could he do? What could she ask for? What traditions did teenage girls have to draw upon as they negotiated first intercourse? Mainly, the popular tradition of true love.

Love's relationship to sex and marriage has varied with the centuries. Victorian ideology treated marriage and eros as polar opposites; early-twentieth-century opinion promoted their union, in effect sexualizing marriage. In the process, sex gained some of the respectability and idealization previously associated with love and marriage. By the time the package began to come apart, as it almost immediately did, the combination of sex and love without wedding bells had gained legitimacy in its own right, especially among those who weren't in line yet for marriage. College flappers told researchers Phyllis Blanchard and Carolyn Manasses in the late 1920s, for example, that love legitimated not only the "sexual expression" of petting but even intercourse "with the man they expect to marry" and gradually this idea filtered down to high school students.[3] By the late 1940s and the early 50s, social scientist Winston Ehrmann noted, "love" increased girls' "desire for heterosexual activities" and their "willingness to flout the folkways and mores," which limited "petting activities to kissing and hugging," although those of his respondents who acknowledged going all the way hastily scribbled in the margins of his questionnaire that they never would have done it if they hadn't been going steady, leading Ehrmann to "discover" that going steady was a "greater determiner" of girls' sexual behavior "than any other."[4]

Subsequently, the average age of first intercourse dropped further and further from the age of first marriage, and engagement became almost irrelevant to the decision to go all the way while "love" in some form became a paramount consideration. Not all girls had sex because of "love," and many girls were cynical on the subject, but at the time Tracy approached it, love was still a generally accepted explanation for deciding to have sex, one widely supported not just by the culture at large but by secondary education. A plethora of sexual education materials, for example, adjured teenagers to "wait for love," rather than, say, for desire, protection, or the money for an abortion.[5] In addition, teenage romance novels were so liberally distributed and promoted in public schools, particularly to girls with low reading skills, that industry-wide annual sales reached $20 million in the 1980s and $60 million in the early 1990s. Even Scholastic Books, which distributes through schools, developed a romance line, the Wildfire series, whose primary thesis, literary critic Linda Christian-Smith contends, was that "love and commitment" were prerequisites to any "expression of sexuality."[6]

Tracy knew this rule very well. Besides, while she and her

friends believed the safest course was to wait for love, they had another idea as well: that sex had the potential to generate caring and love; cure all instead of end all; save a faltering relationship. If this happened, whether or not the relationship lasted a lifetime, they'd know it could happen again. Whenever they needed love, they could get it by having sex. Adolescence and young adulthood would be illumined by great serial flares of sex and love, which would culminate, when they were ready, in one final explosion of sex and love so intense that it would create a permanent fusion (marriage). This exciting possibility was what made them consider going all the way despite their fears.

Accordingly, Tracy decided she was willing to say yes if it was "love" or even if she was just "in love," a state somewhere between a crush and a passion. Being-in-love was a lot easier to achieve than love itself because it didn't have to be reciprocal. You could do it on your own and sometimes you couldn't help yourself. It just happened. For this reason, although it was generally accepted as an understandable reason to have sex, girls frequently called being-in-love—as opposed to loving and being loved—their "downfall."[7]

TRACY REACHED the being-in-love stage after she told Don what had happened to her fifteen-year-old friend and he responded that it wasn't just sex he was after. He *really* cared about her.

So then he told me, "I'll wait till you're ready. I'm not going to push you into anything."

When it came to giving up virginity, Tracy gave a lot of points for patience.

And I don't know why and I don't know how, but somehow I fell in love with him.

Don dangled his eligibility in front of Tracy. If she *was* secretly looking for a "lifetime guarantee," he was her ticket.

He says, "I'm not like those other guys you used to go with." He says, "I'm not like them." He says, "I wish you could believe me. That's not me. I'm not like that." He keeps telling me. He keeps saying—what does he say to me? He says, "What you have here isn't one of those little sixteen- or seventeen-year-old guys you're going around here with in high school. [He was eighteen.] What you have here is a guy who's going to make something of himself." He said, "I know what I want out of life."

If these were honest declarations, he was her dream come true. On the other hand, Julie was back in the picture.

So then I was thinking, maybe I would go to bed with him under one circumstance. I told him, "There's no way you can still be seeing her and I'm going to." Because I figured, he's not mine. Because, like, say, if I did go to bed with him, then he'd just leave me and go to her. I don't know. I'm just confused. I don't know what to think. I really like him a lot. I don't want to lose him. But on the other hand, she goes to bed with him all the time. He's known her a lot longer. I figure maybe she is better for him than me. I don't know. . . . My girlfriends all say to drop him. But somehow I just can't this time. I can't.

Even after he agreed to drop Julie again, Tracy's subconscious stayed on red alert:

A week ago I dreamed about him. I dreamed that I decided to go to bed with him. In my dream, I remember coming up to him and he took me out and we had a very good time and I remember crying and I remember telling him I was pregnant and then him telling me that his other girlfriend was pregnant and that's all I remember. I don't even remember what he said. I just remember waking up. I had to get up for school.

She was, in other words, too young to deal with such a problem—she was still just a schoolgirl. It was all, as the popular press kept saying, too much, too soon.

A couple of months later, Don dropped her. She was disappointed but not devastated. She had remained a virgin. If innocence could be traded for love, she still had a chance. Despite the emphasis she put on virginity, Tracy recognized that teenage romance had changed. She knew that she couldn't condition sexual consent on the promise of a lifetime contract, for example, and she knew she'd have sex before she got married, but she did think it was possible to win love in return for sex. She desperately wanted to: She considered first sex an extremely serious experience in itself as well as an augury. If she had the ability to transform desire into love through the alchemy of sex, she could look forward to a marvelously romantic future and ultimately to marriage. If she didn't, if she couldn't even exchange virginity for love, what was she going to make a life worth living out of? A job at the mall? Single motherhood? Some girls are moved by the expectation of maternity, but she wasn't at all.

In that first sex would give her an idea of her prospects for making a life out of love, it loomed the way College Boards did for classmates with high academic ambitions. But for sex to tell her fortune, she had to gamble what she saw as her most valuable attribute, her virginity. She had seen too many other girls lose this bet to assume the odds were in her favor. On the other hand, she had good cards, in her own view. Hadn't she caught a great guy's attention? If she could do that, surely she could attract a suitor who would answer the riddle that bedeviled her: How can I know before that you'll still love me after?

WHEN I REVISITED Tracy a year after she told me about Don, she was sitting in the living room with her family clustered around her as if she were wounded or dying. Her prominently displayed senior prom photograph showed her in a full-length white dress carrying red roses, looking so much like a bride I almost asked when she had gotten married. Since the photograph was taken, she had gained about fifteen pounds, a fact she mentioned immediately. Her bleached hair was losing ground to shadowy roots, and she was wearing a huge, rumpled sweater. I was shocked. I'd never seen her dressed to anything less than the hilt. That evening she was to start a new part-time job as a clerk in the junior shop of a mall department store. Although she couldn't quite get over not having a three-month summer vacation, she looked forward to the job, which she thought of as "in fashion." She had not made any plans to attend college—a sign perhaps that she had had more hopes for early marriage all along than she was willing to articulate.

When it became clear her parents and sister weren't leaving the living room for their usual hangout, the kitchen, Tracy invited me to her crowded and musty bedroom where the shades were down, the windows closed, and the twin beds unmade. Pink Floyd and Led Zeppelin posters lined the wall. A white-and-gold vanity overflowed with curling irons; blower; bronze, pearl, and silver nail polish; tape deck and stereo; open scarlet lipsticks; glistening vials of blue, green, and white eye shadow; crusted sticks of mascara. Under the pink and purple plaid flounces of her beds lolled heaps of stuffed animals. "A lot of them I won down at the shore," she explained, "or guys won them for me." In a corner of her mirror were ticket stubs for a concert and a handwritten poem. She couldn't remember who wrote the poem but she said all her friends had copied it:

> When I met you, I liked you.
> When I liked you, I loved you.
> When I loved you, I let you.
> When I let you, I lost you.

Tracy opened a drawer and took out a stack of photos. They showed her having a good time with her friends. In the last one, a skinny brown-haired boy in a tee shirt cavorted with a quarter watermelon. Tracy launched into her situation. Again, she talked almost nonstop. She had met another guy. Mark. She had gone out with him a year. They had had a "meaningful relationship."

The meaningful relationship was almost as prevalent in the 1970s and '80s as going steady was in the 1950s. As going steady once had, it contextualized sex. The similarity, however, stopped there. Going steady was a public matter. You had to be asked and he had to give you a sign—an ID bracelet or a ring. Meaningful relationships, in contrast, like being-in-love, could be declared by either party. No one asked anyone else to be in one. They were not necessarily public or exclusive but they were, as going steady had not been, by definition, coital. In meaningful relationships, content (including sex) not promises or exclusivity created value. But content was a matter of opinion. One party or the other declared that the relationship was producing meaning. So far, so reasonable. It wasn't always clear what meaning meant, however.

In describing the first stage of her relationship with Mark, Tracy told almost the same story that she had told about going with Don. Again, she described the physical relationship in terms of things she wouldn't do. Sex was what she didn't do. Whatever she did do wasn't sex. They spent a week at the shore together when he "put up with being in bed" together and "not doing anything," she said, for example. This time she did at last— elliptically—mention desire in commenting that she "wanted to" but was "too afraid of losing him." She *was*, she said in justification, "head over heels in love with him." He wanted to seduce her, he said; he thought he was falling in love with her.

> I said, "Look, you have to prove to me that you care, and this isn't just going to be nice-knowing-you-see-you-later because I'm not like that." He knew I was a virgin. . . . He said I'd be hearing from him. I said, "All right." I said, "I'm not going to bother calling you." He said, "You'll be hearing from me, so don't worry about it." He broke up with that other girl and we started going out.

They had a great time for a while. She really thought she "had him wrapped." She conferred with her friends. A year earlier, she had reported, half the girls where she lived had had sex but most of her *friends* had not. This time half of her *friends* had had sex; but these were not her "closest friends," who had even more conservative standards, she reported, than they had a year earlier. Out of school or going to community college part-time, they now thought a lifetime guarantee a realistic goal.

> They think that if you have sex with a guy and you're not engaged to him or he didn't buy you a ring or some type of proof, you're really rushing into things.

She told them how she felt and they hoped it would "work out" but they "knew" her; they "knew" her "personality."

> And they knew that I'd really be hurt.

Finally she "gave in to him." She repeated her logic, mixing and matching a series of rationales for intercourse she had previously introduced as persuasive:

> I wanted him to be my first. I thought maybe it would make things better if I did. Make the relationship stronger. Like he was a good talker and I was head over heels in love with him, so I did.

She didn't use any birth control because it was "a spontaneous thing." Even after relating months and months of Pro and Con, then, Tracy, like narrators of date rape, held that she hadn't expected sex to happen. In part, undoubtedly, this was a rhetorical claim, but not altogether, I expect. Tracy had talked a lot about her wish to combine sex and love, but she had not talked at all about what she thought sex might be like or given any but the slimmest indication of physical desire, which is, after all, one portent of intercourse. She said Mark said he wanted to "seduce her," but the only seduction she narrated was verbal. She never said she felt physically excited when they were together or that he made her feel pleasure, satisfaction, or desire. Even if she actually felt desire but simply wasn't comfortable narrating it, how pressing could it have been given her exhaustive focus on other aims? And in the absence of both desire and forethought, how was she to have foreseen what sex might be like?

Mark was "gentle" with her, but it hurt, Tracy said. Nevertheless, intercourse "was beautiful" because she "loved him so much." They continued to go together for a while. The sex didn't get less painful and Tracy told of trying to avoid it. Soon Mark chafed at the bit. He wanted to go out with his friends more, he said—to return to the party and the crowd.[8] Tracy didn't accept this explanation for seeing her less, and time proved her right. Soon he was back with a previous girlfriend who committed every infraction in Tracy's book of teenage romance—from attaching herself to him like glue to going down.

> She was really possessive. Really kiss ass. She went to his house every day. After work, she was there. If he wasn't there, she'd sit and have coffee with his mom. She called him every day at work. She made herself available to him whenever he wanted her. She called him

four or five times a day. She really kissed his ass, and I didn't even do that. And she did oral sex and stuff. I never really got into that. Everything was new to me. I never felt that way in my *life* about anybody besides him.

While driving around obsessing about Mark, Tracy had a serious automobile accident. She reported this occurrence with fear and pride.

I almost killed myself over him.

If it happened again, she could really be hurt, she said as if delivering a warning. On the other hand, the accident proved she wasn't "easy," as did her dismal appearance, weight gain, and tears.

IN HER INSISTENCE upon informed consent, Tracy was almost feminist compared with the many girls I talked with who said they were in such a fog about sex that they didn't see sex coming or were so paralyzed with fear or shock they couldn't say no. She didn't prepare for sex—she was too focused on her romantic goals for that—but at least she saw it coming a mile away. They said they didn't see it coming at all:

It was just like—pssst, one minute here, the next minute it was there. It happened. That was it.

Tracy took full responsibility for her own actions. They often talked as if they hadn't been present for their own initiations or explained the whole experience in terms of being drunk.

I'm telling you I did it unconsciously because I wouldn't do a thing like that.

And:

I had a party here and my parents were out. . . . He kind of like—I mean, we were really drunk.

But Tracy's failure to take sexual precautions and her persistent effort to construe her own sexual mores as good and those of more sexually active girls as bad and to trade sex for love indicate how committed to terms and practices of the past she was. Even her version of the meaningful relationship was really just a slight modification of the old idea of one true love that lasts forever; to her it was "love" and endurance that created meaning. But if her terms had a long evocative history, that doesn't mean they weren't still in currency.

Contrary to frequent pronouncements by social scientists and historians, and despite the changes of the 1970s, the double standard, for example, remained virulently alive and well, albeit less strict. According to the old double standard, when boys went all the way, they were just being boys; when girls did, they were bad. By the late 1970s, going all the way no longer definitively separated good girls from bad or boys from girls, but that didn't put an end to distinctions between these categories. Instead, distinctions multiplied. While before, there was a mainstream assumption that the primary dividing line between good and bad was one act, coitus, *after* the 1970s there was no such consensus. Rather, there was "a fine line," as one narrator put it, "between everything," and although groups of girls frequently agreed among themselves as to what constituted good and bad, there wasn't even general agreement among girls in a particular neighborhood or suburb. Tracy held the fusion of coitus and love in high regard but derogated a rival who may well have experienced that fusion but had oral sex in addition. Other girls accepted oral or anal sex but drew a line at coitus or approved of those who had unprotected coitus but scorned those who used contraception or vice versa. Even girls who represented themselves as "bad" frequently derogated those who had a different sexual preference or a more stigmatized identity or practice: drugs instead of sex, lesbianism instead of promiscuity, bisexuality instead of lesbianism.

Fashioned by girls out of the scraps and relics of previous traditions from Victorianism to sex radicalism, these fine lines in effect constituted local and individual sex and gender subsystems. They gave girls maps on which to orient themselves (no small matter in a culture that advertises sexuality as comprising the essence of self) and rationalized sexual losses: As a result,

girls found these constructions extremely helpful, and perpetu-
ated and multiplied them. Tracy, for example, could console herself with the idea that she had upheld her standards and not
played every card in her hand. But which line, if any, would matter to a given boy? Or protect a reputation? It was anybody's
guess. So although the double standard was still alive, dividing
girls and limiting their desires, it could no longer be relied upon
absolutely to perform its most important function from the point
of view of girls who depended on it to uphold their desirability.

As for Tracy's objective of trading sex for love, that bargain
had rested on the idea that girls didn't get the pleasure that boys
did out of intercourse and so had the right to something else;
the reality that girls risked their reputations and pregnancy by
having sex; the resulting scarcity of sex; and the link between
sex, love, and marriage supported by the society as a whole and
the family wage. By the time Tracy tried to bargain sex for love,
however, sex was framed as pleasurable and normal for both genders; pregnancy could be averted; girls who would have sex were
becoming the majority; and while sex, love, and marriage *could*
still be linked, high school students could rarely afford the chains
(the separate household, the diapers, the wedding).[9] As a result,
girls who set their hearts on being able to make the sex-for-love
trade the basis of their lives or at least a primary basis for optimism about adolescence and young adulthood—typically but not
exclusively working-class girls like Tracy—found themselves stale-
mated. Baffled, they circled and circled the problem, looking for
a way to the only future they knew how to dream of.

In the meantime, other teenage girls were developing a different version of the meaningful relationship, which was to gradually gain wider and wider currency. These girls differed from
Tracy and her friends in crucial respects. Although they weren't
all sure where the money would come from, they were definitely
on the road to college and that gave them a vested interest in
separating sex from reproduction. They were also highly conver-
sant with the language of therapy, and the therapeutic model
was much in evidence when they talked about their expectations
for a meaningful relationship.

As Tracy's lament pivoted on the need for love, their accounts
gave dominance to problems like feeling marginal or being
wounded or disoriented by parental divorce. A combination of

meaningful talk and sex could unravel and heal such problems, these narrators believed, and this was the role of the meaningful relationship. Practitioners expected their partners to "work on issues," "deal with problems," "talk things out," discuss pain, alienation, being different or alone or anxious and to be sensitive, responsive lovers. The relationship would last as long as the partners were able to shed a healing or clarifying light on each other's problems or perhaps even generate new problems to work on. Other relationships might also involve meaningful talk; the meaningful relationship simply produced the most meaning. This was the sense in which it was the true love.

Because the production of the most meaning, not intercourse, was what made these relationships central, monogamy wasn't a requirement. Deana, for example, was eager to become sexually active, and although she didn't enjoy first intercourse, she had sex with three different partners the first week she had sex— once with a male friend, once with a girlfriend, and once with the boy she thought of as her "meaningful relationship."

> This was feeling extremely weird because I had never been sexual at all in my life and here I was having sex with Edward, Eileen, and William and I was just turning in circles going, Oh, my god, what's happening to me? But I really enjoyed every sexual experience that I had. Except I didn't particularly enjoy or not enjoy when I first screwed with Edward, but that was quick compared to the whole afternoon we spent together, so I really wasn't thinking about it.

Each sexual occurrence took place more "spontaneously" than Tracy's first coitus—that is, there was no Pro and Con, no waiting and wavering. With Edward and Eileen, it was pure sex, Deana said. Her relation with William was meaningful, and it included a lot of sex as well:

> Oh, ten times a week. After school. After track practice. . . . We would come running home and screw a couple times before dinner and then just in our spare time, we would be having sex.
> Q: Were you liking it by then?
> A: Oh, I was loving it. I really liked it a lot.

But there were two problems: contraception and orgasm. As a converted reader of *Changing Bodies, Changing Lives* and its adult counterpart, *Our Bodies, Ourselves* (the two most widely circulated feminist guides to the female body), Deana knew both were crucial subjects that would require a lot of talk. She started with contraception:

> So that day I said, "If we're going to be doing this on a regular basis, I think that I should have birth control and I think we should talk about it." And he said, "Fine." And I said, "Well, don't you have any feelings about it?" And I said, "Well, I do." And I started going through every kind of birth control I could think of and saying the pros and cons of it because I wanted him to participate in that. I felt that was important, and he didn't. No. . . . And I finally said, "Well, I guess I'll get a diaphragm." And he said, "Okay."

The next time Deana tried talking sex, she upped the ante. She wasn't having orgasms. Here was something important and hard to work on: a sexual problem.

> He said, "You look serious."
> I said, "That's because I am serious. And it's very hard to talk about sex, but I think that we maybe should because I mean we're having it." And I was speaking really poorly, and I was stuttering, and I was being very nervous. Because it's very hard for me to talk about that to anyone, especially the person I'm having it with. . . . And he started saying, "We don't need to talk about it because animals don't talk about it."
> So I said, "Well, I'm not an animal, and I think it's what you think, not just what you feel, and your whole head should be healthy, not just your body."
> And he still didn't want to talk about it. He said, "Well, it's fine."

She dropped her bombshell.

> I said, "Well, it's not fine. I haven't had an orgasm. Not one."

This news did not miraculously transform him into a caring lover or persuade him of the importance of sexual communication.

He, instead of dealing with it like there was obviously something wrong that I didn't have one orgasm ever or even close to one, dealt with it by, "Oh, my god, there's something wrong with me," and reversed the whole thing around and made me feel really sorry for him to the point where I said, "Look, it's not your fault. It doesn't matter anyway." And to the point where the next time we had sex afterward, he said, "Did you have an orgasm?" and I said, "Yes," which I really felt cheap about. . . .

I had to say yes about three times after that and then it was sort of understood that I was having orgasms even though I never did and our sex started getting worse and worse and less and less frequent and our time together started getting more and more rushed.

Deana treated William's artistic interests the way Tracy treated the other girls whom Don and Mark were interested in—as personal betrayals.

He started saying things like "I have to go to the museum." And I'd say, "Why do you have to go to the museum?" Or "Why can't I go with you?" And he would say, "Well, I just have so many things to do and there's not that much time. I'm not going to be alive for that long." And I'd say, "Well, that's the most ridiculous thing I ever heard in my life."

Weren't boys supposed to want to spend all their time in bed? Something was wrong.

I didn't see any of these problems in my relationship as being really that he was completely avoiding me. I just thought that I must be doing something wrong. So every time we were together I would act a little bit differently. . . . Sometimes I would be very quiet and really not say anything, and sometimes I would be open about the fact that I wanted to have sex, and sometimes I would sit across the room and not make it obvious that I was wanting to have sex even though I was secretly really wanting to have sex and sometimes I would think of other things to do and other times I would just say I really can't see you, I'm busy.

They started spending "less and less time together." She saw their relationship going down the tubes. Then she got herpes.

It hurt so much and I still had sex.

Q: Why did you do that?

A: Because I knew that our relationship was going to break up and I knew that I should get in as much—I felt like this was a way to hold on to him and I felt it was going to break up and I sensed that it wasn't going to break up good because I wasn't going to let go.

By the lights of a therapeutic relationship, she should have given up on him as soon as she realized he wasn't willing to "work" on himself or the relationship, but instead she switched to Tracy's terms. She "loved" him, she said, and claimed that working on problems together implied a commitment that wasn't so different from the kind of commitment that Tracy tried to wangle.

I didn't think that it was fair to make a commitment to somebody and then be a shithead. I mean, not deal with the fact that we made that commitment.

In her view, when very severe problems arose, you had the right to get out of a relationship if you made the proper declaration:

But you have to present the fact that you don't want to deal with him anymore.

Short of something that severe and the requisite declaration, "everything" could be "worked out," and that was the most responsible, mature thing to do.

William went away with his family over a school break, promising that he would spend "the whole day" with her when he came back:

And he came to my house at seven-thirty that night and he apologized and then he said, "I have to paint a picture." And I was like, "What do you mean?" And he started going, "Well, there is so much to do and so little time to do it in." This to me was not an acceptable excuse.

She was sure she knew what was wrong. He wasn't talking about what was bothering him and so problems "were building up under the rug."

While he was out of town again with his parents, Deana and

her girlfriend had a fight and broke off communications. At the same time, Deana's mother went out of town on an extended business trip. Deana needed William now more than ever and she had the run of the house. To celebrate his homecoming, she made dinner.

> It was going to be like real nice that he was coming home, and I was very excited. I made chicken and vegetables and rice, and I set the table with candles and everything. It was just very nice, and I was excited. And he pranced in.

He was late, had a cold, and said he had to go straight home. She thought the cold "was just an excuse."

> He really didn't want to spend time with me.

She was very upset. She needed his support.

> I had just spent ten days not talking to anyone, and my period was three weeks late.

She didn't tell him about her period. She just argued that he should stay.

> Finally, he said, "All right. I'll stay. And I really want to be with you." So I made dinner and, of course, he hated it. He was just, "I don't feel like eating this kind of goo." And then at one point he said, "I'm always going to have luck with women the way I had luck with you," or something really awful like that.
> And I said, "That's really disgusting."

They had planned to spend the next day together but he left as soon as he woke up.

> We had sex. I didn't tell him my period was late, and he borrowed twenty-five dollars from me to buy a sweater that he'd lost that his mother had given him.

They had a library date for that Wednesday. She decided they had to talk, and she settled on a strategy: she would take responsibility for some of the problems they'd been having.

And I met him at the library and he didn't kiss me or anything and I felt, I said, "I think that it's really important that we talk about what's been happening in our relationship because I think what's been happening in the last week or couple of weeks . . . is that you've been doing a lot of fucked-up things and I've been doing a lot of fucked-up things and we really have to work a lot of this out."

And I said, "Probably a lot of what you can't deal with is the fact that I hardly have any friends and so it's almost like I expect you to make me happy and when you don't make me happy I get very frustrated and very angry and that's not right." And I started to say all the disgusting things that I did in the relationship. And then he said, "Yeah, you're right. I guess we shouldn't see each other anymore." Which wasn't the point of why I wanted to meet him. The point of why I wanted to meet him was so we could work it out. . . . Our relationship wasn't a heap of junk or anything. It was just that we had a lot of problems that we had to work out.

Taken by surprise, she spilled everything out at once.

And then I said, "Well, that's fine, but my period is three weeks late, and I'm not saying this to guilt-trip you into wanting to stay with me but I'm ninety-eight percent sure that I'm pregnant, because my period is never more than one day late. And he said, Oh, he didn't believe me. And I was just crying hysterically and I paid for his coffee and he got on the train.

She didn't call him after that.

He called me a week later and he said, "I still want to be your friend and I still want to see you because we have a really good relationship."

And I said, "What do you want? Just not to have sex?"

And he said, "Yeah," and I said, "Well, that's just great. You should really hear yourself speaking."

She had an abortion. Then the aftershocks began.

I felt completely nauseated and I felt angry for the first time. I was angry because William wasn't there. I thought he should be dealing with it. . . . The more depressed I felt, the more angry I felt, and the more used I felt. And the more sad I felt, the more used I felt.

It was her relationship, not the abortion, that made her feel used.

> And then there was just one more unacceptable phone call from him and he said, "How are you feeling?" and he called to find out if I was pregnant. This was a week and a half later on a Sunday, and I said, "I'm fine." He said, "You're not pregnant, are you?" And I said, "No, I'm not. I just had an abortion on Wednesday." And he said, "Oh, well, call me sometime. Bye." And I cried for about three months.

"Until last week I cried," she said, breaking into fresh tears. She thought she wouldn't be able to live through anything like that again.

> It makes me very sad because how am I supposed to go into a relationship now ever again? I mean, how can I go into a relationship now?

Like Tracy, she saw this first sexual experience as a bad romantic omen, and although she had experienced sexual pleasure, and had many more irons in the fire than Tracy—a far wider range of prospects for meaning in her life—she joined Tracy in attributing enormous gravity to her romantic loss. It was all very well to look forward to college and travel and some kind of professional career. But what was life without love or with the kind of love that laid one so low?

WHETHER A NARRATOR tried to get true love out of sex or just caring or meaning, expected to make a life out of love or just a shrink appointment, romantic failure was represented as one of the worst "horrors of a teenage life," to borrow the title of one narrator's diary. The more a narrator conditioned sexual consent on romantic expectations, the harder she said she took rejection. Recounting bouts of weeping and fury that went on for weeks, even months after their breakups, these narrators said they didn't think they could ever get over what had happened. Just telling the story renewed the pain. Many wept and raged as they talked.

I was hysterical. He told me over the phone, and if he told me in person, I would have killed him. I would have killed him.

And:

Months and months I would cry looking out my window. I wrote songs and poems about him all the time. I was obsessed with him. One time, believe it or not, after he'd been at our house and was drinking coffee with Tony and my dad, I put his coffee cup in my room on my shelf and I drank out of it after he did.

It was as if someone had died. The experience changed these girls completely, they said.[10] Unrecognized by their lovers, they no longer recognized themselves:

It's really had an effect on me. I've become very quiet. That is not me. . . . I didn't stop living. . . . But I am not the same person. I'm very inactive. I'm eating a lot. I'm gaining weight because of him. But that's only little parts of it. I can't even begin to explain how I feel inside.

Since this had happened, they had lost control of their own lives. Now they were failing in school or were habituated to tranquilizers or overeating. They could hardly get out of bed. They thought repeatedly of suicide.[11]

Not even teenage girls who told of acquaintance rape represented themselves as so damaged. In fact, girls who said they hadn't consented to sex were models of calm and reason in comparison. As if choosing amnesia over hysteria, they reported that they could hardly remember any details of what had happened. Pressed, they responded telegraphically, speaking without adjectives or metaphors, as if they had to pull every heavy word up from a deep well in the mind and the effort required all their concentration and courage. They did not dwell on the experience; they told the tale once. "And that was it," as one said. Some might not have remembered at all, it almost seemed, if they hadn't gotten pregnant.[12]

What, it's fair to ask, in the light of such experiences and anguish was romantic disappointment? What had happened to Tracy and Deana, after all? A teenage romance didn't work out?

How many ever have? They aren't supposed to. They're *teenage* romances. But even if they weren't, even if these were stories told by adults, even if we didn't know that many worse things happen to many other girls, it would be tempting to dismiss the stories these girls told as self-indulgent, overblown, and one-sided. After all, can stories that represent romantic experience in such melodramatic terms (girls as all-good, boys as complete rotters, and romantic dinners as matters of life and death) be accurate descriptions of events as they happened? Might they just be bids for sympathy and absolution based on assumptions about gender differences so conventional that whole genres turn on them?

Further misgivings arise because the presumption of pure female innocence, which is the sine qua non of melodrama, has lost a lot of its viability in the wake of Freud and MTV. Many feminists bring a special distrust to melodrama because it seems to eroticize victimization, virtually training its devotees, some think, to be aroused by loss, exploitation, and desperation.[13] It's a fair point, but there is a tendency to blame the genre for the problems it represents—victimization, unhappy endings, foreclosed possibilities—and to miss its uses.

Melodrama is typically about women's trials and sorrow. It is the traditional expressive form for accounts of spoilage and awakening and for stories of ruinous love. It is also the form for tales about thwarted fusions of sex and love or meaning. To be melodramatic is to tell such a story as it is traditionally told—expressively, hyperbolically. In that serious people often dismiss these stories as unimportant or mundane, their preservation in melodrama is, as Peter Brooks has called it, "a victory over repression," and that is an additional explanation for the overblown quality. (In contrast, we could say that those who claimed they barely remembered having sex failed to vanquish such repression.) Melodramas are also overblown, however, precisely because tellers and listeners feel that the emotion and meaning of events like heartbreak are not likely to be taken seriously.[14]

But why should they be? Even granting the genre's dramatic conditions, and Tracy's wish to make a future out of love, her distress seems disproportionate. Nothing else about the future concerned her so much, no other disappointment so shook her to the core. And why, for that matter, were the boys she became involved with disinterested in love themselves? Understood, there was little call to trade sex for love once sex was plentiful, but why not a reciprocal trade of sex and love for sex and love?

Psychology's account of the role of separation in girls' and boys' development suggests that girls' melodramatic reports of boys' romantic callousness and the damage girls sustain as a result may not be exaggerations at all but rather accurate accounts of a common adolescent romantic experience. As Carol Gilligan has shown, while boys traditionally use acts of separation to develop identity, girls traditionally use acts of attachment. Gilligan's work focuses on friends and family, posing teenage romance, when it comes up at all, as a kind of monkey wrench, separating daughters from mothers and from the bold, inquiring preadolescent self. But identity is not forged through asexual relationships alone. As early marriage was once, teenage romance is a major context for identity formation. Gilligan sees no problem with girls following a different developmental path than boys. Why should separation be *the* model for development? she asks. It's a reasonable question, but her interest in promoting attachment obscures a problem with a two-path system of identity development that girls' romantic stories make glaringly clear: To the degree that they are traditional and treat their gender in traditional terms, girls and boys approach teenage romance at cross-purposes, with boys developing a sense of masculine identity to a significant degree by separating from girls whose identity development depends upon affirming relationships. Boys do this both because separation is simply the act through which boys prove their maturity and because femininity and domesticity are precisely what they have to separate from in order to assert masculinity. In effect, teenage romance faces boys with this contradiction: Having sex proves masculinity like nothing else, but girls' insistence on merging sex with love brings with it the danger of being trapped back in the very homey, mergey, infantilizing world of childhood they must escape in order to be men. (It's not a groundless fear, the narratives suggest. What many girls call true love is domestication—think of Deana's chicken dinner— and narrators like Tracy and Deana did see sex as a contract that gives people possession of each other.)[15]

Before girls became so willing to say yes, boys voluntarily endured a certain amount of merging in return for sex. The late

1970s saw a gradual shift in the balance of supply and demand until so many girls were willing to say yes that boys who didn't want to merge—boys who defined their masculinity in terms of their distance from domesticity—no longer had any real incentive to make good on the promise of love for sex. When they began to feel uncomfortably close to femininity, they could leave the girls whose desires for intimacy made them nervous and start over.

The new script was good for traditional boys but not for girls. In the wake of these benighted romances, boys with any chance to progress raced ahead exhilarated by their sexual triumphs and near escapes from the traps of love while, abased and depressed, girls who staked their hopes on getting love and caring fell further and further behind, weeping and obsessing and looking backward, daydreaming about the day their real prince would come, setting themselves up for another devastating round.

In retrospect, for example, the only mistake Tracy could see that she had made was not waiting long enough. Although she felt she had lost "what was so different" about herself, she added hurriedly: "It wasn't everything that was different." Now what she had to do was to start waiting all over again. In effect, she determined on what's currently being called "secondary virginity."[16] This time, however, if she couldn't have a lifetime guarantee, she would wait until she had at least some proof of reciprocity:

> No one's ever going to hurt me that way again and I'll make sure of it. I'm not saying I'll never be hurt again but I'll try my hardest to avoid it. My idea right now is that I don't think I'm ever going to let a guy touch me again until I'm engaged or married. Until I'm sure that guy means it. I'm not saying that he's going to stay with me for the rest of his life, but until I'm sure that relationship means as much to him as it does to me and until it's positively proven that it does, there's going to be no way that guy is going to lay a hand on me. That's my attitude right now and that's the way it's going to stay.

She had gone back to where she started, in other words, back to the very same convictions that had set her up to become a victim of love in the first place.

A change in strategy could have broken the deadlock: Girls

could have chosen to condition consent on pleasure and desire, for example, rather than on love, or to stake identity develop-ment on another source of intimacy or recognition, such as friendship. Maybe even a vocation other than love, although it's hard for working-class girls without professional expectations to romanticize work all that much. But to understand what they were up against and to stop blaming themselves, they would have needed to be oriented toward—to get an education in—the his-tory of their problem, the history of sex, gender, and adoles-cence. What did they get? They got romance.

As a tide of censorship and sexual conservatism rose in reac-tion to the changes of the 1970s, school districts increasingly replaced realism with romance in curricula, focusing sex ed ma-terials more on "love" and "values" than on sex and replacing novels like those of Judy Blume with romance novels on reading lists and library shelves.[17] To be fair, these pedagogical strategies were based in part on studies showing that commitment in-creased the likelihood of contraception and the assumption that reading anything is better than reading nothing. In addition, though romance novels may *encourage* unrealistic romantic ideas, they can hardly be said to originate them. Girls receive encour-agement to fuse sex and love from countless cues, experiences, responses, and stories that construct femininity—from the tales of Beauty taming Beast and Cinderella bringing her prince to his knees to a daughter's hope for a father's recognition. In fact, girls encourage themselves as they gossip and giggle and day-dream.

They do this, in part, because romances fulfill a need that's just too hard to satisfy in real life. Teenage girls themselves say they love the novels because they teach about "romance and dating" and allow them to "escape." The place they escape to is the land of romance—a place where girls wait for love and get it and boys love the girls who want them before and after a pair has intercourse; a place where femininity tames the beast.[18] This isn't the only way, as literary critic Ann Barr Snitow has observed, that romances fill "a vacuum created by social conditions." They also offer girls the sort of fantastical release that adventures and adventure stories have traditionally offered boys.[19] Until very re-cently, romance was the female adventure or quest. Boys went off to war or on safari. Women conceived a passion for the conflagration of erotic love that would occur when the warriors returned, then stayed home and fantasized about it. This conflagration, Snitow has proposed, was long women's "one acceptable moment of transcendence."[20]

Romantic transcendence isn't just a daydream or a fantasy. Great love and passion actually occur. They are common vivifying pleasures, high, I'd guess, on most people's lists of what makes life worth living. Even the narrators of this sad chapter reported enjoying some of the opening pleasures of romantic recognition. There was, for example, the thrilling moment Don first noticed Tracy. The initial excitement did not lead to great passion but it's been known to happen. And if a fusion of sex and love doesn't often last forever, it doesn't take forever to get through high school. Three years? Four years? People have loved and desired each other for longer than that. But while romantic transcendence isn't exactly impossible to achieve, it clearly isn't always on tap just when it's needed, and it's both very hard to find and extremely necessary in adolescence, as we've seen.

It is, however, endlessly available in the pages of romance novels where boys are moved to love girls who know a hundred reasons to say no, and only one—love—to say yes. Through these novels—and the thousands of movies and songs modeled on the same lines—girls experience the fusion of sex and love that traditional female development through attachment requires. If this romantic fusion is as desperately needed an experience as identity development theory suggests, these novels aren't just diversions, they're absolutely essential reading.[21]

This isn't to say that tailor-made escapism doesn't have hazards. The feminist critic Tania Modleski, for example, persuasively argues that the standard romance plot of erotic passion that brings men to their knees is a fantasy of female revenge.[22] The illusion that femininity will make men grovel with desire, Modleski proposes, entices girls and women to give up any vision of equality for the chimera of female sexual power. Read this way, the plot of the basic teenage romance novel, the plot of the dreams and hopes of girls like Tracy, leads straight to victimization.

To the degree that teenage girls actually absorb such subordinating confusions as part and parcel of intellectual development, teaching romance in school may undermine the whole idea of girls' education—the idea that learning their lessons and doing their work will lead girls to an equality that will best satisfy their hearts' desires.[23] And there's another problem, one with very serious ramifications for sexual education. Although love makes girls and women more likely to prevent pregnancy, it makes them less wary of sexually transmitted infections, because they commonly assume, as most people do, that love is the best guarantee of safe monogamy.[24] Love, however, no more guarantees that a partner doesn't have or won't get a sexually transmitted infection than that he'll love you back or love you after. It doesn't guarantee a thing, and the romantic idea that it does is extremely dangerous. In fact, given the extent of the current danger of unprotected sex and the extent to which girls continue to attempt to fuse sex and love in everyday life or at least persuade themselves that they have done so, love may really now be, as so many girls say, their "downfall."

Abolishing romance is a pipe dream, however, as even the most grandiose theorists know. A plot so magnetized with oedipal material, so eroticized, so ineluctably desirable, can no more be censored out of existence than sexuality can. Fortunately, just as the same plot can be explicated in more than one way, there are many kinds of teenage romance. The ideology of true love draws enormous power from its history and literature, but other dreams have long histories and allure as well. Popularity and playing the field, for example, may not be as venerable as the dream of true love, but their history reaches back to the invention of adolescence.[25] What happened to these practices, initially developed as a way of postponing love and its attendant risk of pregnancy until after adolescence, when intercourse became an accepted part of adolescence? How did girls who achieved popularity integrate the new teenage sexuality into the old game of playing the field?

2

Playing the Field

==========

Sex, Sociality, and Popularity

The ideal American girl is supposed to be popular, which means that she's supposed to have a date with an attractive boy . . . every weekend at least.

—Andrea Boroff Eagan, *Why Am I So Miserable If These Are the Best Years of My Life?*

To live as a girl with many lovers as long as possible and then to marry in one's own village, near one's own relatives and to have many children, these were uniform and satisfying ambitions.

—Margaret Mead, *Coming of Age in Samoa*

In the tradition of the American Girl, popularity has been almost as powerful a vision as true love. "The adolescent absorbs new ideals," psychologists Elizabeth Douvan and Joseph Adelson observed tranquilly in the peaceful time before feminism took gender apart, " 'popularity' . . . for the girl, and 'masculinity' for the boy." For almost four decades, this simple formulation was fairly on the mark. From the 1920s through the 1950s, popular girls animated and dominated extracurricular high school life. Their cashmere cliques kept thousands of clubs going, cheered legions of lettermen on to glory, and inspired cohort after cohort to postpone sex and marriage while they built personalities, played the dating game, and decorated for homecoming. Middle-class girls dreamed and worried about popularity "more than anything else," Douvan and Adelson reported— more than love, more than marriage, and certainly more than college. If they could have changed one thing about themselves, it would have been to become more popular.[1]

In the 1920s and '30s, parents and teachers encouraged the proliferation of adolescent social and extracurricular life on the theory that sociability led to success and satisfaction. As sports and student government prepared boys to become leaders, pop- ularity educated girls to be social assets who could dash off din- ner parties for clients and organize charity balls.[2] Together their wholesome, extroverted families would invigorate communities, pep-talking everyone into the prosperous future. The parents of teenage girls had a more immediate interest in popularity as well. The more girls dated—and well before mid-century, most girls did—the more concerned parents became that going steady would lead to going all the way, and they encouraged clubs, cliques, and playing the field as ways of forestalling that even- tuality.[3]

While many adolescent girls shared the dream of popularity, its practice split them. "Happiness," in one school, reportedly "riddled with cliques," was "being chosen for something"; not being chosen caused "heartbreak."[4] The divide between happi- ness and heartbreak was clear at a glance: Girls who achieved popularity stood pertly on one side of the tracks, sporting batons and pom-poms and crowns and corsages. On the other side slouched tramps and unpopular girls—girls who went too far and girls who didn't go anywhere at all; flagrantly desirable girls and girls who had not even begun to master the art of arousing de- sire; girls who spent too much energy on the body and girls who ground their bodies under while they cultivated their minds; girls whom boys didn't like; girls whom girls didn't like; girls whom nobody liked.

The economic and political implications of the popular/un- popular split concerned social and political scientists as early as the 1920s. Even as manufacturers sought to exploit popularity— actually hiring popular girls to ask for products like Hires root beer on dates—many 1940s and 1950s sociologists regarded pop- ularity as a serious educational problem.[5] The job of the high school, in the view of these critics, was to create equality, and popularity created an elite. Standing at the top of a social and political hierarchy, popular students controlled dance committees, school clubs, and informal social networks. The question was whether to abolish popularity or try to teach its fundamentals to everyone. If popularity were largely a function of external variables like class, high schools had to counter the influence of the cliques and clubs that regulated and consolidated social power. If, on the other hand, popularity was the reward for acquired social skills, high schools had to fill in where cliques left off and teach those skills as part of an education in the ways of middle-class life. None of the many studies conducted to investigate these questions resolved the matter, but they did add considerably to what we know about the making of popularity. A respondent in *Middletown,* Robert and Helen Lynd's study of a midwestern city in the 1920s, explained that popularity depended first on boys liking you enough to accompany you to dances.

> Then, if your mother belongs to a graduate chapter [sorority alumnae group], that's pretty sure to get you in. Good looks and clothes don't necessarily get you in, and being good in your studies doesn't necessarily keep you out unless you're a "grind."[6]

To a substantial degree, then, popularity, like land and money, was handed down from generation to generation. But if you did not earn it, you did have to be worthy of your inheritance. You couldn't be a grind and boys had to like you: you had to have sex appeal. August Hollingshead also noted the importance of sex appeal in his study of popularity in *Elmtown's Youth.* Overall, he found popularity a function of class, enforced in part by parents but also generated by kids themselves, who characteristically sorted themselves out according to what Hollingshead awkwardly but movingly called "self-feeling," an internalized sense of class that largely determined "where an adolescent goes and what he does." But sexual behavior itself also divided teenage girls. A girl who went too far lost all social standing. A girl who wasn't kissable didn't even get the dates that would put her in the running for popularity.[7]

Whether popularity was inherited or earned, a matter of money and class or chaste kissability, it proved resistant to pluralizing efforts. As high schools grew larger and more various and cliques and tracks multiplied in the 1950s, a girl from the wrong neighborhood might not even know the girls in the top clique, let alone have a chance of joining them. Besides, to the extent high schools attempted to democratize high school sociality in the early '60s, popular teenagers withdrew into parent-sponsored networks of cliques and sororities or joined the emerging fast-track elite—those top students who saw a point in acing tests as well as making friends. This development sped up as the pressure of the civil rights movement forced high schools to integrate racially. By the 1970s, many high schools had dropped much of the apparatus of clubs, proms, and student government that had once conferred their institutional power on popular students. The private organization of popularity eroded as well as it lost the support of mothers who had once made a career of fostering daughters' popularity but now increasingly found places in the workforce. Home dinner dances, for example, became out of the question in all but the most rarefied circles. Individual interest in popularity also diminished as girls began to look past marriage—the main goal of popularity—to a professional career. As a result, academic success became more important; social success somewhat less. Even family size changed the rules somewhat: The new smaller family called for a more intimate domestic sociality than the families of ten or more of yesteryear, which were like teams rather than double pairs.[8] Finally, as more and more young people began having sex, they favored social configurations that afforded somewhat more privacy than did the sock hops and slumber parties that popularity traditionally sponsored.

None of these developments wholly spelled the end of cliques and crowds; in fact, historian John Modell argues that adolescence became *more* group-oriented precisely because the previous means of establishing a social network—dating widely and casually—declined. But while hanging out with a crowd may have become a great deal more common as, say, the double date became less so, the two did not have the same social function. On the contrary, for white teenage boys, hanging out was inversely related to a taste for love and marriage.[9]

By the late 1970s, few students remained active in extracurricular affairs. Only 15 percent, a Carnegie Corporation study noted disapprovingly, took part in pep club, cheerleading, debating, or drama. Less than 20 percent participated in student government or worked on school newspapers. The active few, ethnographer Ralph Larkin has suggested, now constituted "a pluralistic elite structure," composed of "the jock/rahrahs, the politicos, and the intellectuals."[10] Of course, popularity had always been elitist, but once it had had a base: a large group of students participating in the clubs and events that popular students ruled. Now the base was gone. The elite ruled and socialized alone, better positioned, perhaps, but no more popular, in the end, than anyone else.

Nevertheless, like true love and marriage, popularity continued to represent connection and acceptance, conditions that remain essential to girls' understanding of happiness. In its pursuit, teenage girls still spend several billion dollars a year and untold hours following the advice of friends and teen magazines to "fit in but be themselves."[11]

GIRLS WHO TALKED about trying to become popular never told success stories. They told "how my attempt to get popular fizzled out." Fortunately, this was not as sad a story as the one about true love lost. Girls could tell it with chagrin rather than tears, even turn it into a joke on themselves, possibly because working on popularity, unlike trying to become the object of love, at least gave girls some sense of agency. It helped, too, that popularity was in decline. Finally, there were pleasures to be found in sour grapes:

> We were scornful. We just liked to make fun of them. We'd draw little pictures of different girls and how they put on their eye shadow.

Jealous observations didn't convey much about popularity, however. It's an insider's tale, and like most insider's tales, it's hard for an outsider to elicit. None of the girls who volunteered when I asked for participants in this project or when I introduced myself in teenage hangouts identified themselves as popular. Popular girls are chosen; they don't much volunteer—unless, of course, a whole clique is volunteering. But when I was lucky enough to be referred to a popular girl by someone she had known a long time, she would usually respond to the sociability of the enterprise and agree to take part, both referring others and setting up an interview for herself so casually that I was never confident that she would show up. (She always did.)

Relying, then, almost entirely on word-of-mouth referrals, I slowly assembled the life histories of two dozen girls described as popular by themselves and their friends. All were suburban and all came from the middle of the country. Most invited me to their homes to talk, and all chose locations that were not private—the living room, the kitchen—quietly but summarily dismissing their parents, setting the stage for a friendly but not intimate conversation. In the flow of memory and empathy, other narrators quickly seemed to forget that I was there. The popular narrators never lost sight of my presence or identity, and despite their friendly chattiness, they gave away very little that they didn't think I already knew. In fact, if other girls hadn't gossiped about them, I would have been led to conclude that nothing ever went wrong in their lives. No interview with a popular girl ever rose to an aria of feeling or suddenly broke out of one kind of representation into another. No popular girl wept over a romantic loss or a disillusion, talked in obsessive circles, or retailed melodrama. Even distraught, they looked persistently at the good side, drew optimistic morals, and kept on smiling. Theirs is a controlled and comedic mode. Gradually, I learned to keep a low profile and wait, assembling revelations by slow accretion.

The popular narrators radiated forthrightness rather than sexuality. Ex-cheerleader Louise Bernikow, a feminist scholar, has referred to the characteristic cheerleader's "Ipana smile."[12] They all had it, and they seemed as if they had just stepped not from the proverbial bandbox but from a Finnish sauna or out from under a hair dryer. Gail's light brown hair, tipped blond, was filled with electricity: it seemed to burst from her head. Jackie had gleaming fresh-cut blond hair, brown eyes, a glowing sunset complexion. Shelley was a Lucille Ball without the red hair. Chris had an edgy cheerfulness. Even sitting down, she seemed to be on the balls of her feet—moving back and forth slightly, ready to strike, leap, plunge, run offense or defense. Patti was low-profile, toned down. It was a part of her power not to seem to care very much.

In the strictest sense, popularity is still for white middle-class girls only. Several teenage girls of color shared the social perspectives of the popular narrators, but with the exception of Jackie, a blond blue-eyed Chicana, not one used the word "popular" to describe herself and no one introduced another girl of color as a "popular girl." In addition, every girl in this group had a high disposable income which she had not had to work for. Several had cars. Bedrooms overflowed with tape decks and tapes, TVs, phones, posters, and clothes, all contributed by parents who were executives or professionals.[13] Popular girls are often athletes and all these narrators were physically active—swimmers, runners, cheerleaders, tennis players. Unlike most high school students, all reported attending school dances and proms, but they said they came late and left early unless they had a special role to play, and—good-time girls that they were—they typically broke high school rules against drinking and drugs.

JUST AS SCAPEGOATING begins with difference, popularity begins with similarity. Popular narrators said they and their friends had "something in common"—"a feeling" of mutual understanding, of being on the same wavelength. Here Patti is typically vague:

> Well, the girls that became friends it was just, you know, we just found likenesses and became friends, and the boys pretty much the same. Pretty much the groups came about because the girls were trying to get dates with the boys and the same with the boys. So.
> Q: What were the likenesses? What made the girls find likenesses?
> A: Uhm, oh, that's hard. Uh, I don't know—ohhhhhh, you found a group of girls that—you know, you could go out and have fun with and giggle with because that's all you did in junior high. . . . It's hard to put your finger on it, you know, why you become friends with somebody.

Within their age group, popular girls spend most of their time with teenagers who share their views, history, and position, but there's clearly something beyond such similarities at work in their bonding. Often what separates the popular from the unpopular, members of one clique from those of another, is attitude: body language and style; a casual presumption; above all, a gift for having "fun"—the primary vocation of popular people (and Americans as a whole, some have insisted).[14] Popular girls have a talent for being easy "to go out and have fun with," for making friends feel that being accepted, recognized, and included also makes them special. In addition to nodding and smiling at the right place, appealingly mixing sympathy and wit, they also had the skill to make it all seem effortless. The narrator of Alix Kates Shulman's *Memoirs of an Ex-Prom Queen,* one of the great novels about popularity, describes concealing her ambitious efforts to be beautiful and smart.

> I hedged all my bets . . . With a vanity refined to perversion, I cut school to hide that I cared to be smart, telling no one about my books, and I affected sloppiness to hide how much I wanted to be beautiful, locking away my beauty charts in my desk drawer.[15]

If a popular girl felt melancholy or had a problem she couldn't master or laugh off—say, an eating disorder or a tendency to panic attacks—she didn't look to others for help. She just put on a brave face and willed it away.

Commonality accustoms popular girls to communicating allusively, even wordlessly. They rarely say anything concrete, anything that might pin them down or get them in trouble. Within the culture of popularity, to transmit knowledge is to give away the keys to a secret society.[16] The exceptions to this rule are cheerleaders, who make a tradition of teaching their skills to the next generation. "The older cheerleaders teach you everything," Gail said, looking back fondly. "They put you through an initiation that's supposed to make you a close-knit group and it does, because they make you do the most embarrassing things in the world."[17]

Many adolescent girls I spoke with magnified the problem of making themselves socially acceptable. Popular girls, on the other hand, downplayed the difficulty of conforming—an art they practiced with consummate, offhanded skill: "You had to change yourself a little bit to try to be this so-called popular," Gail said indifferently, as if the matter were hardly of interest. They exhibited a matter-of-fact, no-nonsense attitude toward conformity: Of course they went "along with popular opinion." They didn't "mind." It suited them. And it did. Popular opinion was their opinion. They represented hegemonic adolescence or at least thought they did. They took every requisite change—from fashion to attitude—in stride, saying things on the order of "I like clothes, so I don't mind dressing in any kind of way." Or: "Mainly, I think it was more your attitude was what you had to change."

Popularity requires conforming for the most part while making and publicizing an occasional distinction—being "your own person," expanding the ground of conformity rather than crossing the boundary. A girl who can't make a distinction doesn't have the social power to be popular. A girl who makes too many can't fit in. Popular narrators used the word "strange" frequently about other teenagers, and they had many categories of girls who were "other," but they didn't devote much time to talking about them, although they were volubly cynical about the purportedly rosy futures of the girls at the top of their class. Chris:

> I've seen a lot of people . . . that when in high school they were getting straight A's and taking all the hard classes and got into Northwestern and Stanford and Yale and stuff like that, and now they're frybrains.[18]

It's not easy to be simultaneously friendly and exclusive. They pulled it off with a waxy casualness and a second sense for distancing themselves from trouble. Gliders not divers, popular girls stayed close to the surface. They said "hi." They made optimistic inquiries. (Have fun last night?) They talked about appearances. (New haircut? Looks nice.) The reward for this amiable conformity was a pool of friends and boyfriends, while diffuse sociality created a secondary pool of potential friends and boyfriends.

Conformity has its downsides, of course, but it served popular girls well. Because they conformed, they didn't have to go to a lot of trouble to cultivate friendships. They "fit in" and others fit in with them. It was as if their personalities were large common denominators, divisible by any whole number. Problems could come up, however. Other girls frequently mistook their generalized friendliness for an invitation to form a best-friendship. It was a particularly humiliating error to make, and those who did often responded defensively by building a case against the two-faced phoniness of popular girls. Partly what was occurring was a clash between two subcultures—one based on intimacy and one on sociality—subcultures as strictly divided as good girls from bad. Popular girls solved the problem the same way they provoked it: by continuing to act friendly. In most cases, the approach ultimately worked. Persistence, like an ongoing smile, pays off.[19]

The party and the group, not the lover and the friend, were the shaping material in these accounts. In friendship and in love, popular girls rejected the ideals of permanence and pairing off. They referred to "my best friend at the time" instead of "my best friend forever," "my first boyfriend," "my summer boyfriend," "my boyfriend at school" instead of "my one and only" or even the one "who really meant a lot to me." They said: "I have a lot of best friends" or "I know a lot of boys who are friends." There was no one person they couldn't stop talking about. Gail:

> I don't like having one best friend because it seems to me like a best friend is more like a boyfriend. You know, if you fight or whatever, it's just devastating and . . . best friends get jealous. And so . . . I try to have a lot of really good friends and a lot of acquaintances.

While the female clique was basic—the launching pad—popular girls stressed that they also had friends who were boys.

> And I have a lot of close boyfriends as friends, and really close.

Jackie had almost always felt "more comfortable with boys than girls." Gail, too, "had a lot of friends that were guys." In fact, "some of my best friends are guys."[20]

Those outside the group often complained that insiders socialized only with each other:

> You know, they can only have boyfriends and girlfriends in that group . . . You can't possibly go with another group.[21]

But frequently, popular girls talked about groups as they talked about individuals: They didn't stick with one.

> I'm in kind of a clique but I have a bunch—I have about four different groups of friends. I have one from camp. I have one from

temple. And I have my old friends from junior high school. And then I have people I met this year.

The impression was one of abundance: of many friends, "groups of friends," boyfriends. They talked often about being "socially active," applying the term literally.

Perhaps preempting adults' fear that peer pressure can lead to trouble, they made a point of saying that they were independent affiliates, not "followers":

> You have to be strong for yourself. You're not going to have a thing to hang on to forever or depend on, because that's impossible. You can only depend on yourself. That's the only sure thing you have.

Obviously, this representation differed a great deal from that of narrators who depended on love for support and recognition. Popular girls didn't see lovers as teachers or models either.

While these narrators said they could take care of themselves, they liked to be part of a team—literally as well as figuratively. They were good sports. Instead of exchanging tomboyishness for femininity after puberty, as many girls still do, popular girls added "femininity" to their prepubertal identities. Even those who went from playing baseball to cheerleading often continued to practice a sport of their own as well as cheering on a boys' team—swimming (Chris), running (Gail), tennis (Jackie). To a degree, being athletic worked against the repressive effects of conformity and femininity, enrolling them in the action-packed realm of masculine adolescence.

The story of their first sexual and romantic forays was not about looking for love, intimacy, or even trust. Rather, in the context of the energetic social activity they valued, popular narrators talked about playing the heterosexual field—one boy after another, many boys. They turned boyfriends over more frequently and certainly more intentionally than any other girls, and instigated breakups as a means of maintaining social freedom. Their cliques matched up with boys' cliques, and there was a marked exchangeability about who went with whom. Often they went to proms and parties with boys who were friends rather than boyfriends.

They preferred first love in a controlled dose. A vacation was a good length of time for a romance, for example. The limited time frame and change of venue lessened the tension between having a close relationship and keeping faith with the group, although even spending a "whole summer with just one boy" seemed to one popular narrator like losing opportunities.

UP TO THIS POINT, this is a 1950s story transposed to the 1980s, unaffected by the changes in the book of love wrought by the 1970s and '80s. But what happened when the press of intimacy, desire, and history added "making love" to the list of activities included in going out and partying? How did popular girls handle the contradiction between sexual intimacy and friendly sociality? Did they break the long-standing connection between sex, intimacy, and love? "Popularize" love? Or treat sexual relationships differently from other relationships—specially, intimately, lovingly?

There were two "popular" answers to the problem of sex and seriality—two kinds of popular girls. "Old-fashioned" popular girls played the field but did not go all the way (or at least said they didn't). Indeed, they reported less sexual activity than virtually any other group. In earlier periods, playing the field did not preclude making out and heavy petting. In this period, some girls actually restricted sexuality to kissing alone to hold the line against coitus. The new school of popular girls, in contrast, extended the characteristic social practices of popularity—seriality and multiplicity—into the realm of sex: These popular girls played the field *and* went all the way. Despite this divergence, both kinds of popular girls tried to keep true love at bay.

Old-fashioned popularity's solution to the problem that sex poses for casual sociality was the time-honored formula: play the field; keep your friends; wash your hair every day; steer clear of passion; say no to intercourse. If the prescription had always been harder to follow than to dispense, the fact that more and more girls rejected it made it that much harder for most girls who wanted to heed it. But popular girls narrated hardly any trouble.

The romantic histories of Gail and Jackie begin to describe how old-fashioned popular girls maintained the old-fashioned way of love and friendship, managed sexual pressure, and retained—or turned over—their boyfriends. Gail was a cheerleader who traced much of what she knew about sociality to the lessons older cheerleaders taught her. Jackie was perpetually in transit: Since her parents divorced, they had shared custody and she had had to move back and forth from one house to another on a weekly basis. She had many friends. Groomed to be a tennis champ by her father, she cited "dad" as the source of much of her social knowledge.

Both Gail and Jackie had "going out" relationships in junior high school. Gail didn't remember much about hers. It was just "nice to have." "Fun." The relationship broke up of its own accord. The first time Jackie went out with a boy, she was confronted with the problem that marred popular girls' romantic experience: the difficulty of reconciling "going out" or romance generally with the ethos of sociality. It all started with a kiss after volleyball:

> He pulled me over to the side and he goes, "I have to talk to you." . . . I was, "What is this? Oh, this is it! This is what everybody's been talking about."

He wasn't "very good" but she had been waiting for her first kiss, and she was "happy."

> Because it was finally happening, and it was with a guy that I really liked, and we had gone out for so long.

They went together for a while but he soon became very possessive—a tendency she didn't respect or enjoy.

> He'd be telling me how jealous he was of any guy that talked to me. And he didn't want anybody to talk to me.

He made his ownership obvious to everyone:

> He had this thing where he had to tag on to my hand and hold my hand and walk me to every class, and it bugged me, and I couldn't do it and I would pull away from him.

Sociality was her way of life, and his possessive effort to regulate it made her very angry.[22] It was important to her to have friends who were boys as well as friends who were girls.

> In fact, I had more boyfriends as friends and girlfriends as friends before I started having boyfriends.

His dependency was making life "monotonous" and finally she broke up with him. She got a new boyfriend from the popular pool right away ("You had to go to the dance with somebody"). Her new boyfriend didn't last long either.

> He was the one to say "I love you" on the first date, and that kind of set me off because he'd just like hold my hand and stare at me and go, "I love you." I'd go, "I've got to go catch a bus now."

In high school, both Jackie and Gail belonged to the shrinking numbers of girls who attended high school dances. (In the late 1980s, the high school prom became a cherished event again.) Gail wouldn't consider going "stag," as some girls did, but she could very well go with someone who wasn't a boyfriend. "You'd just go with a boy," she explained; all her friends did the same. The cheerleaders were a "tightly notched" group with a monopoly on the football players, and beyond that it didn't matter a lot who went with whom. But when the captain of the football team picked Gail out at a party at the end of ninth grade, that was special.

> He was following me around like a lost puppy all night, and all my friends were like, "He likes you, he likes you."

She didn't make it easy for him but he persisted, and they began to go out. Cheerleader and captain of the team, they seemed perfect together:

> The little storybook couple. Everybody thought we were so cute. And it was a big ego trip because everybody thought, Oh wow, you know, she's dating the captain of the football team.

She spoke with unusual irony for a popular girl, probably because hindsight had cast the relationship in a harsh light, but the excitement of remembering soon overtook her: "And so . . . and so."

> That was the summer . . . he had a school license so he could drive to and from driver's ed and so he picked me up and we'd go to driver's ed together and—um, we saw each other until about October of the next year and then he started getting too wild for me.

"Wild" didn't refer to sexual pressure. Sexually, their relationship was "nothing major."

> You know, we'd cuddle and kiss, but that was about it. You know, he probably would have liked more but . . . you know, I didn't want it. I wasn't ready.

She had enough power in the relationship to signal "no" indirectly and have it stick without struggle. She didn't think he had even touched her breasts.

> I'd probably remember that. It was more just your hugging and . . .

When he did press for more, it still "wasn't anything major." Attraction, which she mentioned as a minor given—"Oh yeah. Yeah. I was attracted to him"—was not the heart of the story to her. Rather, the heart of it was the image of an ideal couple they projected. Privately, however, they were anything but ideal. Increasingly, he seemed more interested in drugs than in her:

> We'd have dates and he'd forget to come get me or he'd call up at the last minute and say he was going out with the guys.

Describing those developments, she focused on the resolution of the problem, not its humiliating and unnerving duration. The whole thing "worked out for the best."

> And so we realized that, you know, it was stupid to keep the relationship up.

She did feel terrible, she acknowledged, albeit with irony. "I thought it was the end of my world," she said, laughing abashedly. But her disappointment faded fast. In a characteristic popular girl transition, she made the best of an unhappy experience in her very next sentence:

> Now that I look back to it, it was the best thing that we broke up, because I've seen girls he's gone out with lately, and they've turned into clones of him.

I asked how long her feeling that breaking up was the end of her world lasted. "About a week," she joked. I said, "Come on." She said it was true. "One thing . . . I get over guys real fast." I asked if she had to work at that. She said there were some tough moments.

> Let's see, with him—well, I remember it was right around the time of homecoming, okay? So I wasn't going to have a date for homecoming, because everybody thought I was still with him. That was pretty hard because all my friends were going to the dance and I didn't have a date.

But if Gail missed the first dance after her breakup, she had no problem finding guys to go out with after that:

> I'd been going out with the guys forever. So you know in that group I could just find another guy.

Because seriality and multiplicity are the principles of popularity, a big advantage of belonging to a popular crowd is that it contains a good number of like-minded, like-positioned candidates for dates. This is also an advantage of maintaining a group of friends who are boys. Gail understood how to make good use of these advantages. She went out briefly with a boy two years her junior. She went to the dances with "friends who were boys." She didn't become really involved, though, for another year— partly because, she admitted, with the same ironic distance, she was fantasizing that she and the football captain would get back together and she would help him reform:

I can cure him and make him better. And you know I knew that was stupid.

Most girls would have talked and cried their way through a period like that, collecting sympathy and support from everyone they knew. Gail didn't. She didn't "want to be somebody who goes around, you know, always whining and crying" and so she became "pretty good at concealing a lot of the emotions."

She gave no outward indication, other than her failure to begin another relationship, that she may have been burned more badly than she acknowledged. Unlike Tracy, she didn't wait in a social vacuum or advertise her pain. Cheerleading had taught her she had "an image to keep up."

> You're supposed to be the ideal girl. . . . Most of it, you don't keep up, you know, but you try.

JACKIE ALSO KNEW how to keep up an image although she had a more psychological take on life than Gail and talked somewhat more candidly about the pain in things. Whenever she began to talk about a particular boyfriend, she rapidly veered off into generalizations about her style of having a relationship or about someone else in her group. But when she finally got down to her feelings, she spoke pointedly. Like Gail's, her first relationship was very public. Like Gail, she ultimately decided to break it up. The first boy who genuinely interested her was older than she was—a college guy. They both played tennis. "In public we'd act like a couple, and we were always in public." When they went to tournaments together, they pretended they were married, but their relationship barely involved sex at all, not even petting. The end came when "he started wanting more." What was "more"?

> Um, touching me, all over. And I began getting scared, right away. Gosh, right away. . . . It was kind of like he never did anything until this one day he decided he wanted a lot. And that kind of set me back, because I wondered, Gosh, he's been holding himself back then.

She fidgeted and "tensed up a lot."

And he'd say, "Don't you, don't you like this?" And I told him, "I don't know."

For once she was at a social loss. She "stopped taking his calls." She couldn't help it. She guessed "he deserved it." He had come in too close, without any warning.

Although they had gone everywhere together for over a year, she "put a stop" to the feeling that she was "going to miss him." She had the ability to "build a wall," she explained.

> I can put stops to feelings. . . . I consider it kind of a power that I have. . . . It goes to a point where I feel that I'm in danger of being hurt. Or invaded. I can, I can make a wall. I can, I can stop it.

She saved herself "a lot of hurt," she thought, by blaming him "for everything instead of blaming myself." She went to the prom "as friends with a friend," a senior whose girlfriend had just broken up with him. He had already gotten a tux.

> I just happened to have a dress, and he asked me, and he said, "We'll have a great time. You know, I made reservations and everything." So we just went as friends. And that's . . . we're still really close.

These friendly dates made the time between one real "relationship" and another much easier to get through.

The boy with whom cheerleader Gail next had a relationship —"a summer boyfriend" met at art school—was the antithesis of her crowd. Once the much better half of a storybook couple, now she was with a freak—a guy who was both wild and fun—a Deadhead and a practical joker.[23]

> Maybe deep down inside I was trying to find a guy that would shock my friends.

Or maybe she was looking for another guy to reform. He was, after all, her second druggie. Her sexual relationship with him "was more than with anybody else."

> I don't know how to put it. We never slept together but we pretty much did everything else.

That was all she volunteered. I began to ask questions. Had he touched her breasts? Yes. Her genitals? Yes. Had she had orgasms? No. "It was, you know, it was perfect for what we wanted," she said, cutting off another question on that subject.

She gave two reasons for not going further: They were going to part at the end of the summer; having sex might make separation harder. Second, while "fun" and "sex" were opposites— fun was social, sex was intimate—it was hard to leave someone you really had fun with.[24]

> I don't think we could have handled anything more, because it was still hard enough when we had to leave each other. You know, because we had a real fun summer.

Gail knew other girls believed that sex, intimacy, even love belonged in a teenage relationship, but she disagreed.

> I think it's all a lot of fronts. The girls I know that are in serious relationships . . . when they're around everybody else they have to act like they're in love and you can tell that they're not. And they talk about "Oh, I'm so in love, I'm so in love," twenty-four hours a day, and you know that if they really felt that way, they wouldn't have to keep dwelling on the subject.

JACKIE'S STORY contains a number of comments that suggest she may have had an unusually strong aversion to sex—her feeling of being invaded the first time she was kissed, for instance; the abrupt way she ended her relationship with the tennis player as soon as he indicated his desire for her. In her high school, most Chicana girls got married or pregnant before their senior year. She was only half Chicana, and both her parents had modern views on gender and reproduction, but she may nevertheless have felt she had to avoid sex altogether to escape that destiny. Gail, too, knew from her cohort what kinds of romantic and personal disasters lay on the other side of the disciplined lines of popularity. Her successor as the football captain's girlfriend— another cheerleader—became, as she had not, a co-dependent, finally getting to be "as bad as he was."

But whether their reasons for not having sex were psycholog-

ical or social, both Gail and Jackie eschewed the new sexual freedom that many of their peers found so compelling, steering clear
of both sexual pressure and romantic obsession. They saw sex as
the coup de grace in intimacy's struggle for exclusivity and away
from a wider sociality—against fun and freedom. They saw the
popular way and the sexual way as antithetical and they valued
friends and family over sex, romance, and intimacy. It's easy to
slight the "fun" they prized so highly, but it is not such a small
matter, especially in comparison with the misery of despised love,
a fate that not all popular girls manage to avoid completely.

THE NEW SCHOOL of popularity extended the traditional practices of popular sociality to sex, repositioning sex within the
realm of fun. (Love remained with seriousness—at the opposite
pole. They avoided it too.) To girls who practiced the new school
of popularity, sex, like fun, was social. It could be acknowledged
publicly as long as it didn't come to the attention of adults who
might disapprove or make trouble. It was neither intense nor
exclusive. It didn't have to mark its participants with longing,
desire, or regret. If old-fashioned popularity used social power to
keep to the old ways of love and friendship, the new school used
it to make a new way. First, Shelley.

Shelley represents an early stage in the new popularity. She
described herself as "socially active" and viewed cliquishness as
"immature." Maturity, by contrast, was high school's more open
sociality, and membership in a number of groups instead of just
one. Her parents discouraged her from becoming too involved
with any one boy. They told her to "play the field," and she
boasted about how well she followed their advice. The previous
year she had enjoyed "just all little flings."

> A "little fling" is like when you go—like I went to a weekend or a
> dance or something, I'd be with just this one guy. Just like for a
> couple of minutes in the coatroom, and that was it.
> Q: The coatroom?
> A: I mean, where else were we supposed to go?

She relished these flings and "just fooled around the entire
year."

She didn't go very far on those occasions, no further than "second quote unquote base." When her parents let her travel to a religious youth conference for the holidays, however, she had the opportunity to go further. The first day there, she met a boy she liked. That evening she went to his room, where they made out for an hour and a half. "Then I fell asleep." She laughed, relishing the memory.

> His roommate came in and found me lying there in the bed. Really. And he didn't say anything. This roommate had a different girl in his room every night. But it was funny. I left my lip gloss in the room . . . and the roommate had to give it to me the next day, because for some reason the guy I was with the night before didn't feel like talking to me.

She had a pretty good idea of the reason: "Because he was just using me or whatever you want to call it." She also had a way of thinking about "being used" that spared her from feeling terrible about herself:

> But that was okay. I was using him too.

Toward the end of the conference, she spent the night in a guy's room.

> So like that last night, I was—I really liked him. His name was John. The last night I was with him, I went very, very, very far with him. Extremely far. If I had gone any farther with him, I would have needed birth control pills!

She explained what she had done in terms of sentiment, situation, and desire. They had talked for a long time. She really "felt like a part of him." She "wanted it." And she wouldn't have to face him later on. The conference was ending the next day. In sum, she said: "I really liked him and I was leaving the next morning." After, she "felt good."

Since then, she had engaged in heavy petting many, many times. Desire and choice, in her sexual perspective, protected her against "hurt." She felt fine about everything because she stuck to her principles:

I've never let it get that far where it's like I've not wanted it myself
or . . . I've never gotten to where I felt like I was really used, like
really hurt. . . . It's always been something I've wanted also. So it
hasn't been too bad. I've never gotten into a position where I felt
really terrible afterward, like a piece of—like a toy.

At the same time, she repeated, she wasn't "that indiscriminate."

I mean, if I knew them, if I liked them, we kind of liked each other
a little, then we would.

As proof that she wasn't "really indiscriminate," she cited her
recent fidelity:

Like I was with him all night.

But she was already impatient, as she soon indicated, using terms
very like the ones that Jackie used in explaining why she broke
it off with her first boyfriend, the tennis pro:

I have to, like, talk to him because I'm not one to be pinned down
to one guy for a long period of time.

IN THAT it involves skirting adult prohibitions against forbidden acts like drinking, popularity has an outlaw aspect as a peer
ethos; but while outlaws flaunt their transgressions, popular girls
hide them behind a healthy good-citizen image. In Alix Kates
Shulman's fictional memoir of the 1950s, Sasha Davis dares to
go all the way the night she is crowned prom queen because she
feels her reputation is secure. Who would believe the prom
queen is a slut? But she quickly realizes that even a prom queen
is vulnerable to rumor, and she buys her boyfriend's continued
silence with continued sex. When she visits Ohio State for a college weekend, she makes the mistake of having sex with a boy
she has just met, only to find out he has another girlfriend. He,
she knows, has no reason to keep her secret. If she attends Ohio
State, she'll start out with a bad reputation. She resolves to keep
her grades up so that she can go away to a distant school.
    In comparison with Chris, Sasha Davis was a model of honesty.

Chris mixed the old and new in her history and appearance: She wore staid plaid Bermudas, a solid cotton top, and twelve earrings in both ears, including a safety pin and a skull. At her own school, she acted like an old-fashioned popular girl; belonged to a leading crowd; went to dances; maintained a "good reputation"; had a series of boyfriends. Out of school, she followed the practices of the new school of popularity.

She met the first boy she went with—Stephen—at a party given by one of the "mean" and "rich" popular girls. She and Stephen left together and made out "under the streetlamps." As much as she enjoyed their relationship, she hardly noticed when they broke up. "He went out on me or something like that." While a girlfriend got furious on her behalf, she was only mildly "offended."

> Ellen just glared at him. And I was like, "What are you doing? Why are you so mean?"
> She said, "I hate him so much."
> And I was like, "Whyeeeeee?"

She got another boyfriend soon, and then another, and she continued to see Stephen from time to time as well.

> I kind of liked him. I didn't like him more than I liked anybody else, really. A little bit more maybe.

She didn't see the point of staying mad. She played around herself. Besides, she never entirely dropped any boyfriend, just saw them less or more at different times, and not seeing any boy all that much during the school year.

Unbeknownst to her school friends, Chris had a second social life altogether that she shared with her rebellious and adventurous older sister. They went out together practically every night to parties on the other side of town, where they "just used to like get wasted" on Everclear punch (190 proof grain alcohol mixed with Hawaiian Punch, 7UP, and fruit), grass, and hash. Wasted, they "scammed," which she defined as not going "too far," just flirting with guys "and kind of pulling them off" to a corner somewhere.

And it never got too far. I mean it was basically kissing, maybe a little farther than that, but I mean it happened often. Like maybe even I guess it's happened like three guys in one night or something like that. I—it was pretty bad for a while.

She used the language of judgment—"promiscuity," "bad," "too far"—when she talked about sex, but basically her analysis was the same as Shelley's. She never felt bad about her sexual experiences:

Not at all. I was doing what I wanted to do. It didn't bother me. I didn't figure it was hurting them any.

Anyway, she was often so drunk she didn't even remember what she'd done.

Junior year she stopped getting high and started to work at school. Like many other popular girls, she could see the wall at the end of the tunnel; after all, she was out for a good time, not to burn every chance in the book, and she had always intended to go to college. She even stopped smoking after she took up synchronized swimming. Not that she gave up partying altogether; she simply reserved it for Saturday nights.

That year Chris and still-present Stephen began to sleep together at his house when his parents were out of town sometimes but they didn't "make love."

I mean, we slept together nude but that's it.

Swathed in sheets, she didn't look at him below the waist let alone touch him.

The first time she finally had sex she was "really drunk." Nothing specific made her decide to go all the way. It was "just go with the flow," and she was curious. "Really curious."

She didn't like it at all. "At all."

It didn't really hurt—it hurt a little bit—it was uncomfortable. I was pretty bored actually. I didn't see anything very nice about it at all.

She didn't use contraception, figuring she'd get an abortion if she got pregnant. Nothing came of the experience—no deeper relationship, no change. She hadn't expected it to. They did it again after spring spree. They weren't "quite as drunk" the second time and she liked it "a little bit" but "not that much."

That summer she had two summer boyfriends. One of them was so possessive it drove her crazy but she couldn't bring herself to break up with him because:

He was a really, really good kisser.

Senior year she slept with him a couple of times. "I liked that," she said, adding she also liked it when her other boyfriend went down on her, although she still hadn't had an orgasm.

SHELLEY AND CHRIS used multiplication to resolve the problem of attachment that plagued the true-love narrators so acutely. With many friends and a pipeline of potential boyfriends, breaking up was hardly even an issue. How hard is it to separate from one boyfriend when you have a dozen on call? Besides, boys didn't run from popular girls, didn't threaten them with separation, perhaps because popular girls weren't trying to act out their need for attachment on the life of one boy. Love didn't seem to occur to them, and the boys they saw didn't press them. Evidently the similarities that attracted them to friends and boyfriends went far beyond those of taste or class to a consensus about the body, the heart, and the other.

Not all popular girls were as armored against love as these narrators, but none set out to get it the way Tracy did, and none indicated before they fell in love that they needed it at all. Those who nevertheless came under its sway shed some light on popularity's changing forms and powers. Susan was an old-fashioned popular girl. She grew up in a far midwestern university town. In her high school, popular girls split between athletes and cheerleaders in freshman year. Skill rather than popularity won her a spot on the top cheerleading team. Her fellow cheerleaders, the most popular girls in school, seemed "snotty," but she went along with them. Her old friends became increasingly jealous and cutting. Fortunately, she made many new friends on the boys' athletic teams, and she began to date one boy steadily. He was a classic popular guy—more comfortable in a crowd than in a couple, in public than in private, with casualness than with passion or love. Less socially at ease, she soon came to rely on him, making some mistakes popular girls usually avoid—the mistake of intimacy, the mistake of pressure, the mistake of love. As she pressed in, he started to get cold feet.

> Well, he was afraid that he wasn't going to get his high school life in. He was afraid he was going to miss out on all the dating and how many girls you can date and all that stuff like they do for fun in high school before they start settling down.

When he broke up with her, she felt her old girlfriends gloated over her downfall. Her male friends were first and foremost friends of his, and she had never felt really comfortable with the girls. It all left her feeling depressed.

> I don't know, I just feel really low sometimes.

But she had what it took to be a popular girl. She put on a brave and optimistic face: Now she understood about playing the field, she said with a forced laugh, "because you want to have fun in high school before you get married to one guy."

Patti had an exceptionally permissive attitude toward sex but love got her into trouble all the same. A little more extreme in her sexual practice than other popular girls, she became a cautionary tale among her classmates, especially those on the fast academic track, who criticized her in order to define their superiority. They cast her as the ultimate popular girl—a girl who once had everything but who began to falter around junior year when her academic carelessness caught up with her. She brought out their tendency toward "we knew it all along," and "we told each other so." Lynn said she and Patti had been good friends freshman and sophomore year. Junior year, Lynn abandoned the "popular crowd" for the upward-bound fast track. Safe in that aerie, she looked down on Patti and tattletaled, devoting most of her own interview to Patti's deepest secrets, which she had clearly spread widely.

When Patti answered the door, her offhanded greeting and relaxed demeanor communicated an ease that verged on indifference, but every stroke of informality—the unironed cotton blouse, the short sleeves turned up just so—bore a relationship to her dating and clique associations as well as to media images. She could have been on the advisory board of *Glamour*. She didn't express herself easily but, caught in the throes of romantic disappointment, she talked more than any other popular girl. It wasn't sexual initiation that did her in. She had had sex for the first time when she was in seventh grade, she said.

> Let's see—I was with my cousin and one of his friends came over and we liked each other and we started messing around. . . . It was just sort of something that I wanted to get over with, 'cause . . . at that point it was seventh grade and all the older girls I looked up to weren't virgins.

"It was sort of the in thing to do," she explained. "It wasn't supposed to be a big deal. It was something that you were supposed to do."

From then on she had sex casually with boys she "played" with. The group was important to her. Individual relationships were not. Just before she entered high school, her family changed school districts. She continued to see her old friends and play with them by the old rules, but in her new school she soon had a "serious" boyfriend who introduced an older and more restrictive view of sex. Trust and commitment were important, in his view. He waited until it was "time."

> After about six months or so we talked about it and we felt that we knew each other well enough and it was right. We cared about each other enough. And so that's when we started.

She did not tell her "serious" boyfriend about her earlier sexual experiences, or that she still sometimes went all the way with other boys. Lynn—who called herself Patti's "best friend"—claimed that when he found out, he put his relationship with Patti on hold and began having long talks with Lynn. Soon Lynn and he were boyfriend and girlfriend. Patti became desperate and began to threaten suicide.

Patti's account of the change never mentioned Lynn at all. Her relationship with her boyfriend had become a "duty," she said,

and they decided to see other people. She didn't find going out
with other people the fun it had once been, however:

> Because with him, there's nothing really that he doesn't know that
> I can hide. But with other people, you don't know them, and they
> don't know you, and so you feel kind of nervous actually.

She didn't entirely leave her world of casual sexuality—where
nothing meant anything in particular—but she thought about
her relationship with him in the conventional terms he had introduced into their relationship: Sex symbolized trust and eter-
nity, love was forever, he loved her, and nothing could change
that. Patti expected him to cherish her and to forgive all her
lapses while she treated him with indifference and played the
field. If her expectation seems one-sided, it made sense given her
high opinion of her own sexual value.

In her version of the story, when he learned of her past—and
of her different perspective on sex and love—he shifted ground.
Now he wanted what she had had: freedom, casual sex, a clean
break in the link he had forged to her. Telling about his reac-
tion, she spoke ruefully about her cavalier sexual past. At first I
suspected this was a rap that she had used to try to persuade him
that she had changed, but then she expressed an ambition so
difficult that suddenly I believed her:

> I'd like to be able to see him and not be jealous when he's with
> other people, because I really don't—I mean, we're only going to
> be seniors and we shouldn't be tying ourselves down right now. We
> should be able to do what we want and experience things. And so I
> really—I don't want to tie him down. So. I'd like to let him do that
> and not be jealous. 'Cause it upsets him when I get jealous. So I
> don't want to be jealous about it.

Did she have an idea of how to rid herself of jealousy? Mourn-
fully, she shook her head. No wonder she wished away her past.
Not knowing the typical fate of true-loving girls, she thought that
if she had been as sexually inexperienced as he thought she was
when they first became lovers, she would never have had to face
the daunting task of integrating the ideals of casual sex and true
love. At the same time, her sense of her own place in the world

had come into question in other ways as well. For all her sexual adventurism, Patti was a very old-fashioned girl who had approached adolescence as if she thought marriage and social life were to be her only vocation. In junior year, the "smart" members of the popular crowd like Lynn began to work harder in school and spend more time with top students—those in accelerated and advanced placement classes. Patti couldn't. She was too far behind and too confused about what she was going to do next—romantically, academically, generally. What life would she make for herself after high school?

GIVEN THE TENDENCY of popular narrators to accentuate the positive, it seems remarkable that no popular narrator recounted much fun. They said the word all the time, and it was a high value; but they rarely described having it. Popular girls are supposed to be girls at the center of a social whirl, generating a wider high school sociality. In a bygone era, they would have set the extracurricular pace for their schools as juniors and seniors and generated a sense of community. But only one popular girl I spoke with held a student office. None was involved in an academic club. Gail didn't even train the next cohort of cheerleaders. She got a job instead. Chris went to her school's dances but she never took part in any other high school activity; neither did Patti. Susan kept on cheerleading, but she didn't have a boyfriend and she didn't have a clique. Jackie hadn't stopped managing the football team when we talked, but it was summer, and she didn't seem likely to pick it up again come autumn. None felt any social responsibility at all, not even the most banal or normative.

In the 1920s, dating and petting represented sexual permissiveness, and adolescent sociability cut wider paths for life outside the family. Popular girls were the seductive wave of a future that beckoned women forward toward increasing freedom and pleasure. By the 1950s, they were the right girls at the right time—perfectly socialized for suburban homogeneity, social mobility, and the double standard. But in the late twentieth century, the practice of popularity was out of synch with the times and with the future. These narrators dropped their pom-poms and batons for the same reason many teenage girls get pregnant: They realized that they weren't on their way to anywhere worth going.[25]

As long as they steered clear of love, however, the popular narrators racked up notably high scores in sex and romance. They met boys almost as equals, and they didn't let anyone get the better of them. No accounts in this group involved coercion or even blurred the line between volition and coercion. Popular narrators didn't report much sexual pleasure, but that may have been just one more sign, from the group of girls that understood the social rules better than any other, that though it may have become acceptable to acknowledge having sex, it still wasn't cool to talk about liking it.

Because of their social and sexual power and their remarkable imperviousness to the persuasion of love, most popular girls could say yes and get sex, or say no and make it stick—and since a girl who can make those decisions can also set the conditions of sexual encounters, most were in a position to keep a rational distance both between sex and reproduction and between sex and danger. After all, a girl whose first priority is playing the field can hardly be talked into having a baby or having unprotected sex to prove her love or trust. Popularity also made them less desperate: there was no sense in these histories of fixing on a boy obsessively because of a fear of a boyless or loveless future.[26] This strength increased with numbers. Pairs of friends—best friends—can't establish and enforce local sex and gender systems. A group of fifteen or so highly desirable girls who share the same view of sex and gender can. But what makes a particular group of fifteen or so more desirable than another? In one study of premarital dating, Winston Ehrmann considered why boys rave about some girls "as having 'wonderful personalities.' " He observed that "physical attractiveness" wasn't "the essential element." Rather, "the basis of their great popularity," he deduced, "rests in the way they talk, smile, and laugh so that the male is made to feel alive and important."[27] But plenty of girls hang on every male word, only to have the boys they flatter grow increasingly uneasy or distant.

One secret of popular girls' success was their ability to develop nonromantic friendships with boys. This gave them a choice when they went through a breakup and made high school social life tolerable between relationships. They developed these friendships easily because—for all their uncritical femininity and heterosexuality—they had some important things in common with boys. They, too, preferred comedy and action to romance, and they strove to live—as boys traditionally have—in the public (albeit not the professional) rather than the private sphere. They, too, were ambivalent at best about intimacy and about being tied down. But if sportiness and a gingerly approach to intimacy were all these girls had going for them—if they were simply boys in girls' bodies—they would have been boys' buddies, not their girlfriends. Rather, they met boys halfway across the gender gap, probing subjects that boys do not characteristically discuss, like feelings. This worked as long as their questions were neither loaded nor aimed at the heart.

In that popular girls knew they could always get other dates, popularity armored them against the depredations of love and against sexual pressure, while playing the field gave them two alternative approaches to teenage romance: one noncoital, one coital. But these approaches to sexuality didn't consist of a set of principles on which to base a sexual decision. Rather, they came down to either/or: Either have sex with no one or have sex with anyone in your clique. (In comparison, Tracy's reasoning was extremely nuanced.) For a while either/or worked well for these girls, because it took the weight off sex and detached it from loaded concerns like love. This both lessened the emotional impact of adolescent sexual experience and increased the likelihood that they would shield themselves against the most dangerous practical consequence of love: its tendency in making girls feel safe and trusting to also make them feel they need not protect themselves from pregnancy or sexually transmitted infections.

Once popular girls entered the magnetic field of love, however, the practices of popularity offered no guidance or protection. Popularity rehearses sociality not intimacy, being desirable not desiring. It doesn't offer a way to talk through or out of heartbreak. Its genre is situation comedy, not melodrama; its method is accentuating the positive, not dealing with the negative. It's a decent tactic as long as there's something positive to accentuate—something to look forward to, something to take the mind off disappointment. But what if there isn't? What if the future looks dim? Perhaps it was their lack of prospects other than love, in other words, that finally caused the downfall of the few popular girls who had to deal with heartbreak. One way to assess this is to consider the accounts of girls who put work before love, fast-track girls headed for the best colleges in the country. How did they hope to arrange sex, gender, reproduction, and adolescence in the wake of the changes of the 1970s? And how much success did they have?

3

Infinite Possibilities of Doing

Sexual Opportunity and the Capitalized Self

> It may in fact be a defining characteristic of the modern novel (as of bourgeois society) that it takes aspiration, getting ahead, seriously . . . and thus it makes ambition the vehicle and emblem of Eros.
>
> —Peter Brooks, *Reading for Plot*

As popular girls began to lose steam in mid-high school, the studious girls they had dismissed as grinds and future fry-brains were coming into their own. These buoyant competitors saw building a knowledgeable, well-rounded self as "good" and becoming sexual as a process of accumulation. Far from sharing the common boredom with secondary education, they experienced freshman and sophomore years as laps in a thrilling race they planned to win. They took gender equality for granted; viewed feminism as a strident movement whose relevance had passed; and treated the changes in the rules of love as additions to the curriculum of adolescence. Reason, intelligence, and optimism would gain them entry into the highest professional echelons, they believed, as they raked in high school prizes, and even peers came to think that if anyone had romantic promise, they did. This was an amazing turn of events.[1]

Europe has long had an adolescent intellectual tradition, but brains have generally been suspect in the United States. From the vantage of adulthood, writers or artists may trace the origins of their work to mid-adolescent concerns, but the country hasn't had a self-sustaining adolescent intellectual subculture. James Coleman's 1957–58 study of ten high schools found that brains barely weighed in as a factor in the composition of a leading crowd even in schools that instilled Ivy League ambitions in a majority of their students.[2] Of course, intellectuals were beginning to gather influence as early as the 1950s: the bohemians in black tights and turtlenecks; the science brains whose stock skyrocketed right along with Sputnik. Such groups just hadn't reached a sufficient critical mass to show up statistically.

The history of the relationship between brains and femininity is a particularly checkered one, and race adds another complication. As late as the mid-1950s, the presumption was that from adolescence on boys would outstrip girls intellectually as well as physically while students of color weren't even considered in the running. In 1966 Douvan and Adelson referred to girls who "reached late adolescence"—that is, sixteen—and did not "yet date" as representing a "deviant pattern." This "very late dater" of sixteen was "missing one of the critical experiences of adolescence": Not only would she miss the developmental necessity of socializing with boys, but she would also have fewer and fewer girlfriends. "Too dependent" on her family, she'd never begin a life of her own.[3]

Then came feminism, the growth of high school intellectual subcultures (from freaks to hacks, politicos to poets and painters), legislation barring discrimination in education, the excellence movement, and, finally, the toughening job markets. Together these increased the ambitions and intellectual preoccupations of students who had previously seen academic effort as futile or dull. This isn't to say that all students came to respect academic success. Many popular students still scorned grinds for working harder than privilege and popularity required, and many impoverished students of color despised those gifted, ambitious peers who seemed to think they could leap clear of the conditions of their birth by "acting white."[4] Such anti-intellectual currents, though, no longer went unchallenged. The generational zeitgeist had clearly shifted.

At the time of this study, many senior high schools had powerful intellectual cliques, whose members had a highly charged sense of their own enviable promise. The gender parity of these cliques was the product of the legal requirement that schools educate boys and girls equally and girls' belief that life held many opportunities for their generation of women, not just a token chance or two.

BRIGHT AND VAULTING OPTIMISTS, Elise and her friends—the main narrators of this chapter—were honors students in the best senior high school in the upper-middle-class western suburb where they came of age.[5] In the educational vernacular of their time and place, they were fast-track. Their parents were computer scientists, professors, psychologists, and communications specialists, many of whom still embraced the ideals of social justice, spiritual enlightenment, and holistic living that they had found persuasive in the 1960s. (So many lived on organic produce that the local health-food supermarket was larger than the average Pathmark; there were almost as many ashrams as churches in town; and computers outsold household appliances.) These parents supported their daughters' educational aspirations on a combination of idealistic and pragmatic grounds: Theirs was the generation of second-wave feminism; they were more or less progressive; they *believed* girls should have an equal chance. At the same time, they were acutely aware that two professional incomes were now the minimum guarantee of a middle-class future for a couple and there was a good likelihood their daughters would end up the sole source of support for themselves and their children. Parents weren't the only ones reading the writing on the wall. Many teenagers themselves could see that divorce, and the new desires of suddenly single parents, had made money tight. In response, these students scrambled to win scholarships.

For them school was the real romance. They experienced decreases in rank the way their peers took romantic disappointment. They flushed at the words "Harvard" and "Yale." Academic work was not, however, just a competition for approval for them. These students had a passion for the camaraderie of intellectual life: the discussions, the shared fervors and challenges. Despite their rivalry, they put into practice the paradoxical educational ethos of cooperation and competition, working as hard as they could to be the best while helping each other through:

> I had a lot of help from my friends. I used to call them up, "I can't do this assignment," you know, I'd be crying, in tears, "I can't do this. This is too hard for me." "Oh, you can do it. I know you can. Now open the book. What page?" And they really helped me out a lot.

I had a lot of help from them as well. Several generously brought documentation to their interview—diaries, letters that they clearly thought they might use themselves someday. One introduced herself, sat down, and began dictating from her notes. Another riffled through her papers after each anecdote to compare her written version with the one she had just told. They also took the project of referral very seriously. Other girls referred a friend or two; Elise referred her entire peer group. With one exception, however, no one referred beyond the group, and other evidence as well suggests that they kept fairly high boundaries between themselves—a very homogeneous group—and students who were not in accelerated classes.[6] They spited enemies of seriousness and academic success, especially the popular girls whom they had envied and emulated in junior high school.

> Oh, they were the good-looking ones, and the funny ones, and the ones who I wanted to be just like, who I now know are big jerks. . . . They're superficial. They're not smart.

The one referral they made outside the boundaries of their group was a popular girl they all thought exemplified the popular crowd's mistake in giving too much priority to sex and other varieties of teenage fun and too little to work.

In contrast, they felt the danger of making the opposite mistake: working too hard and not learning how to have fun, how to get along with boys and elicit and enjoy the pleasures of sex and romance. For them, the newly established right to contraception and abortion generated the same kinds of responsibilities that academic opportunities did. They saw sexual experience as one of their generation's college requirements. But they had more than their résumés in mind as they sought out sexual and romantic experience. They saw work as properly the highest adolescent priority, but they knew firsthand that all work and no play produced depression.

Almost all these narrators reported feeling lethargic as puberty passed, adolescence began, and romance failed to come their way. As exciting as their classes were, they wanted some indication that there would eventually be more in their lives than work. By late sophomore or early junior year, those who had not even held anyone's hand since third grade started to worry about themselves. The word "paranoid" came up frequently.

> I have friends who are freaking now because they're seniors and they've never fooled around with a guy and they're getting really paranoid.

Ellen offhandedly remarked that she planned to commit suicide in college if her situation did not change by then.

Elise's eloquent testimony described her long wait for romance. A pixie with dark lashes and a serious demeanor, Elise dreamed of chivalry—"like in the Westerns"—from early childhood on. "He'd protect her . . . and then gradually they'd start sleeping together." Her longing intensified with her parents' divorce. Year after year, she told of waiting and plotting for romance. She gave herself pep talks, set objectives—be more social, get to know some boys first, then get a boyfriend—gritted her teeth, but "nothing happened." At the end of one talk, when I asked what we had missed, she replied that we hadn't talked about how she really spent her time.

> I would just find myself staring into space and, um, dropping down on my bed and lying there for hours and wishing that I just didn't have to think about anything.

If she wasn't too tired, she daydreamed. If she was "just exhausted," she would sink "into oblivion." As the year droned on, she lost interest entirely in crushes and daydreams:

> I'd think, Well, what's the point of getting a crush on somebody? They'll never like me. . . . I wasn't really talking to people very much. . . . Why should somebody fall in love with me if they didn't know me? . . . I—I had to start being more outgoing and get to know people or I would just be like this for the rest of my life.

Next year was always going to be different. With her characteristic managerial optimism, Elise focused on the lessons she still had to learn: "So that's an unknown variable I'll just have to consider next year," she said repeatedly. The "unknown variable" wasn't sex; it was the male mind. Though she had a younger brother, she wrote him off as a monstrous anomaly. "They all put up a front," she observed. "You don't know what they're really thinking about."

To help me out, she filled in the vacuum of her experience with fragmented anecdotes about her own dashed romantic hopes; tales from her family romance; reports from other girls. Encouraging games of Truth and Dare to find out what we both wanted to know, she became almost an associate researcher. But like most girls, she mainly knew girls in her same situation. For almost all of her friends, Sleeping Beauty had been gender-reversed: it was the boys who were comatose and the girls whose kisses and come-on's didn't work.

One line of thought explains the academic success of talented students in terms of the very sexual retardation Elise bewailed. The mind is built on sublimation, this argument goes, or on late menarche. But within this crowd, that theory was not borne out: one of the fast-track friends had experienced a precocious puberty, developing breasts in second grade, and not all the girls came late to romance. What they did have in common was the view, strongly supported by their families, that puberty didn't reflect destiny.[7] To the extent that they believed in biology's importance, they looked to sex to make them more knowing rather than to complete or transform their lives. They viewed intercourse as the kind of growth experience that produces cognitive leaps; romance was window dressing (nice but not necessary); and love was hardly even in their lexicon during freshman and sophomore years. It was for parents and pets, but mostly it was for later, and they derogated classmates who became wholly absorbed in intimate experience early on in high school:

> I thought it was extremely frivolous . . . that my classmates would think that they were mature enough, developed enough, to fall in love.

Love, at least, was worth mentioning. Maternity wasn't. They pushed the subject away with distaste as something so far in the future it was totally off the point.

While they did not share the absorption with intimate responsibility traditionally attributed to girls and were definitely not making plans for marriage, they did appreciate the idea of romance—both in its own right and as a pleasant accompaniment to sex. Many fast-track girls become speed readers by gorging themselves on romances and preserve a romantic inclination long after they turn from the best-selling romance writers to pure mathematics. Even those who stuck wholly to classic or textbook fare found the idea of romance appealing. The difference was that they saw romance itself, as well as reading romance, as an avocation or leisure-time activity—the equivalent of golf to a doctor perhaps. It never occurred to them to try to make a life out of it, to go pro. Like medieval courtiers, they were prepared to practice it for its own sake—that is, without any aims beyond romantic experience itself—as interlude, gesture, token. In this sense, they were among the few pure romantics in this book.

In these accounts as in so many others, the preparation for sex and romance began with personal appearance. These teenagers, however, made the connection explicit by discussing at some length remaking themselves in order to attract sex and romance. As if describing the progress of a prizewinning science project, all but one told a story of successful self-transformation. These frequently included:

Before:	After:
Occasionally mistaken for a boy	Long-haired and feminine
Snarly, grungy hair	Trendy cut, brushed to shine
Wore ugly glasses	Wore contact lenses
Shy	Aggressively flirtatious
Pansocial	Member of exclusive group that rivaled and ultimately surpassed the popular clique

The bane of their post-makeover existence was Julie, whom every girl in the group criticized even more caustically than they criticized popular girls: She didn't care what she looked like and lopped her hair off without even glancing in the mirror when it got below her ears; she was ostentatiously careless about her work, regularly handing in compositions she had scrawled on the bus, for example; she flouted gender norms and flagrantly propositioned female classmates. Once she went so far as to messenger Valentine candy to another girl during French class. Furious, the recipient told not only all her classmates but also a school counselor about Julie's "problems," in effect putting Julie's deviance on record and formally registering the recipient's own allegiance to hard work, styled hair, and heterosexuality.

Against Julie, on one end of the spectrum, and popular girls, on the other, the narrators in this group defined and worked toward normality (heterosexuality) and excellence. Their heterosexuality still a platonic ideal, despite their makeovers, they began to train for the triathlon of career, marriage, and maternity they would take up years hence. They began with research—consulting the few girls they knew who had always had boyfriends (mainly those popular girls who switched to the fast track when it became apparent that popularity was a dead end) as well as older sisters, even mothers, and, of course, books. One or two succeeded immediately at getting boyfriends. The others continued to study, analyze, experiment, and learn. What happened next depended on who was telling, who their friends and lovers were, and how they viewed the possible relations between—responses to—sex, love, and pregnancy.

LIKE ANNE of Green Gables, Meg had thick, long, wiry redgold hair and a tendency to use large words and foreign expressions. She ended breathy, nervous sentences tentatively with questions or half laughs, but alluded often to her own remarkable intelligence. Meg was reputedly the genius in the group, the teachers' favorite who beat everyone else out. Her abilities made her friends feel inferior—two or three decided against trying for Yale for fear of being surrounded by Megs—but they felt privileged, they all said, to know someone as smart as she was. Sophomore year, Meg decided she wanted—well, you couldn't exactly call it romance. She wanted experience with boys, and down the line a bit, she wanted to have sex. She only had one friend who had had any romantic experience, Judy, and Judy's concerns and romances came to greatly inform Meg's own—and, through Meg, those of everyone else in the group—despite the many differences in their histories.

If Meg had had even more intellectual opportunities than her peers, Judy had had fewer. In addition to attending the excellent local schools in her area, Meg had traveled widely with her parents and gone to school in Europe. Judy, in contrast, had barely even had the advantage of the suburban school she attended when I met her. Her parents had had to get married right out of high school because her mother was pregnant, and for most of her life, they'd lived in a blue-collar town with mediocre schools. She'd been at the top of her class in elementary school and junior high, but she had never really faced competition before her father received a promotion and her family moved to Meg's suburb. She just made it into advanced placement in her new school, and she had to work long, long hours to keep up. Her determination and effort moved the other girls in her classes to help her—Meg among them—and ultimately the difference in their histories seemed to matter less than the intention they all shared not to let anything get in the way of the future. Especially not anything as trivial as love.

Although Judy had to work harder than any of her peers and talked a great deal about the pressure, she had a relaxed way about her that made her seem more accessible than her friends, and perhaps that's why boys flocked to her as they did not to any other member of the fast track. As her friends looked on with bated breath (half envious, half as afraid for her as she was for herself), Judy began to go out well before anyone else. They needn't have worried, at least not at first. Petrified of making the same mistake her mother had, Judy kept the boys she dated well at arm's length throughout freshman year. "I was a cold fish," she recalled. Then late in freshman year, just about the time her mother and father split up and her father announced he wouldn't contribute any money for her college education, she met Doug, a junior. When Judy first went out with Doug:

> This was going to be like my other three boyfriends in the past where you just go out and do something and if it works, it works, and if it doesn't, you blow it off.

After their first couple of dates, "he was almost in tears . . . because he needed more of a commitment." Judy was "really stunned." She thought "men do not show strong emotion."

> So I said, "Oh, okay, I'll be your girl. Fine."

But she was uncomfortable and she moved to give herself more room.

> For the next couple of days, I was thinking, What did I just say? What did I just do to myself? . . . I said, "You know, I sort of jumped into this and it's not that I want to back out but we're going to have to see how this works because I've never done this before."

I asked what she meant by "this."

> Well, just having commitment of any kind . . . where you have to be responsible to this person.

Her notion of a commitment suggested how little she liked the idea of intimate responsibility.

> If you say you're going to call, then you should call, not just because you said you were gonna but because the person's going to be hurt if you don't.

But she also feared intense involvement because she associated it with her parents' fate. Over time, however, she came to an understanding of how two people can reinforce each other.

> Where . . . you actually draw off another person's strength.

The knowledge served her well. While her parents raged at each other through divorce proceedings, Judy and Doug made their relationship into an emotional home.

> That was such a bad year for me. And . . . he could give a lot as well as receive.

Still, when Judy summed up the relationship, she sounded halfhearted.

And so—that, that was fine and that worked out pretty well. It was a confusing time for me, though, because . . . even though I was getting a lot from the relationship, it was a strain too.

She and Doug went to a family-planning clinic together before they had sex. Alone among this group of narrators, she chose the pill because it was the most effective option. What if, like her mother, she couldn't go through with an abortion? She didn't want to find out. She wasn't ready for pregnancy. She had to get through school and she envisioned a few years on her own after college.
In no time, sex took over their relationship.

Neither of us had any money, so there was nothing to do but sit home . . . so all we did was have sex.

She didn't tell Doug she didn't have orgasms.

I could not bring it up and talk about it. . . . I was just too insecure about it.

Doug finally began leaving his bedroom door open sometimes when she came over, a signal that he too thought they could give sex a rest.

It was real subtle but it was real obvious too. And so that sort of ended that.

As she "began to depend on him more and more," the tables turned in a traditional direction. All of a sudden he wanted space. Like many girls who give up their lives for love, she told this part from his point of view.

He was really worried about it because he had been in a relationship where he had become very dependent like that and where he went out with this girl every single weekend and they were always together. And then pretty soon things started not working out and then they broke up and he had no friends at all anymore. . . . And so he was really worried that this was going to happen to me.

She filled in excuses for him.

> He had senioritis, and I didn't really understand all of it until this
> year. . . . It's like getting ready to leave home more than anything
> else. It's—it's getting rid of the parents. For the final time.

Still, she felt gypped, "because 'Well, *you're* the one who wanted
this big commitment.' "

She got through junior year without becoming pregnant. He
went to college. She got her college applications in and persuaded her father to pay part of the cost of college after all.
When last we talked, she was halfway there, past what happened
to her mother, past her father's financial curse, heading for her
own future.[8]

Inspired and educated by Judy's experience, Meg began to understand a sexual relationship more as a valuable extracurricular
activity than a dangerous distraction—that is, as something that
might supplement her development rather than harm her academic work: increase her energy and make it easier to work.
Besides, she thought she should experience sex before she went
to college, she did have some spare time, and if she had a relationship too, she and Judy could talk on a more even footing.

All in all, Meg decided, it was time to get some experience.
She arranged her first date by getting an assignment to do an
article for the school paper about a boy she was attracted to. She
made a point of telling all her friends she would ask him out
after the interview. "That way I couldn't back out." After one
date, she felt uncomfortable and broke it off. She concluded,
however, that hers was a "good way" to get things started and
she prodded her friends to take similar initiatives.

The next year she decided on another try. Again, she told her
friends first. Again, she took the initiative, asking Hal, who had
written something promising in her yearbook, to *The Rocky Horror
Picture Show.* He had "good legs," she explained. Again, she
praised her own approach, describing it in the traditionally male
terms of taking a date out: The movie was "a good thing to take
a first date to? Because you find out what kind of person they
are by the way they react." She judged that "he reacted very
well." They saw each other for a while and began to talk about
sleeping together.

> I was always the one who said, "Well, we can sleep together. That's
> okay." And he was sort of, "We have to have true love."

He was like Doug in this respect. But like Judy, Meg kept her distance from love. Finally, Hal concluded that for him it *was* love. She didn't reply in kind.

> I didn't want to say I was in love with him, because I didn't know if I was. And so I said, "Well, gee, I really care for you a lot." And he was sort of disappointed.

The next day after a movie they went to his house "and everything sort of happened at once." They used condoms, and the sex was "okay." It didn't hurt, as she had expected, but it was "not like Hemingway, no fireworks." It wasn't like Judy Blume either. "I didn't go home and feel that I'd experienced something and been very changed and immediately write in my diary for a long time. It was sort of a letdown." "Chocolate cheesecake and artichokes" were better. Nevertheless, on balance, sex was "worth it," meaning, it appeared, worth the time. She boasted to her close friends about being the first to have sex, but she didn't want any students outside her circle to know. She had an image to think of.

> People that I don't know very well . . . I feel that they would look down on me if they knew that I'm not a virgin anymore. . . . I'm like the sort of very honor student and getting more awards than anyone. And I sort of like that image and want to keep it.

Since condoms, the only form of contraception they used, aren't perfectly reliable contraception, I asked what she would have done had she gotten pregnant. "Oh god, I would have died," she said first, but she followed up with a plan:

> I'd go out and get a pregnancy test as soon as possible and, if I was pregnant, have an abortion right away.

She was much too young, she thought, for motherhood.

Benefiting from Judy's experience, she never let herself depend on Hal or allow the relationship to narrow her extracurricular world. Rather, she kept up all her activities and friendships. Hal began to feel hurt that she didn't love him. She gradually "became more sensitive maybe." He was the one, then, teaching her to love. But unlike Judy, she didn't seem to be learning. Gradually, the sex got better. They developed a routine of starting with partial oral sex (no ejaculation) and then going on "to do other things." They had "a bunch of positions" he had learned from *The Joy of Sex.*

> I think the first time it was missionary. But now we've tried me on top, and I don't know. That is nice too.

She began to have orgasms during intercourse and after a weekend apart, observing that she missed him, she decided it was love. "It was like he was important," she said with surprise.

> He'd made a place in my life, you know. And so I decided, Well, this seems as much like love as I can imagine. So I said, "Okay, I've thought about it and I've decided I love you." And he was really happy.

He grew possessive. She found combining love and work "exhausting." As another fast-track student observed: "This courtship stuff, it's just like so time-consuming." (Imagine how little time popular girls had for school if fast-track girls had trouble juggling the responsibilities of *one* relationship.) He got angry she didn't have more time for him. She got angry at his nagging. Getting ready to go away on vacation with her family, she remarked that she assumed they could see other people but not sleep with them. He went crazy. Meg reconsidered.

> When I'm really upset, I write everything down. I just sit there and try to do my math homework and I can't, and I open my math notebook and find a clean page. I write everything I'm thinking and everything I'm feeling and what I think I could do and what I think I couldn't do and then I read it all over and see if I make sense. And so I did that and . . . basically I thought it was too awful for him to think that I wouldn't be faithful to him. Um, and I cared enough for him that I didn't want to hurt him. It was something like that. And so I thought, Well, I will make the promise and I will keep it and we will be happy. And it's true. I have and we are.

She agreed not to go out with anyone else, but advised him to keep their romance in perspective. They still had many years of education ahead. "We'll look back on this and say, 'Oh, what a lovely relationship it was,' " she prophesied.

Meg's success encouraged the other girls in the fast track. She drove them on, setting romantic targets: going to the prom; taking part in a necking party; having sex, which they coded as "buying a computer." But it wasn't so easy. Even Lynley, who had had plenty of boyfriends when she was a member of the popular clique, couldn't come up with one now. Frantic by the middle of senior year, they began casting their lines at random, prepared to do practically anything to gain sexual knowledge. Anything, that is, except masturbate. No girl in this group, sexually initiated or not, respected masturbation. In part, this simply reflected the continuing power of the taboo against masturbation. But also, it revealed the extent to which their interest in sex was an aspect of their interest in sociality. They had spent enough time alone with their fantasies. They wanted action.

Following Meg's advice, they threw themselves at the boys they knew. Often they were turned down or stood up, or a date would go unbelievably badly. Jane spent an evening in a coffee shop with a computer nerd who didn't talk at all.

He was taking a knife and *stabbing* all the creams.

Another got a boy as far as her bed:

We were lying on the bed kissing, completely dressed, and . . . all he did was lie there! On top of me! Like sort of a rock! And he— didn't—do—anything! For ten minutes! And I just thought, Hmmm, I know that there's supposed to be something different happening.

That spring the girls all dedicated themselves to sociability. Lou gave the first big event—the Waltzing Party. Every narrator told a version of this, the first really romantic event their group pulled off. Beforehand, they divvied up who would get which boy. When the boys arrived, the girls got them drunk and waltzing. There commenced a game of Musical Boys. Eliot wasn't interested in Lou, so she went after Lars, whom Jill had dibs on. Jill, meanwhile, turned her sights to Mark, who was technically Lynley's. Elise pursued Cal until Cal put his arm around Lynley. After the party, they all went walking, arms interlocked, harmonizing "Singing in the Rain."

The next party took place in the summer. It too began awkwardly, but as if the first experience of actually interacting in a romantic framework had reoriented them all in a more erotic direction, it was sexier. I heard about it first from Elise, who showed up late, hungover, and excited for an interview the next day. At last she had something to report:

> If you want me to start somewhere interesting, I could start with last night.

She went to the party expecting to connect with Cal. She knew he flirted with everyone, she says, and then adds, giggling, "Just girls, I guess."

> He's really physical. He's—he's like a playboy. And I could never imagine myself liking him.

To substantiate the claim, she went on, "In fact, I once told him I thought he was insincere, sort of jokingly. . . . And he told me, 'No, I'm not insincere. I really do like you.' " Another time he told her he was "really attracted" to her.

> And I said, "Really?"
>   And he said, "I don't know why, but I really like you."
>   And I said, "Well, I don't really believe you."

He told her he never lied.

> I got the feeling that maybe I was offending him . . . I'm so perceptive.

She was eager to pick up this conversation at the party. When Cal showed, she "didn't know what to do," so she left. A few minutes later she came back and talked with him. He said he had to leave soon. They went for a walk.

> He said he did sort of feel romantic about me, but . . . he didn't want to get into something with me because when he goes out with

somebody he wants it to be intense and very committed, and he wasn't ready for that right now. And all these great lines, you know. So basically, after all this nice stuff, basically he said he didn't want to go out with me.

No one else's luck was any better. As the evening wore on, all the girls got "depressed" and drunk together. Then everybody went to a lake. They opened a bottle of champagne. Elise:

> As soon as I drank that champagne, everything started spinning. . . . And then Lynley came and sat next to me and we had a little whispering talk and she said she didn't know what was going on with Mark because he was sort of ignoring her and I said, "Oh, don't worry about it."

Mark came over and the three passed the champagne back and forth.

> Lynley was lying on the other side of Mark and I sort of noticed that I was very close to Mark and I sort of noticed that I had put my arm back and he was lying on my arm and I realized that . . . that he was intentionally being near me and we just kept talking for a while and occasionally Lou would come over and hug me and we'd congratulate each other on getting so drunk.
>
> And then—let's see. This is the point where things get rather fuzzy. From the champagne. Okay. We sort of spread out and I seemed to be lying alone with Mark. And I was incredibly sleepy. And I think he was too. And I was sort of lying on top of him. Not on top of him but sort of on him, I guess. And we weren't doing anything at all because I was too tired and drunk to do anything. And so we were basically just sort of lying there . . . and we just got closer and closer and closer until we were hugging each other and it was really nice and it was cold anyway.
>
> And then all of a sudden Jane and Lynley and Lou were leaving . . . and I got up to talk to Lynley and . . . She's a really close friend of mine, so this was sort of bad . . . and I said, "Well, I'm not doing anything with Mark," and then I went into the thing about how I just wanted to snuggle up with somebody and I—really wouldn't do anything . . . And she said, "Well, he might take advantage of you." And I said, "No, he won't take advantage of me." And she said, "Well, okay, stay here but don't let him drive you home."
>
> And she told me that while we had all three of us been lying down

earlier, she had talked to Mark and she had told him how she had
liked him all year, and she didn't understand him and what was he
doing and he hadn't really said anything.

They chased Mark down to the lake to get his car keys, which
they gave to Elise, before they left.

And basically the rest of the evening we just did more of this hugging
business.

Eventually Mark sobered up, she gave him back his keys, and he
drove her home. Elise summarized:

So basically in the course of the evening, I had lost the chance of
going out with somebody I really wanted to go out with. I had somehow sort of stolen away a potential boyfriend of a really close friend
of mine. I had gotten massively drunk. (I even fell down the stairs
once.) And, um, I got home and I went to bed and I woke up this
morning and I felt really awful and my glasses were broken.

IN THE NEXT few weeks, the girls—now more educated about
sex and experienced in sociability—introduced themselves to
pleasure and to the masculine body:

Well, it was interesting to touch one. I've heard a lot about them.
. . . I guess it was the same as what I've heard but when you hear
about it, it's appealing to your sense of hearing. . . . This was definitely touch.
    Q: Well, what about—did he get an erection while you were touch-
ing him?
    A: Yeah.
    Q: What did that—how did that strike you?
    A: It was kind of interesting. It was soupy down there. Lots of soup.

Mary didn't realize, and wasn't particularly interested to learn,
that this meant he had come. It was not the mechanics but the
power dynamics of sex that interested her: "The idea that it's *me*
who does that to him." Other narrators acknowledged having
more than one lover, and they didn't think twice about taking a

cool comparative view. Beth, for example, said she was going to point to "this difference" between Bill and Jason.

> I'll be completely graphic here. Okay, letting him take off my bra . . . with Bill it was just natural. It was just like things would go that way. But with Jason it was more like the central parts of the body are the sexual parts of the body, instead of the whole body.

She had told Jason:

> I—I would—I liked it when he would, you know, stroke my body and kiss my neck and things like that. And, um, so he just started doing that and it was really nice.

Almost alone among narrators, the fast-track friends described making out as a sexual experience in its own right. They also made a point of revealing—again, as few girls do—that sex improved with experience. Partly they were claiming that sex was yet another lesson they had mastered, but they did not claim a mastery they had not yet earned. They did not report orgasms, for example, and they didn't hesitate to ask for pointers on how to achieve them.

The firmness of the resolve to have sex before college, in combination with inexperience, led to a number of pitfalls, with some girls ending up having sex without feeling any desire or affection at all for the boys they chose as sexual objects and others pursuing sexual intercourse aggressively with boys who had no desire for them. A year older than the others, Ellen had never enjoyed their strong sense of belonging to a group of peers with whom she could share her sexual and romantic longings and initiatives. Throughout junior and senior high school, she had felt completely isolated. Her deepest attachments in high school were to the hamsters, snakes, and fish she still reared in her room. She looked upon her mind as an obligation, as if it were a creature she had created, or a pet, or her own child: she had to keep taking care of it, feeding it, giving it the experiences it needed for development.

> It is my responsibility to see that I am educated in necessary ways.

It was an oddly long-range view for a teenager who was thinking of suicide at the time.

Between junior and senior year, she lost twenty-five pounds of "baby fat" and began to brush her hair a hundred times a day and practice the arts of blusher and eye shadow. That year her brilliant academic success made her an object of admiration among younger fast-track students. By the time they began to cultivate her friendship, Meg and Judy had already had sex and talked about it. This left Ellen, a year older after all, feeling behind. She didn't like the feeling and she didn't like the idea that she would arrive at college a virgin. Social life was hard enough for her without that handicap. Besides, she felt, she owed it to herself—to her mind—to have a sexual experience.[9] The sexual horizon looked bleak until a cousin came to visit:

> Not bad-looking, a kayak champion, you know. Anyway, he was very pushy. Oh, not *very* pushy. He was nice, but emphatic. So since for so very long I had been reading about sex in the most exalted terms and all. In novels. I mean, I didn't go out of my way to get dirty books. Like *The Sun Also Rises* is where I got the phrase "the sun stood still." Oh, not *The Sun Also Rises, For Whom the Bell Tolls.* Because Hemingway gives this description of his hero and his hero's girlfriend. It is so good that the sun stops for him three times. So I thought, um, humanity, I mean, how can I possibly understand mankind never having participated in this. And it is quite possible that I shall die a virgin, I thought. Really. So I felt—I mean, I seized the opportunity.

Her family had gone out for the night. She and her cousin went into her bedroom and began making out. He was twenty-five, she said. I probed for coercion:

> Q: You said at first he was pushy and then you said he was emphatic.
> A: No, not emphatic. I'm sorry. Okay . . . Well, he just slowly moved toward, you know, kissing and all that. We talked for a while. He didn't strike me as particularly intelligent or admirable but I had only known him for a morning. I had heard of him by reputation for a long time because he was a very, very good kayak champion, and I thought that having the opportunity, I really ought to, I mean, I might as well find out what it was like.

I continued to try to go beneath the surface of her explanation. Was she attracted to him?

> Not particularly. It was really more out of curiosity, which was probably unfair to him. He seemed to have a reasonably good time. Personally I felt it was very painful and unpleasant.

She assured me that they had not made the mistake of going too fast:

> We didn't rush at it, we led up to it.
> Q: How was the leading-up-to-it part? Was that equally unpleasant?
> A: It was all right. At points, I felt I enjoyed it. But, um, yes, I wasn't highly excited or anything.

He left on schedule a couple of days later. The day after she had her wisdom tooth pulled. For that reason alone, she said, she "didn't feel too good." She had found her first sexual experience "rather sordid," she confessed, but she nevertheless considered it to have been useful. She had fulfilled her "responsibility" to the self she was rearing, and she had learned something.

> I mean, that was my experiment. I had the results of it.

Her mother was probably right, she concluded. For sex to be worth the trouble, "probably you would have to love someone or like them quite a lot. . . . You should at least be physically attracted to them." Why was attraction so absent this time? On this point she shared the opinion of another honor student who dropped a boy she desired because he wasn't advanced-placement material: "He was really not a very together or intelligent person."

ELISE DIDN'T just want to get sex out of the way. Her mother's circle included a few women—two in particular—who loved to recall their thrilling sexual adventures in the 1960s and their recollections had made Elise eager to have her own passionate exploits. In addition, Elise found her few experiences of heavy petting extremely pleasurable and that too made her want to go all the way. But with whom? Mark had never looked her way again, and despite their interlude at the lake, he didn't really feature in her fantasies. Cal, on the other hand, did—in part, because he kept propositioning her. His propositions always had a joking quality, but Elise kept taking them literally. One time, for example, Cal said to Elise:

He said, "So, Elise, let's go off and have casual sex in the bushes."

She was bored and needed some "diversion," she claimed, belying the interest in him she had previously expressed, so she agreed. They went behind a building. She tried to start a conversation.

He didn't want to talk, though, and so we just started making out, and it was—it was really—nice. I mean, I felt really attracted to him.

After a while they went back to the group. Later, he propositioned her again.

He was sort of teasing me and so he was saying, "Well, I think we should get together and have sex." And I said, "Okay." And he said, "How about Saturday?" And I said, "Okay." So I was—ecstatic. I was so happy.

They started seeing each other. They talked a lot about sex, birth control, attitudes about sex, positions, "anything you can think of." Elise enjoyed this and liked being with him, but she began to sense "a veneer."

He was so into sex and talking about sex and being sexual all the time. It seemed unnatural to me.

Finally:

I—I was—I felt completely ready and I also just felt I wanted to do it. Now.

Elise had trouble catching her breath as she told the rest of this story. Saturday afternoon she went to a drugstore and bought a contraceptive sponge. That night she and Cal went out to eat and then back to her house.

We started as usual, and he seemed to me to be going quite slowly. You'll hear why in a little while. This is a bombshell. Anyway, he seemed to be doing all the sorts of things I told him I liked him to do, and I was sort of wondering why everything was going so slowly, but eventually we got there and we took off our clothes and—and, um, he actually started, and then he kind of stopped. . . . I thought that, you know, it was difficult because I was a virgin and I was small and it was going to be hard and—but he did seem to sort of be hesitating. And I said, "Well, let's turn over and I'll be on top and we'll see if it works." And, and, um, he seemed to be losing his erection, and finally he was just lying there and talking to me and he said, "Elise, I have something to tell you." And I said, "Yeah?" And he said, "I'm gay." So that was, that was, that explained everything, you know? And he—we just talked for a really long time and he told me everything and he told me how he thought it was going to work with me . . . that he just liked me so much and was so attracted to me that he thought it would work.

And he said that he truly—he never faked anything . . . and was really attracted to me all the time and really did physically have the inclination to have sex, but when it finally got to that point, he just didn't feel right doing it. And—uh—so—he—that explained— why—he had this sort of—what seemed to me—unnatural—way of behaving at school.

She appreciated what had happened as a sentimental education.

It was the most incredible night . . . I'd been going out with him for quite a while and I thought I knew him. . . . Yet there was that thing I couldn't get to. And all of a sudden it was sort of like a revelation. It was just like I saw this person—as he was.

It was the first time she felt she could love him, but, she said, "of course, at that very moment, I couldn't."

He felt he had let her down. "He kept saying that." As for her:

I was just in shock. . . . It completely—um—overturned all of my notions about everything.

It changed her understanding of homosexuality. During the contretemps about Julie and the Valentine candy, she had wanted the school counselor to help Julie come out so she would stop bothering girls who were not like her. Homosexuality was fine in its place. Healthy, that is, self-consciously gay people understood the boundaries.

I basically felt that you're either gay or you're straight.

As girls looking for true love are thrown off when they realize how hard it is to tell true love from false, Elise was disoriented by realizing she couldn't recognize—or even define—desire or homosexuality. She also felt used.

Why does he have the right to just go out free to see if he can try to get it together to be able to have sex with a girl. I mean, that should not be my purpose.

It didn't occur to her that she had looked on him instrumentally as well, but perhaps her motives had been more romantic and personal than she had indicated. In any case, she reinterpreted his motives:

But then I thought, No, no, that's completely wrong. He really cared about me as a person.

Elise saw sexual rejection as an extremely serious injury, but she had a bit of the popular girl in her and looked on the bright side: They hadn't had much in common anyway. Breaking a promise to Cal, she told her best friend everything; she "felt better" for a little while, but then came "another bombshell." Her best friend heard Cal giving another friend "all these intimate details" about his night with Elise.

But you know what he said? He said that we started to have sex, but we didn't because it hurt me because I was a virgin.

Tracy, of course, would have been proud to have a boy say that about her, but it was the worst thing Elise could imagine. She talked over what to do with her friends. Half of them thought, just forget it.

> Forget about trying to be friends with him. Forget about even telling him off for what he was doing. Obviously he was so screwed up if he would tell a lie like that, completely disregard my feelings, tell a complete lie to someone who wasn't even pressing him for information, just because his own ego was so weak and he has to keep— keep up his false macho image.

But the thought that they "would never speak to each other again" gave Elise a "terrible, empty feeling." She didn't think "anything should end like that." She told Cal:

> That it had humiliated me utterly—I mean to the soles of my feet. . . . I had no dignity left. . . . And he said, "Well, I'm sorry. I wish there was something I could do." And he kind of half lied to me and he said, "Well, you know, I had to. . . . They were asking me, so I had to tell them something."

Then on a field trip "all of a sudden we were coming on to each other again, and it was very strange."

Elise's account is the story of her own sentimental education and development. Sexual experience forced the fact of another's existence upon her, awakening her to the reality of others: percipient, powerful, changeable, and unpredictable. Difference and surprise proliferated even in the most seemingly homogeneous crowd—all middle class, all Ivy-bound. No matter how attentive you were or how hard you worked to learn, there was no way to know what another person was like from external signs like appearance or grades. This recognition cut deep into her sense of herself as distinctly separate from stigmatized teenagers like Julie. Before, she had mouthed tolerance but held herself rigidly apart from those who needed it. After, she knew they were in the world right next to her, they were kissing her. For all her studied normalcy, even she might turn out to be different. If she still hadn't bought a computer, she had tasted knowledge.

THE EMPHASIS that runs throughout these accounts on accumulating experience and learning from setbacks and victories places them in the tradition of the story of development or *Bildung*, a tradition that has sorely lacked female examples, and the accounts make the usefulness of this narrative stance apparent.[10] In a melodrama, to be a victim of love is to suffer endlessly. In a story of development, it's to learn a lesson and move on. This approach both acts as an extraordinary protection against pain and estrangement and turns everything that happens into grist for the mill of self-improvement. Even without this narrative protection, however, it's hard to imagine any of these narrators becoming victims of love. In fact, they hardly seemed vulnerable to love or passion at all, largely because, like runners at a starting gate, their eyes were on the race ahead and on their splendid futures.[11] Considering the danger of becoming totally obsessed with a high school romance, giving work and the future precedence over love and the present seems almost too sensible to fault. Still, the fast-track narrators' pragmatic willingness to seize any sexual opportunity, to put career and the self before anything, was sometimes unsettling. Often they barely recognized intimate obligations. Frequently they described themselves as so miserly with their affection that I wondered if they weren't as blinded by the discourse of self and success as other narrators were by the discourse of love. Had ambition become the "emblem of Eros" in their lives?

Psychologist Alice Miller has movingly depicted children who become so dependent upon adult approval that they use almost all their energy and intelligence to make themselves into representations of what adults seem to want them to be. In the process, Miller argues, they lose spontaneity and autonomy, a sense of connection with peers, and satisfaction in an accomplishment rather than in the praise it may garner. When the supply of approval diminishes, as sooner or later it must, these children are desolate, she says, because it's all they've lived for.[12] Perhaps this begins to explain the depression several of these narrators reported when they left behind the comparatively indulgent world of elementary and middle school and entered the highly competitive stratosphere of their high school. In elementary and junior high, there's a lot of room at the top, plenty of possibility for sudden improvement, and even shaky students often receive a lot of praise. In high school top tracks, praise is doled out much more abstemiously, top students are increasingly identified, and there's far less room at the pinnacle. There's only one valedictorian, only one editor of the paper. Meg and Ellen consistently topped their classes, for example, winning the lion's share of praise and prizes. The others made it clear that they couldn't imagine challenging such prominence. As early as sophomore year, they seemed to have come to terms with this, but that doesn't mean it was easy. Meg did not suffer any injuries to her pride in high school—quite the contrary—but she did foresee that college might bring a significant reassessment of her unquestioned supremacy. In addition, she, like the others, recognized psychological dangers in relying on academic success alone.

But there's also a simple explanation for the girls' depression. They wanted romance and it hadn't come their way. In any case, they stopped talking about depression when they started talking about reaching out for sexual and romantic experience. At first these experiments were carried on with marked detachment and seemed to have more to do with achievement than with feeling —with accumulating such key experiences as being attractive and attracted, trying sex, and using contraception. Love didn't spark much interest. If anything, these girls feared it as something that would take too much time away from work, their true passion. Gradually, however, their narratives took on a different focus— learning to love. Judy told of beginning to rely on Doug's support; Meg recognized that Hal had "made a place" in her life and decided she "loved" him; Elise got just a little crazy, albeit mistakenly, about Cal, and ultimately came to recognize him as a totally separate person rather than a manifestation of her fantasies. And, finally, Ellen decided love or at least strong liking might have a place in sex. But although they talked about beginning to love, they never considered slacking up on work. At most, they were prepared to make a small place for love—to begin to learn to balance feeling and ambition, love and work. The importance of learning to do this is one of the strongest arguments for beginning sexual and romantic experience in adolescence.

A major purpose of adolescence is to prepare for the juggling act of adulthood. That's why high school students are encouraged to take up a host of extracurricular activities in addition to challenging academic schedules. But one of the hardest aspects of being an adult is balancing personal and professional life: love and work in all of their myriad forms. The idea that this task should be postponed until adulthood is based on the idea that learning to be an adult is more consuming than being one. But, in fact, it's difficult enough for adults to balance one set of urgent professional demands against another, let alone suddenly to have to learn how to leave room for, or manage, love and passion. It's particularly difficult for girls, who must overcome the long female history of giving up work and passion once love and family come to the fore, to become adept at this task.

In addition to recognizing the importance of work, pleasure, and ultimately even love, these narrators had extraordinary clarity about separating sex and reproduction. Every one of them used contraception every time she had sex—condoms at the very least, which are fallible but do offer the best protection against sexually transmitted infections.[13] Besides, these girls didn't have to fear pregnancy as much as narrators who had doubts about whether they could go through with abortions. They all agreed that abortion was the only responsible recourse if pregnancy occurred. After all, they had certain obligations to fulfill: an obligation to complete their education, which they owed to the parents who had invested so much in them, and an obligation to fulfill their own potential, which they owed to themselves. Their enormous confidence in their abilities did not extend to the presumption that they could handle maternity and education. Just keeping up with each other was hard enough, and they weren't out of high school yet.

Ever competent, they backed up these ideas with know-how. They all knew where a clinic was and how they'd get the money if they felt too nervous about telling their parents. (Meg, after all, didn't even want her parents or anyone beyond her best friends to know she was sexually active.) Parental-consent laws were under discussion in their state, but if any teenage girls could stand before a judge and prove the competence to make an abortion decision, these were among them. Only Judy, haunted by her parents' lives, had any sense that an abortion decision might be rough but she had surrounded herself with friends who would make sure she didn't make the mistake she feared.

In their sexual and reproductive agency, their emphasis on professional opportunity and heterosexual equality, these narrators realized the mainstream feminist vision for female adolescence. But although they seem to fit the feminist model perfectly, they described themselves as postfeminist, and that term fits as well. They were just over a generation—a mother—away from the conditions that gave rise to second-wave feminism. Ellen's parents had to get married straight out of high school; Judy described herself as "a big mistake"; only about half of their mothers had made it through college, and all were mainly homebound during child rearing. This is important: On the one hand, these narrators learned from their mothers' experience to defend themselves resolutely against love and to extend adolescence long enough to ensure financial autonomy. On the other, their ability to do this made their ambition less rebellious than that of the previous generation. In achieving mastery and equality, second-wave feminists became women that no one wanted them to be. Even becoming a professional was a rebellion—a subversion of the constraints of gender. These girls, in contrast, did not associate professional aspiration or sexual initiative with any sort of rebellion. In aiming for successful careers, they were complying with parents' and teachers' express wishes. The new social ideal they were realizing was simply a by-product. Even their sexual assertiveness was compliant and ambitious. Through this conservative strategy—the belief that they would triumph by being good—they at once put themselves in line for power and reconstituted gender difference and hierarchy generally. Like the educated young women at the turn of the century described by literary critic Catherine Stimpson, they aimed "to project an ideal woman" who added "a disciplined and agile intelligence to . . . traditional functions." Way down the line—say, in their thirties—the "synthesis would be the all-round woman: a sturdy, healthy, interesting wife, mother, and worker."[14]

One obstacle they did not take into account in conceiving of this all-inclusive ideal was the persistence of gender inequities. We know, for example, that the right to confidential abortion, on which these girls would have to count throughout their aca-

demic preparation and professional careers, was severely cur-
tailed throughout the period. In addition, many of the most
promising female high school students of this cohort would not
attain the ambitions they set for themselves in high school.[15]

It's not hard to understand the problems fast-track high school
girls face in college. To begin with, the competition is often
much tougher, and of a different order, than that in high school.
Narrators of this chapter, for example, were well prepared for
college but other students may have been better prepared—or
more talented, for that matter. More significant, gender discrimination is clearly still in play in college and graduate school. It's
not as decisive as it once was, and many young women overcome
its traces. But it's there and its ability to retard female students'
progress has been well documented. Finally, sooner or later,
something stronger than the relatively dispassionate relationships
these narrators managed so adroitly was likely to move them.
Although they gained some practice in balancing sex, love, and
work, passion is a harder counterweight to handle, and they had
no experience at all with it.

Thinking that you're equal and coming up against discrimination, thinking that you have the right to separate sex and reproduction and having that right whittled away, expecting
success to be rewarded with romance and finding that female
desirability does not age as well as male: these are the kinds of
painful experiences that generated second-wave feminism. If by
some amazing chance these narrators escape them, they won't
need feminism. If they do, they know how to learn from experience.

THE FAST-TRACK friends could not even conceive of combining
maternity and education; the idea never occurred to the popular
narrators; and Tracy and Deana wanted romantic not maternal
love. But for many girls the most significant change that took
place in 1970s was the passage of Title IX of the 1972 Educational
Amendment Act, which enabled pregnant or married students
and mothers to remain in school.

4

Having My Baby

===============

From Sex to Motherhood

No human society has as yet developed a style of expectation that does not weigh heavily upon some members of the younger generation, hurrying them forward into a life for which they are unready or holding them back when they are ready to go forward. . . . The simplest device is to marry all girls off at puberty.

—Margaret Mead, 1959

If all teenage girls had had the fast-track friends' infinite uses for adolescence, and if the right to abortion had not been hobbled almost as soon as it was established, teenage pregnancy might nearly have disappeared in the 1980s. As it was, teenage girls took sufficiently swift advantage of contraception and abortion's new accessibility for birth rates to decrease to their lowest point since the 1940s despite the fact that coital and pregnancy rates rose. Nevertheless, as the fast-track friends compared the merits of Yale and Stanford, diaphragm and pill, about one in twenty teenage girls debated what to do when the baby came: stay with her family, move in with his family, or strike out on her own; stay in a regular high school, enroll in a special program for teen mothers, or drop out for a while and devote herself entirely to her child.[1]

Just over a decade earlier, it was unthinkable for a high school girl even to acknowledge being pregnant in high school. To do so would have at once made her a social anathema and forced her to leave school. It didn't matter if she were married or at the top of her class. It didn't matter if commencement was a month away. She wouldn't graduate.[2]

Instead of producing a society in which no girls went all the way until they were over twenty-one and married, the practice of expelling pregnant girls from school simply forced them underground, concealing and exacerbating the devastating choices they faced. Concluding that the best choice was secrecy, untold numbers of girls resorted to unlicensed abortion providers. Adoption offered a less dangerous, although also less secure, way to conceal a pregnancy, and this alternative was so popular in the 1950s that homes for unwed mothers proliferated. Few such homes, however, served girls of color, who usually had to turn to their families for help. Often an aunt or a mother agreed to raise a girl's baby as a cousin or sister but many girls of color found themselves with no choice other than to raise their babies on their own. Without a high school degree, this was extremely difficult, and not surprisingly, most pregnant girls who had and kept their babies opted to marry if they possibly could. As a result, the teenage marriage rate soared through the 1950s.[3]

This untenable situation finally began to change in 1972 with the passage of Title IX of the Educational Amendment Act, which forbade the expulsion of pregnant teenage girls and teenage mothers from federally funded schools. Six years later, Congress passed the Adolescent Health Services and Pregnancy Prevention Act, which further helped pregnant adolescents and adolescent parents become productive, independent citizens through a variety of services, including family planning and abortion counseling and referral.

Teenage mothers seized the new opportunity to combine education and maternity that Title IX provided. As their rate of high school completion tripled, their presence within the ranks of adolescence became steadily more visible in communities across the country, and teenage pregnancy went from being a terrible secret no one dared talk about in public to a frequent subject of girltalk, high school term papers, and political debate.[4] To many adults it was all proof that the country was suffering from a sudden and terrible breakdown in morality. Alarmist cries were largely in vain, however, because teenage pregnancy wasn't a new problem that could be quickly eliminated with a quick fix or two, let alone with rhetoric. It had a long and complex history, embedded in shifting patterns of gender, family, and work. Its emergence as a social problem in the 1970s was related to the larger sea changes in the lives of girls. When only bad girls were thought to have sex, it could be dismissed as a just punishment meted out by fate to a smattering of deviants and sinners. But as sex became more and more common among girls, pregnancy had to be reconceptualized as an ordinary risk all girls shared, something that could happen to almost any girl—even a white middle-class girl—and that just about everyone had a vested interest in thinking and talking about.

Lawful abortion, as established by the Supreme Court in *Roe* v. *Wade,* (1973), reduced the birth rate even as the risk of pregnancy rose. This significant accomplishment was not enough to safeguard the fragile right, however, and in 1977 freedom of choice was again impeded with passage of the Hyde Amendment, which restricted federal funding for abortion, putting the service beyond the reach of the very girls traditionally most likely to become mothers—poor girls. Since then states and localities have placed one restriction after another on teenage abortion. Thirty-six states had parental-consent or notification laws on the books by 1991, for example, despite clear evidence that girls confide in their parents about pregnancy unless doing so would put them in grave danger. Soon the only girls who really could get abortions were those who lived in the right cities and had plenty of money. Just getting judicial approval could involve an overnight trip and in many states it was a day's drive or more to reach a provider. (Not easy to explain when you're expected home for dinner.) Further, controversy and scarcity sent the cost of abortions skyrocketing: the cost of second-trimester abortions went up 25 percent in one state that put parental notification into effect, and a third-trimester abortion went for as much as $3,000.[5]

In addition, antiabortion forces worked tirelessly to influence the process of choice itself, bombarding girls with pleas to make the "right" choice—to redeem the sin of sex by unselfishly and responsibly giving up their freedom to nurture another. This message came from the pulpit and over TV as well as through a variety of local mediums, including organizations that represented themselves as neutral counselors but actually subjected callers and visitors to antiabortion scare propaganda such as *The*

Silent Scream, a film designed to generate empathy for the fetus. Antiabortion friends, family members, even distant acquaintances felt it was their moral duty to interfere in the lives of girls they suspected were pregnant by lecturing the suspects and their parents on the evils of abortion.[6]

In 1981 the U.S. Congress enacted the Adolescent Family Life Act, and thereby joined the chorus of voices encouraging teenage girls to become mothers. Commonly known as the Chastity Bill, AFLA funded abstinence education as well as prenatal and postnatal care but—unlike previous legislation—largely prohibited participating institutions from offering any family-planning counseling or services at all, let alone abortion referral.[7]

Anti-abortion rhetoric and regulations undermined girls' sense that they were important in themselves by stigmatizing and limiting their right to put their own futures first in deciding what to do about a pregnancy. But they also had another effect: They valorized maternity, communicating that far from being something to be ashamed of, maternity was heroic. A few remarkable teenage mothers felt empowered enough, as a consequence, to sue for the right to be cheerleaders and prom queens, and almost all became convinced that their situation was something to talk about publicly, as did the society at large.[8] But if, after decades of silence, all of a sudden the mainstream press could not get enough of the story of teenage maternity, something happened in the translation. At least, the tragic scenario repeated most often in the press—the story about children having children—was not the one I heard from teenage mothers. It's not that I didn't meet any girls who looked back longingly at the innocence of a childhood over at fourteen or fifteen. It's not that teenage mothers didn't narrate their lives as hard. But just as very few teenage mothers are elected prom queen (although I did meet one valedictorian), most are well into mid, even late adolescence by the time they become mothers, and they are more likely, I found, to talk in terms of transformation rather than tragedy—about "how I went from there"—a rough childhood or the downhill slide of puberty and the shock of pregnancy—to "here"—motherhood, the pleasures and rigors of adulthood, and in the wake of Title IX, continuing education. In between come dozens upon dozens of explanations for pregnancy and for rejecting the possibility of abortion and the great saga of labor and delivery.[9]

IT's COMMON to talk about teenage pregnancies as "unplanned" and, for a staggering array of reasons, they often are. Many teenage mothers tersely explained that sex "just happened."[10] Iris was visiting her father's family for the summer when she got pregnant. She hadn't been planning to have sex, hadn't ever even had a boyfriend, when she met a boy in the park. She seemed less to have made a choice than to have fallen into a trance but in any case they had sex:

> I tell you, I don't know why or how I did it. Maybe I just did it unconsciously.

Toby was at a party. She met a boy. They danced and talked for a while, then went into a room.

> I don't know what came over me that night. I really don't. I mean, I can't really answer it. But it happened.

Maybe it was desire, maybe it was fear. She couldn't say. When I asked about pleasure, she looked at me as if I were crazy.

Other teenage mothers couldn't imagine putting any distance at all between the capacity to bear a child and maternity. To them, pregnancy was simply an inevitable consequence of puberty. Asked how she felt about first menstruation, for example, Alice answered with a statement that assumed the fusion of biology and destiny: "In a way I regret it because now I have my son." Such narrators answered inquiries about contraception almost dreamily as if the very idea were a marvelous fantasy. From a childhood Christmas wish to the desire to avoid rape, they had almost never gotten what they wanted.[11]

Other girls had more trouble explaining themselves. Somehow they'd been too preoccupied to think of contraception, it seemed. Love was clearly one major preoccupation; the chaos and trauma of daily life another. Loretta had run away from an abusive father. She lived on the streets for a while, then met a boy whose family let her move in with him. They had sex "all the time," and she blamed her pregnancy on the frequency of their intercourse, still apparently vague on the basics. Then there was Violet.

Violet could have been any age when I met her. Twelve. Thirty. But she was nineteen. She had dark circles around deep-set beautiful eyes, which gave her a withdrawn but intent expression. Tired out, I thought. Wasn't well, I learned later. She had a quiet voice in which flat tones predominated. "Didn't bother me," she said repeatedly. And: "I didn't worry about it." She answered questions about chronology with weary precision. She "stuck to herself" from the time she was little, she said, especially after she was molested by a roomer. "It came kind of lonesome after a while," but she "got used to it," and she always had her family, unlike Loretta. Violet stopped going to school when she ran into trouble with a group of violent girls there. At home with nothing but time on her hands, she became sexually involved for the first time with a neighbor, Howard. After he was sentenced to prison, she went back to school briefly for her GED but she became involved with a boy she met in class and, well before the final exam, she was pregnant.

WHILE COERCION, ignorance, romantic confusion, and the sheer trauma and chaos of their circumstances caused many teenage mothers to become pregnant before they even thought of using contraception, most narrated at least some effort not to get pregnant and several told of having tried almost every contraceptive in the book—an improvised version of the rhythm method, an array of over-the-counter methods, and finally, the pill and the IUD. Between methods, some girls resolved on abstinence, but abstinence only works when you don't have sex, and while early sexual activity may be sporadic, almost all girls who've done it do it again sooner or later—sometimes when they don't expect to, don't even want to, don't have a thought of it, except to just say no, sometimes when they are really moved, if not swept away, by desire.[12] But although plenty of teenage girls had plenty of stories about why they didn't use contraception or their method failed, some teenage mothers gave a very different explanation for their state: they got pregnant on purpose—because they were in love or because they were in despair.[13] Ana and Carmella staked their young lives on the dream of combining first love, first sex, and first pregnancy. Chicana, from a poor southwestern family, Ana was tiny with long, slightly waved black hair perfectly parted in the middle. There was a porcelain density to her, and she was less shy than reserved. Ana had a vivid sense of community: she said "we" as often as "I," and she meant "we Chicanos," not "my family" or "my baby's father and I." The few times she did use the first person singular, she quickly cited community standards to support the opinions she expressed. Everything she thought now, she and her community had always thought.

Just as she saw her community's life as a continuous tradition of pride and honor, she narrated her own life as an unbroken thread. Everything she wanted now, she had always wanted. Generations of girls before her had dreamed her dreams of fusing sex, love, and pregnancy right after puberty, as she understood social history. The choice she made was ancient and traditional, not some new and aberrant phenomenon meriting social scrutiny. She saw adolescence as an intrusion into the normal life course, an artificial postponement of the womanhood—and marriage and motherhood—that puberty naturally brought. The phrase "children having children" made her very angry.

They're all, "This generation. Children raising children."

Not only was she confident that her youth didn't indicate a lack of maturity—she considered it an asset. After all, how could an old woman keep up with a young child as well as a young one could?

I'll say, "Well, you know, that's your opinion . . . but you never know, I might be a better mother than you.

Ana recalled playing "wedding" when she was a little girl, and she warmed to the memory as if the game had set the direction of the rest of her life. She stressed the continuity between the past and the present, including a contract between childhood and adulthood:

We always used to play a lot about how things would be when we were older. My mom's wedding dress, we used to always try it on and say we were going to get married in it. And I did get married in it. And my friend and I used to promise each other, "When you get married, I'll stand in your wedding, and when I get married, you'll do the same." And she did come down for my wedding.

She had never liked school or wanted a career, she said, although she was back in school when we talked. All she had wished for was marriage and maternity. Her husband was her "first," the only one she had ever had sex with. They started to go out when she was thirteen. Her parents let her get "promised" that same year but insisted she was too young to marry.

And then Greg would tell me, "Well, have my baby. Then they'll have to let us."

She didn't have intercourse for pleasure; she had it to get pregnant, so she could have a baby, so she could get married.

My daughter was wanted. You know, she was no mistake. She was wanted to be there, and she's here.

SLIGHT AND INTENSE, Carmella wore a flame-orange starched cotton dress with a thousand tiny starched pleats. Her blanched-almond face was perfectly smooth, but often her eyes radiated fury. Her story was very similar to Ana's, but she represented herself as a different kind of child: a good student and a "tomboy" whose father taught her to fight after an older sister was battered by her husband. Like Ana she stressed that her baby's father was her first lover, and she was similarly insistent that having babies young was a sensible choice. You had to be young enough to remember childhood and adolescence to be a good mother:

When the time comes, I'll know what drugs is to him, and I'll *know* what he's talking about . . . and when the time's come for him to go to party, I'll know where he's coming from and I'll know why he wants to go.

She met Johnnie at the mall.

> And I went home and he called me that night. . . . And we went out
> and we started talking, and we just really talked that whole night.

From then until he betrayed her, she was more taken up with
Johnnie's story, his life and problems, than with her own. His
mother, who had had the first of her ten children when she was
fourteen, was "a mom who was not a mom." Half the time he
slept "under the bridge," a hangout "where nobody goes, where
just us kids go." When he went home, "they didn't tell him
anything." Carmella could have him, in other words, for her
own.

That summer she used to wait until everyone in the house was
asleep and then creep downstairs and call Johnnie. "And we
would talk till like five in the morning." In the fall Carmella cut
classes to be with him. One Saturday she took her dad's truck—
"and I didn't know exactly how to drive"—and went to see Johnnie. Her parents found out:

> And they got very upset and everything, and we got into a big ar-
> gument and my mother told me, "If you want to go, just go. Just
> leave. Just go." And I said, "Okay. Fine." He had already asked me
> to live with him and I had told him, you know, "I can't. I'm still in
> school." And I called him back and I told him, "I'll be there in a
> minute," and I went in to my parents and I said, "I love you but I
> love him more." And they told me right before I left, "If you leave,
> it's like you don't have any more parents."

The couple still hadn't had sex and didn't, she said, until her
parents began to talk about forcing her to come back home.
Then she got pregnant to stop them. It worked.

Ana and Carmella, it seemed, had dreamed all their lives of
falling in love and becoming mothers. Many other teenage mothers, however, said they chose maternity because they couldn't see
anything else to do. The longer they had avoided pregnancy, the
better it had come to look in comparison with their present condition. Even girls in fairly stable and supportive homes experienced depression as adolescence went on and on and on.

I always felt so lonely. I used to try to kill myself from like age ten. Ten to about age fifteen. I'm surprised I'm not dead. Honestly. . . . I used to take Excedrins, Anacins, beers, alcohol—one hundred percent alcohol, the rubbing alcohol, that's what it was. Witch hazel. Witch hazel's nasty. Um, what else have I taken? That liquid, dishwashing liquid. . . . I have tried everything. Everything. It was like I just saw myself as having no reason to live. I thought my mother hated me, you know. It looked like I could never do my thing right. I thought I was a misfit. I didn't belong here.

And then as high school got harder, students at risk of being left back began to feel they'd never finish, while girls who did foresee graduating became conscious of how little good a high school diploma alone would do.[14] Many girls packing bags in the supermarket for minimum wage, they noticed, had diplomas and so what.

Discouraged teenagers often reported depending on partying to lift their spirits, but even the biggest partyers found an endless round of sex, drugs, and rock and roll depressing sooner or later.

I just felt so—not even a boyfriend can help me.

What's life about? What's it for? Many girls reported thinking along these lines around the same time that their boyfriends were beginning to say it was time for a baby. It would prove her love, he often said. It would prove his manhood, he may have thought.[15] In the turmoil, many, like Suzette, gave in.

Turner was just begging, begging, begging. "I want to have a baby, I want to have a baby, I want to have a baby. By you, by you." He begged and he begged and he begged and he begged. So the next time we had sex, I put my pills away. . . . And I mean, the feelings we were having, the emotions, the contacts and everything—I just looked at him, and I was feeling so high. I was so blind to reality and what the consequences may look like. . . . I was just so involved in this, this one relationship.

Samantha implied that she began to consider pregnancy when her boyfriend's father was "making it hard" for them to be together. She needed her boyfriend. Before she was with him she had been committing slow suicide. Since she'd been sleeping with him, she'd stopped drinking and smoking, and had even gone back to school. She had hope. She couldn't lose him. She just couldn't.

TEENAGE GIRLS who planned pregnancy rarely looked back when they found out they were pregnant. Their eyes stayed fixed on the future: on the day they, their true love, and their baby would all begin to live more or less happily ever after. Some, like Ana, quickly won their parents' permission to get married. Others had to or decided to wait for their lovers to prove themselves. A few teenage girls who didn't plan their pregnancies were similarly unwilling to treat pregnancy as merely a choice. Violet was appalled when her lover argued for an abortion, saying he wasn't "fit" to be a father. Word for word, she repeated to me what she replied to Franklin, as if when she spoke to him she had found a voice and a mission she would never give up:

> I said, "Well, nobody thought about that when we laid up here and when we had sex, right? You didn't think about it, and I didn't think about it. So don't come to me with your problems now."
> He said, "I can't take care of it. I don't have the money to."
> I said, "Franklin, nobody has the money to do anything. But we can at least try." Right? So I told him, "If you don't want the responsibilities of being a father, there's the door."

That was all there was to it, not just for Violet but for many teenage mothers. If it was going to be hard, wasn't life always hard? Where would they be if their mothers hadn't been willing to have it hard? Besides, pregnancy offered a future—something useful, something important to do—and although Violet was in a GED program when she got pregnant, she didn't have any plans beyond passing the GED test, and it wasn't clear she would. In this sense, as hard as it was going to be for Violet to make a life for herself and her child, her pregnancy was, as anthropologist Ruth Horowitz has suggested, "fortuitous." Brenda, in contrast, had a brilliant future ahead of her.[16]

As ambitious and brilliant as any of the fast-track girls, she no more expected to become a teenage mother than they expected to drop out of high school. Unlike them, she never longed for

sex or courtship, although she too loved "romantic books."
Where she lived, boys were forward, and despite all her studi-
ousness, she had to dodge rather than elicit sexual overtures.[17]
She remained more interested in reading, studying, and playing
football than in fooling around with boys until she met Raymond,
a basketball player three years her senior and "the last person
on earth" that she thought she "would ever be with." At first
their relationship increased her academic confidence and ambition, and it was after they became involved that she set her
mind on winning a scholarship to the best prep school in her
region. She wanted to prepare for Harvard Law.

Dreams like going to Harvard are almost a tradition among
young poor kids. The ideal of becoming "somebody" and enjoying "all of the material possessions" of a middle-class life,
Joyce Ladner observed in her 1960s study of ghetto preadolescents, is what almost all poor kids hope for, but while many
can "only verbalize" the ideal, as Ladner noticed, Brenda had a
real shot at it.[18] The best student in her class, she had "that
'grrrrr,' " she said about her relish for playing football, and she
clearly had it in relation to school as well. She'd wanted to be a
lawyer since she was a child:

> They say a lot of kids change their mind, from being a fireman to
> being a schoolteacher. But from as far back as I can remember, I've
> always wanted to be a lawyer.

Just as being top students was the real romance for the fast-
track circle, getting into prep school was Brenda's most romantic
story, the part of her life she loved to tell about. "So many kids
try to get into that school every year. So many kids are turned
down. For me to be accepted, that was a *big* thing for me."

> We had a large, pretty campus, open land, like just miles and miles
> around just open, pretty land. Lakes and rivers and—it was so pretty.
> Horseback riding. Everything.

Brenda didn't say she found the transition to a more rigorous
school hard going, nor did she express the pain and irritation at
white insensitivity that other African-American prep school students have reported. Everyone was "pretty friendly," she said,

but she never mentioned a single conversation with a new class-mate in prep school or a teacher who had befriended her.[19] Her close friends were still the kids from her neighborhood. As a result, she never got the fast-track take on sex and reproduction. All her ideas on the subject came from the girls she'd grown up with, many of whom were already mothers, although she saw her-self as so different from them that she didn't believe that what happened to them could happen to her.

Love was all she remembered having on her mind when she and Raymond started to have sex, but clearly she was thinking about her academic work as well since she did well in prep school. She was also absorbed in the process of adjustment and readjustment involved in going back and forth every day from one world to another. In any case, instead of constantly assessing how well she was balancing sex, love, and work (as Judy and Meg did), or looking out for pregnancy, she put sex completely out of her mind. The longer she had sex, the less thought she gave to the danger of pregnancy. If she hadn't gotten pregnant yet, surely she wouldn't. She wasn't the first girl to make that mistake.

Near the end of the second semester of sophomore year, Brenda fell seriously ill. At first she thought she "had the flu."

In a way, you know, I knew, I'm pregnant.

Her family rushed her to the hospital.

And sure enough . . . "You're pregnant."

She was as dazed by pregnancy as many girls are by sex, but while the last thing she ever thought she'd be was a pregnant teenager, she also thought of herself as the kind of girl who wouldn't have an abortion—the kind of girl who met challenges and respon-sibilities rather than ducked them. As to the right to happiness and self-development, assumptions that strengthened fast-track girls' ability to look out for their own interest, she'd framed her hopes in terms of her responsibilities to others rather than her own rights or happiness, and she couldn't help thinking now in terms of her responsibility to the next generation. Anyway she couldn't really convince herself that she was "too young" to be a mother, an unquestioned assumption among the fast-track girls. If her friends were old enough, so was she. Hadn't she always been more able than they? She was the one who could do anything, and although her mother urged her to have an abortion, she knew not only her mother but her large extended family would help her if she needed it. She decided she could have her baby, stay in prep school, and still make it to Harvard.

Neither Brenda nor Violet seemed to feel the need of counsel beyond their own steely resolve, but many teenage mothers narrated turning to their friends and family for advice about whether to have an abortion. What followed was something akin to the Pro and Con debates girls have about having sex, but while those debates mainly took place in the company of other girls and suitors, the question of whether to have a baby involved family above all. Often the first thing that happened was a family drama. Then shock set in and abated. Then the debates began. Many girls narrated having thought and thought and thought about abortion, changing their minds repeatedly as they asked themselves questions about the future. How lonely would they feel if they did not have the baby? How would they take care of another person when it was so hard just to take care of themselves? What would make them feel good about their lives? Would they get help? Could they get through school with a baby? A lot depended on whom they listened to and when. Family and lovers became more or less supportive. Girls were welcomed back to homes that had expelled them. They were thrown out. Friends who said the wrong thing were dropped. Fights erupted. Love swept in and out. Everyone thought and thought again. More and more time passed. What seemed most definitive in the end was, Would he or his family be there? Enough for her to finish or go back to school?

Like Brenda's mother, Victoria's wanted her to have an abortion, finish high school, and go on to college before she started a family. At first Victoria was inclined to follow her mother's advice, but then her boyfriend and her boyfriend's mother began to pressure her to have his baby.

He told me if I really cared anything about him or myself, I should have the baby, because if my mother had aborted me, I wouldn't be here. And then his mother showed me a film of an abortion. That turned me off. It was on the TV show that the 700 Club was showing. She had it on a videotape, and that turned me off. I couldn't do it.

Her mother had taught her not to make a decision until she was sure. Generally, it's good advice, but pregnancy has a deadline. Torn between her mother's desire that she postpone maternity until after college and the religious values of her boyfriend and his family, with her sympathies split as well, Victoria vacillated for over three months, almost as if she was waiting to see if her boyfriend would stick with her. When he remained stalwart and his mother promised to help financially, she began to feel better about her pregnancy.

> I was unhappy the first time that I found out, but when I saw that he was sticking with me and everything, I was okay.

After three months, she made up her mind.

> I *was* sure. I *was* sure.

She would have her baby and she would stay in school too.

Josetta stipulated that she would become a mother only if her own mother agreed to help. She and her lover had gotten engaged a year before she was pregnant.

> See, that's what makes me feel proud too.

Her lover acknowledged he couldn't support her yet, but he really wanted her to have the baby. Josetta was inclined to do what he wanted because she felt he had shown her that she could trust him.

> When you see a man cry, he really cares. Not some guy who's, you know, talking that man stuff.

Her mother begged her to have an abortion.

> She said, "You're not ready. You don't have no job. You're too young. Don't mess up your life like that." And I think she was right and everything but he wanted me to have the baby because he had a girlfriend before he met me, and she had got pregnant but she didn't have the baby. . . . He begged for me to have the baby. He even cried. He said, "Well, if you don't want to take care of the baby, I'll give the baby to my sister until I come from work." . . . So I told my mother, and she said, "Well, what's going to happen?"

He had a job at the time. She did not. He asked her mother to help them.

> He said, "All I ask is let us stay there for a year to get myself together and we can get an apartment."

When, finally, her mother agreed, Josetta agreed as well, but just in case he didn't turn out to be as good as his word, she signed up for a GED program at the same time.

Lorna had gotten pregnant while trying to become heterosexual, realized that she was pregnant as she was planning to move in with a teenage girl she had met in a youth shelter:

> I thought, Oh boy, I have to get an abortion now, now, now. I have to get it over with before she finds out. Everything's going to go wrong. For about two weeks, I was just basically at war with myself. And I told her. And I said, "Well, are you ready for me to have the baby?" She said, "Look, this is your decision."

Quarrels and infidelities followed, but ultimately Lorna's new lover, Allie, agreed to support Lorna and her baby. The first couple of months, they made out okay. Then Allie lost her job and Lorna had to turn to the mother who had driven her out of the house for being gay. Parents often shift to tolerance in the face of a pregnancy and welcome back an errant daughter, and Lorna's did.

> That Tuesday we ran out of money. . . . I said, "Look. I'm going to go home and ask my mother if you can come, if you can stay there," and she said, "Yeah. She can come and stay."

Deciding how to proceed was so difficult, confusing, and perilous for many of these girls that there were many moments when they could be forced or manipulated into carrying to term by lovers or parents with their own set of interests. Turner used the knowledge that Suzette's mother opposed abortion to force Suzette to have their baby. She had become pregnant in the first place because Turner begged her to, and she was one of the very few teenage mothers who said they planned their pregnancies who did consider abortion. She raised the subject in an attempt to get Turner to promise support.

> Okay, I went to him, I told him, right? And I asked him what was we going to do. So he said, "You better not kill that child," right? He said, "You kill that child and I'll kill you." I said, "What you talking about?" I said, "You going to help me take care of it?"

Instead of offering guarantees, he went to her mother. Suzette was trapped. With or without a baby, she needed either her mother or her boyfriend to survive. If she had an abortion, she'd lose both.

ONCE THE DIE was cast, all any of these narrators could do was watch and wait—for labor, for delivery, for the baby. Usually they didn't have to wait long. Because it typically took so many weeks to recognize pregnancy and decide on motherhood and because delivery was frequently premature, sometimes less than three months remained before the baby came. But a lot could happen in three months. Exactly what did happen depended mainly on what a lover did: take off, play cat and mouse, remain stalwart, or become abusive. For girls whose lovers refused to have anything to do with a pregnancy, the weeks passed slowly and sadly. When Violet saw Franklin walk out, she expected he would reflect on her forceful words and come back, but he did not.

> As time went on, I used to sit up and look at myself in the mirror and I would just cry because I would say that my baby had no father. It would be hard for me to find somebody to love me and my child. And my mother told me, "Don't ever think about that. Don't ever."

Her mother reminded her that she had raised *five* children on her own:

> "Plus other people's kids. Alone. If I can do that, you can raise your one." And my mother, I got to give it to her, she did a good job.

At least Violet had her family. "They were always there, right?" The family lucked into a decent apartment for once. "Five rooms." Her usually flat voice warmed, remembering the pleasure.

> We painted that up and fixed it up. . . . Put in new furniture and everything. Furniture for the baby.

Violet's lover didn't take responsibility, but he was honest and straightforward: He hadn't asked her to have his baby or promised support. But many girls said their lovers vowed they'd be there for them until it was too late for abortion, jerked them around for a while, and then vanished. That's when "the man" in a lover came out, one girl explained. Men had "to be away" to come to terms with fatherhood. "They have to think about things, you know. I don't know what they really be thinking." Sociologist Elijah Anderson suggests that young men see the project of manipulating girls to have their babies as a "game." This would explain why they lose interest after they've won, but other studies indicate that boys view becoming fathers much more seriously—as a way to establish masculinity. Not being able to support a child calls that masculinity into question, however, and perhaps the only way to maintain the feeling of pride that fatherhood engenders, given the extreme difficulty of earning a living, is to make themselves scarce.[20] Whatever the explanation, girl after girl reported that boys talked them into having sex and getting pregnant and then abandoned them.

When a boyfriend walked out on a girl who had happily planned her pregnancy with him or acceded to his pleas to have his baby, she was totally devastated. Belinda, for example, who planned to have her first baby on her lover's birthday, was in torment when we talked a few weeks before her delivery. Her family's car had broken down not long before we talked, and when she asked Chris if he would drive her to the hospital, he said he wasn't sure. Her eyes brimmed with tears at the memory.

> I always tell my mom . . . "What is it going to be like when I have the baby?"

And as resilient and hard-nosed as Brenda was, she wept when she recollected the way Raymond ran out on her after she learned she was having twins and the doctor put her on full bed rest. So much for prep school. There was no going back with twins and no help from her babies' father.[21] She had to withdraw. That must have been heartbreaking, I said. She made a sound like the air going out of a cushion.

Brenda turned away from Raymond forever. She would never give him another chance. Other girls couldn't bring themselves to give up on their baby's father while they were pregnant. Suzette was furious when a mid-pregnancy case of crabs proved that Turner had to be two-timing her.

> I thought I would die! . . . I told him off. He just, "Hey, how do you know it was me?"

But once she got treatment, she also got "softhearted."

> So I helped him get rid of it. Then it took me only one month and I was back having sex again. . . . He had apologized and everything, so then I put that all in the past.

She construed her forgiveness as a proof of true love: She had a permanent weak spot for him.

If boys often stayed with girls who were so all-forgiving and sometimes even married them, this was not necessarily a boon. Ana swore her young husband was perfect, but if so, he was an exception. Most boys who married or moved in with their babies' mothers continued to play a mean game, throwing girls into a state of turmoil that made it very difficult to stay calm and purposeful enough to keep on going to school as they had planned or using contraception consistently.[22] When Andrea's lover disappeared, she knew he went to another lover. Sometimes he took her engagement ring with him.

> He was from me to that girl, from me to that girl. . . . The part that hurt me worst was when he was passing that ring between the both of us.

Teresa had a boyfriend who stuck by her. At first being pregnant was a dream come true.

> I was real happy about being pregnant, but he wanted to do it every night and when you're pregnant, it doesn't feel so terrific. . . . To top it off, he was—I guess he got real scared, and he wanted to be out cruising and drinking and partying with his friends. I'd end up staying home by myself.

Then he was out of work and that made things a lot worse. It was hard to keep on being understanding.

> I started getting this hate toward him. I used to take everything he used to give me, you know. I used to wait up for him all night when I was pregnant. And whatever time he came home, I would feed him and we'd go to bed like it was nothin'. Finally, I got tired of that.

Sylvia had had it weeks before she gave birth. She put her foot down.

> I told him, If he didn't shape up himself by the time I give birth to the baby, he could forget about it after I give birth 'cause I don't want him back.

But despite Sylvia's and Teresa's tough words, and Brenda's defection, most of these narrators still kept on trying to work things out before they had their babies. If they could possibly achieve the dream of fusing sex, love, and reproduction, they would.

Meanwhile, they had their families, usually, and they had the fetus. While teenage mothers described the fathers of their babies mainly as trouble, they talked about the fetus as fun, often representing it as a companion, a playmate—a quixotic, humorous, beloved trickster with a mind of its own. Even Violet found her fetus fun and she talked about it with the only humor she displayed in her interview. This was something she could narrate without sadness, shame, or guilt:

> About three months, I was sitting up in a chair. . . . And something rolled across my stomach, right? We were watching TV. And I looked down, my mother looked at me, my brother turned around and looked. What was that? I said, "I don't know." We waited. Something rolled its way across my stomach, right? My mother looked at me. She said, "You don't know what that is?" I said, "I think it's the baby, right?" She came over and started pushing my stomach all kind

of ways, and the baby started squirming and rolling across my stomach. I said, "Lord." She had that baby going.

Occasionally, they even quoted the fetus:

> You'd look at my back and you'd see a little bulge back there. I'm saying, "Push it." "I can't see nothing." "You see that little knot back there? You see a knot?" And they'd say, "He's moving." "Would you please touch it?" So they'd touch it and he'd move right on back out of the way, saying, "Who's touching me?" Boy, he scared me.

They also attributed motives to the fetus and quoted others attributing them:

> They was saying that I was putting too much pressure on it . . . and he was putting stress back on me. They said, "This baby believes in payback. He doesn't like you." I'm like, "Where can I hide him?"

In part the humor was sparked by the happy expectation that soon they would really have someone. Not a lover, true, but in a way a baby was better. You could hold on to a baby for a long time. He or she would never replace you. A maternal bond was permanent. Andrea was pregnant when we talked:

> Someone else enters the world, you know—and knowing that it's going to be yours.

Doreen:

> I do have this dream. One day I'm going to get married, live in a big house with a big yard, and have a bunch of kids. So. I was glad about it. I loved the feeling of being pregnant and knowing he was there, you know.

They began to make plans for raising this child so that his or her future would be better than their own.

Lamaze training raised morale even though most girls delivered before completing the program. None narrated expecting any trouble with their babies. They assumed that delivery might be difficult but that their babies would be fine.

SOON ENOUGH the waiting was over. They were in labor. Suddenly, everyone—at least, everyone who was family—seemed to act in concert. Even the worst on-again, off-again boyfriends showed up for the big moment, although, by that point, girls, mad and bitter, didn't always welcome them. Mothers, brothers, sisters, neighbors, all pitched in—getting a bag packed, bringing a car around, rushing to the hospital. Margarita had her mother with her instead of her baby's father because she wanted someone to be "calm" with her. In the very few accounts that narrated going into labor with a boyfriend around, he was a joke.

> I was sleeping and my water broke. I said, "Now, Dave, you have to get up." He said, "No, leave me alone." I said, "Dave, my water broke." He fell apart. He didn't know where his pants were, he didn't know anything. . . . Now he's looking for his friend, right? To drive us to the hospital. I said, "Dave, go in my wallet." I had carfare in my wallet for the cab, but he didn't want to listen. So I just sat there peeing on myself.

When the baby came out, Antoine fainted.

> I said, "Get up, boy." And I was crying.

Victoria's boyfriend "couldn't take it" either.

> At first he said he wanted to be there. He's going to be there. He's going to be there. . . . He wanted me to hold his hand and all these stupid things. When he saw I was really going into labor, he said he couldn't see me through all that pain.

Mothers and other relatives played an extremely important role in labor and delivery. Violet's mother "went all the way . . . for five and a half hours." Brenda's boyfriend wanted to be in the delivery room, but he had done her wrong once too often and besides:

My aunt, she was just determined to get in there. She said she didn't care who didn't go in, she was going. My mom said there was no way she wasn't going, so . . .

Suzette and her mother went to "classes" and to the hospital together. Her boyfriend snuck in after them and caused an uproar.

He was like, "What is all this about? Cover yourself. Cover yourself." I was like, "Leave me alone, leave me alone." . . . And he couldn't understand it, right?

Even during labor, some boyfriends continued to play cat and mouse. Teresa, the teenage mother whose boyfriend stayed out till the early-morning hours and then blustered in demanding a meal, went into labor on a Saturday when she and her boyfriend were out driving. As they headed toward the hospital, they saw a friend who needed a ride back "home," a town about fifty miles away. Her boyfriend decided to take him first.

I was in labor, and I kept telling him to hurry, and him and his friend kept walking around his house, "Oh! look at my other car," and all this stuff. And I was over there in pain. . . . So finally he took me home. Then on the way home on the highway, there was a road-block . . . and I had to sit there. For hours. . . . Finally he took me home. Then he went and took the spark plugs out of our car. . . . He was checking them. . . . And he couldn't put them back in. And I was already ready to go to the hospital . . . and I was real uncomfortable and I felt like biting him.

Once she finally made it to the hospital, her husband told her "to hurry up 'cause he was sleepy."

An occasional good guy was reported. Antoinette's Luis, for example:

After I had her, he just stood there in shock, and I looked up at him and got my arm and pulled him down to me and hugged him. I was all, "Gosh." And then he looked at my mom and he says, "Can I go tell everybody?" . . . And his sister told me that when he went out it looked like he had tears in his eyes. . . . I remember that perfect.

But for all the talk about mothers and boyfriends, it was teenage mothers themselves who starred in this part of the story. Anthropologist Emily Martin has observed that women frequently talk about everything from menstruation through birth in the passive voice.[23] Accounts of labor and delivery by white teenagers replicated Martin's observation; those by teenagers of color reversed it. While white teens talked much more freely about abortion than African-American, Puerto Rican, or Chicana teens, they barely narrated labor and delivery. Ruth said so little about delivery that I presumed she had been asleep. She said no. She was awake.

> They weren't giving me nothing at first. I told the doctor, "You've got to give me something. I can't take this." So they gave me something, and I slept for a while, and then they woke me up and told me that the baby was coming and they could see the head and all and that I had to stay awake. So I did.

I waited for her to go on. Silence. Teenage mothers of color, in contrast, talked freely about the process and made themselves its subjects. Representing themselves as *having* babies, they expressed a sense of importance and efficacy. They were public, visible, centers of attention; individuals doing something well; efficient and successful laborers, deliverers, and negotiators of the medical system, bold, curious, observant, energetic, and active—beings they might have been all the time had life dealt them a more powerful hand. In the process, melodrama and tragedy gave way to comedy and adventure. Perhaps because they were at last confident of achievement, for once they represented life as under their control. They were having a baby; doubling; getting something without having to pay for it.

Some reported trying to delay delivery, but this experience couldn't be postponed.

> I was playing cards and my water broke. I didn't have any pain, so I thought I was peeing on myself. My mother said, "No, your water broke." And I said, "Git out of here. I'm not even going to have this baby tonight. I'm not in the mood." And it was like, "Get lost. Don't come now because I don't want to get dressed."

Finally, they called an ambulance. When it came:

> I said, "I'm too tired." 'Cause I had just taken a bath. And I was
> tired and I was watching television.

At the hospital:

> I was in labor for fourteen hours but it didn't hit me till the last two
> hours. I was in labor all night long and didn't even know it.

Labor and delivery often occurred faster than anyone expected. A girl who arrived at the hospital crowning felt jubilant
as if she had managed to outwit the world.

> I said, "He's here." They said, "No, he's not." I said, "Yes, he is."
> I said, "His head is already out." They stripped me and what did
> they see? A face looking at them.

Suzette had found sex an interesting learning experience, and
she responded to labor with the same interest and curiosity. She
saw it as a revelation about life.

> I was like, "Mm-hmm. So this is what it's all about."

Like many teenage mothers, she thought the job was to deliver
a baby as rapidly and efficiently as a human could.[24]

> Everybody was yelling, "Breathe! Don't push!"

Finally, she had "breathed" until she couldn't "breathe no
more."

> And I pushed and I pushed and I pushed and I started yelling, "I'm
> ready, I'm ready, I'm ready." Nobody believed me, right? I'm in the
> hallway and my baby is coming out. They went to strap one leg and
> she just, wheeew, came right out! I didn't even split myself until
> afterwards when they went to take out the afterbirth. I said, "What
> you all doing?" He said, "We're stitching you up." "Stitching me
> up? What happened?" It took them so long and it was so frustrating.
> They were digging in, and I was like, "Come on. I just had a baby.
> I'm tired."

Many reported fascination with the experience of delivery, which frequently received a much better report than first coitus:

I wasn't really that scared. . . . It was neat.

But not for everyone, of course.

When I got to the hospital I was like in labor, but I was only open, I'd say, about two centimeters. They told me just to walk around the hospital for a couple hours. . . . So we walked for two hours, and, you know, we came back and they checked me again. I opened about two more centimeters, or three more centimeters. . . .

They said, "Well, you can walk a little more. Something will happen soon probably." And I walked for another two hours. My water didn't break. It just leaked and I was beginning to get wet and I didn't feel comfortable walking around the hospital. So I sat down and, you know, as my contraction came, I'm sitting there telling my mother, "Another one," you know. And people are looking at me like, "Oh, look, she's having a baby." And now it's beginning to get painful, right? It's close to I'd say about three o'clock now, and I'm like, "Oh boy, Ma, I'm getting all wet." And I'm sitting here. And she's like, "Well, maybe you should go in and get it checked again." You know, so I go back in and I'm about seven centimeters now and he says, "Okay, you can put her up on the, you know, examining table." So I get up, and now the pains are coming on strong, and I'm like, "Oh, Mommy, you know, this is killing me," and my mother is rubbing me on my back and she's like, "No, it's not killing you. It's not killing you. You'll be all right."

As soon as the nurse put me up on the table and told me to lay back, one contraction came so strong, I just wanted to jump up and sit up and curl over and hold my stomach. And I just had to lay there and take it. Then the nurse came and wanted to put the IV in my arm. I'm really shaking now, and I'm trying to hold on to the bar of the bed, and she's trying to put the IV in and I'm telling her, "Could you wait a minute until this contraction's passed?" because the labor pain was making me really shaky, and she was still trying to put it in. She missed the vein. Had to do it again.

And I'm getting upset now. I'm not thinking about the pain because they're like sticking me with needles. And then the doctor comes in, like the assistant or whatever, and he's like, "Take some deep breaths . . . This will help the pain." So I started doing it and it *was* helping. But as soon as he walked out of the room, one hit me, and I called him and he ran back and I was like twenty centimeters open and he was like, "Come on, let's get in there." And pretty soon her head was coming out. And he was like, "I can see the hair! I can see the hair!" So they run me into the delivery room . . . and the nurse looked at me and said, "Don't push." And I almost had a fit. . . . And I was—I just looked at her like in a trance. Okay, I'm not going to push. I guess that must be something really important. Don't push. So I didn't push.

And she's looking at me like, "Oh, you're a good mother. You're a good one." You know, because most girls if they feel like a push, they're going to push, you know. And I'm trying not to push. But I feel, you know, like I just want to push. But then she just looked at me and she said, "Okay, you can push now." And I pushed and I looked up in the mirror and I watched my baby come out. And then the doctor pushed my stomach and I watched the afterbirth come out.

She was all scaly-looking, you know, and I was just looking at her. And then I thought about what my mother said. My mother said, "When she comes out, count her fingers and count her toes." And I just looked at her hands and looked at her feet.

The baby had emerged. It was a new day. Or was it?

FOR A FEW, at least for a while, against so many odds, the dream of founding a new and better family actually came true. Vicki, an engaging, outgoing Puerto Rican teenager, told the story of meeting and marrying Sammy, who was to become her baby's father, and she told it with gusto, relish, and realism. This was a good time. This counted. This wasn't a fantasy. This was her life! The first time she and Sammy tried to have sex, she had changed her mind as he started to penetrate and decided she didn't want to do it after all. He said, "Okay, forget about it," and then asked her to marry him. Since that day it had been "pleasure all the way." Sammy had to be in school during her delivery, but he'd been there for her and the baby ever since, not only making her happy but enabling her to continue with school. Both he and his family had become very involved in the baby's care:

He's only five months but . . . he wants to teach him right. He wants him to be very healthy, athletic. He wants him to be everything. So we're taking it step by step. When I come home, I talk to him. See

what he wants. Play with him. I teach him how to walk. I teach him
—I give him the newspaper. He tears it up when he reads it. I give
him books. I give him the *TV Guide* so he can enjoy the pictures. But
in the meantime, I talk to him so he knows what things are around
him. He looks around to see what's new. And I show him the refrigerator when I take him to the kitchen. I show him his uncle, his
grandmother. His father. He—he enjoys everybody. I enjoy having
him. That's the best thing that happened to me so far in my whole
life. He's everything. You know what I mean.

Lourdes took a quiet pride in her good fortune. She had been
a problem student ever since she was named Queen of the May
in eighth grade, she said. From then until she met her babies'
father, she was fighting and cutting school all the time. Her own
father's heart about broke when he found out she was pregnant,
and she had a second baby soon after her first. She didn't think
she'd ever finish school, and she was right to be pessimistic. A
second baby usually spells the end of education for a teenage
mother. But after the birth of her first she went back to school
and she kept on going through her second pregnancy and
birth.[25] When we met she was valedictorian.

Lorna and Josetta stayed with their mothers after they gave
birth. At the end of a year, as promised, Josetta's baby's father
came up with an apartment he, Josetta, and the baby could move
to. Lorna, her lover, her baby, and her mother were still living
amicably together when we talked. Her mother was no longer
touchy, let alone violent about Lorna's lesbianism, partly, perhaps, because Allie turned out to be so helpful. A union brick-
layer, she made good wages, for one thing, and she consistently
handed over her paychecks to her family while Lorna finished
school.

As encouraging as these few happy endings are, they aren't the
norm. Rather, their narrators represent a very small percentage
of the girls who set out to realize the dream of fusing true love,
first sex, marriage, and motherhood. Many, many of the boys
who talked girls into having their babies dumped, betrayed, or
beat them up long before their babies were born. In addition,
there's reason to believe that some of the optimism of these teenage mothers might be short-lived. Although teenage mothers'
high school completion rates increased substantially throughout

the 1980s, many, especially those who married, found they soon had to leave school again to give birth a second or third time. Finally, teenage marriage is at least as likely to end in abuse and abandonment as in happiness.[26] Nanci's boyfriend José stuck by her and his family let the couple move in, but her sisters-in-law soon treated her like a servant. She couldn't go home; her own family had been abusive even before she got pregnant. They had to find somewhere else to live and they did—a shack that the owner offered rent-free in exchange for fixing it up. Nanci was eloquent about making a home, but once she and her husband were on their own, he picked up where his sisters left off:

He was fighting and pushing me all over the place.

Carmella's Johnnie stuck with her through the anxious weeks after her premature delivery until their baby was ready, finally, to go home. Then he split, and her subsequent account detailed her efforts to get him back, which she felt compelled to do because for her, as for many teenage mothers, puberty, gender, sex, first love, and reproduction belonged together.

Although a few teenage mothers, Carmella included, continued to try to live the dream of maternity and marriage no matter what, most others finally gave up on their babies' fathers once they had their babies to stake their lives on. Some said they gave up not just on their babies' fathers but on love. They'd never fall in love again, they said. They'd experienced too much male callousness to find the idea of romance credible, let alone attractive. Anyway, for now, they were too busy with school, work, and motherhood. They told a good girl's story of quiet independent responsibility. Their "days," as one mother of a teenage mother put it, "were over."

But most girls weren't ready to give up on sex and love totally at so young an age. Many started looking for love a few weeks after delivery. Occasionally "someone else" turned up right away, a new and better man who was everything the baby's father was not: kind, faithful, supportive. Before, they were too wild to exercise good judgment when it came to partners, these narrators explained. Now they knew better—a relationship wasn't about love or lust; it was about reliability and concern. It almost seemed like a plan: one wild romance, one settled relationship.[27]

Others gave up on love but not on sex and fun. They *were* good mothers, those who went this route said, and they would always provide for their babies, but that was it for them with goodness. With slow glimmering smiles and sharp laughs, they bragged that they were difficult to pin down—moody and slick—and proudly described being beyond romance and the reach of fatal attractions.[28] As one said:

> If love is that blind, then I don't ever want to fall in love.

They had given up on romantic expectations altogether. As a matter of principle and practicality, they acted as if they couldn't care less. Belle wouldn't lift a finger to keep a lover enthralled:

> My mother said, "What do you do to them?"
>   I said, "Nothing."

That was her secret. She never practiced the passive arts of attraction or made affirmations of love.

> He says, "You're no fun. You're not romantic."

That's right, she said. She wasn't. She was "cold." When these narrators said they could "take or leave sex" or "romance doesn't faze me," they were saying they'd learned to be impervious to emotional and erotic blackmail. They knew how to see sex and boys for what they were, and to bother with them only so long as it was pleasurable. "Sex is fun to me," one observed. They were "slick"—fast, smooth, hard to hold on to, quick to wriggle out of trouble. Above all, they were strong. When they talked about abuse, they focused on their courage and imperviousness.

> And, you know, I don't care who I get, they can't hurt me.

And:

> So he's like, Mmm. Nothing I do to this girl hurts her. I got to find me a higher step for her. You know, because, I mean, things he be thinking be hurting me, they don't hurt me.

Belle described a fight with her lover so brutal that the police had to break it up. Yet as she told it, she emerged unscathed. "He had scratches! He had a black eye!" Nothing could hurt her. Not romantic disappointment. Not assault. She had been through it all and where was she now? Back at home, back at school, back at work—living to tell the tale.

VERY, VERY FEW teenage mothers told stories as triumphant and hyperbolic as Belle's, but even the most clearly victimized or fatalistic shared her indomitable will to rise above poverty and despair. If all they had to work with was disappointment, deprivation, and the body, so be it: Out of these materials they would create lives of commitment, meaning, love, and even, for the very strong, pleasure. No matter what, they would turn setbacks into promising futures by absolutely refusing tragedy. Their particular insistence upon making the best of a bad situation in part explains how they *all*, even Brenda, came to say if they had it to do over again, they would.

For their children, however, they wanted very different lives. Having thrown their pitons into the next generation, they all had advice at the ready to keep their daughters from making the choices they had.

Take pills and think about the future.

Take the precautions, because you can't count on anybody else but yourself.

Don't be in such a rush to grow up, because it's not all you expect it to be and I have known that from experience.

Only thing I have to say is get your education before you have a baby. That's the best thing for you.

Stay in school no matter how hard it is, no matter how boring it is, no matter how fine your boyfriend is and he's telling you to cut class, stay in school. That's the best thing. You will never regret staying in school. You will only regret dropping out. And get birth control before you start because having a baby just adds to your problems.

If they really had it to do over again, these passages suggest, perhaps they *would* choose differently. Certainly they intended their daughters to do so. In the end, this would be the hardest of all the challenges these girls faced: parenting their babies so they could have a better chance than their young parents had. Their success will depend both on them and on social policy. On the whole, teenage girls are much better mothers and much more self-sufficient than they are reputed to be. Few spend their lives on welfare, as many ideologues contemptuously accuse. On the contrary, under the most difficult circumstances, most combine maternity, work, and, education. Historically, a very damaging outcome of early parenthood, however, is that the children of young parents do much less well in school than those of older parents whose lives are the same in every other respect.[29]

There's a chance that these teenage mothers will better prepare their children for school than previous generations because of the preparation they've had. Not only did they take advantage of the chance Title IX and other programs offered to continue school, but many also attended supplementary educational programs focused on improving parenting skills. Moreover, it's reasonable to guess that for all their disappointments, these girls felt better about being mothers than their own mothers, who, after all, had rarely had any choice at all about whether they would expend their youth on diapers, colic, and nursery rhymes. In addition, if they didn't believe in separating sex and reproduction for themselves, they clearly believed in it for their daughters. Of course, many of the mothers of these very narrators urged their daughters to have abortions. But they hadn't laid any groundwork for this advice, and decisions about sex and reproduction are highly influenced by early childhood socialization— all those games of wedding, marriage, and Run Catch Kiss, those assumptions about the relationship between puberty and destiny. If, from earliest childhood, the children of these young mothers are raised with assumptions about sex and reproduction approaching those of, say, the fast-track narrators, they will be far less likely to vacillate when faced with an abortion decision. Finally, the eagerness on the part of these young mothers to finish school and go to work—the expectation that they will work— suggests that they may well manage to be more self-sufficient than their own mothers—if they have the chance. This is critical, because the evidence suggests that their children's success will depend very greatly upon their own.[30]

It's not clear, however, that these mothers were being as well prepared as they deserved to be. The GEDs so many pursued are both less widely accepted and harder to get than regular diplomas. And although some of the schools set up specifically for teenage mothers that I observed were extraordinarily well-funded demonstration projects, most programs were both separate and unequal—located in a few dingy rooms at the back of a school building or miles away from the regular school. True, even the worst of these programs seemed lifelines for teenage mothers too frightened of humiliation to attend a regular school, and there's actually considerable evidence that intimate low-key settings increase the likelihood of consistent attendance. But attendance is only half the battle. Teaching is the other half, and those who attend schools with language, science, and computer labs, large libraries, and more than one teacher have a clear advantage. Of course, many programs for teenage mothers have very limited practical objectives: to teach teenage mothers to be electricians, carpenters, or data processors, for example. Some such programs are brilliantly conceived; others, however, are neither effective nor strategic, and their students' hopes are all too frequently dashed when they enter the job market.[31]

Even the prospects of the best-situated students depend upon the economy itself as well as upon social support. Without Aid to Dependent Children, these mothers won't be able to keep their families together during the periods that will surely come when they simply can't work: when there are no jobs, when they're sick or a child is sick. Yet we know that young children need to stay with their parents to thrive. In addition, teenage mothers do much better when they have only one child in adolescence. Without abortion as a backup, this will be almost impossible to manage. Moreover, if their daughters are not to become teenage mothers, they, too, must have access to abortion, which, more than anything else, reduced the teenage birth rate during the period of this study. Many girls and women become convinced it's futile to even try to get an abortion the moment a state begins to debate limits on the right, and teenagers who live in states where abortions are still relatively easy to obtain are twice as likely to have them as those who live in highly restrictive states. Nevertheless, restrictions are proliferating, with the result that in 1992 the abortion ratio fell to its lowest level since 1977.[32] Unless this changes, demographers may finally see the population explosion so often raised in the 1970s come to pass. Certainly, it's no way to enable teenage mothers to raise children who will not become teenage parents themselves.

To realize that goal, mothers and children alike must have relevant, invigorating educations and meaningful, well-paying vocational opportunities as well as continuous, free, unimpeded access to contraception and abortion and support during the times when they cannot support themselves. Opportunities alone won't be enough, however. Most important, the daughters of these narrators must hear—from their families and the culture at large—that it's fine to put their own goals and even their pleasures before reproduction, for only when most girls believe that they have a right to, and an ability to achieve, forms of happiness that do not depend upon the fusion of sex and reproduction will teenage maternity become as rare as conservatives so often mawkishly pretend it was in that great fabled past when nice girls supposedly didn't go all the way until they were grown and married.

5

Years of Hell and Freedom

Sex, Anger, and Remedial Socialization

Where is the female *Catcher in the Rye?*

—Patricia Spacks, *The Female Imagination*

She's a pretty good student, maybe a very good one. Around second semester freshman or first semester sophomore year, she gets cynical or depressed or just plain bored. Maybe she's been abused, maybe she's lonely. Maybe she's confused by new desires or just doesn't feel good about herself. Maybe the human condition's on her mind—mortality, injustice, the general lack of social responsibility. Could be a lot of things; probably a combination. But she falls in with a group of kids whose relationship to school is ironic or marginal and the next thing anyone knows she's going with a guy who's sliding off the track, or she's sleeping around, drinking, doing drugs, cutting classes, staying away from home for days, even weeks at a time.

Parents fear behavior like this as they fear almost nothing else. Even pregnancy almost pales in comparison: One way or another, it's dealt with and life goes back to something like normal. But this? There's no reaching her—she's the one fucking up, yet she's so damned righteous. Still, you can't give up on a kid, after all. She could ruin her mind forever with designer drugs, and the clock is ticking; records are piling up for college. She doesn't care, she says, looking down on her counselor, dad, mom, insinuating that aiming for a good college or job is as venal as marrying for money. She always did well enough in school before. Her teachers say she has the ability. They suggest an appointment with a shrink or a family therapist.

THIS STORY has become so familiar that it's almost archetypal—a part of the lore of teenage life. During the 1950s and '60s, panic flared with each new manifestation of teenage outsiderhood—from the delinquents of the mid-1950s to the beats and bohemians of the late '50s and early '60s through the hippies of the late 1960s and early '70s—and each new panic generated a spate of theory. Very little of this theory had anything to do with girls. As British feminist Barbara Hudson has noted, adolescence has been primarily "a 'masculine' construct."[1]

In the early 1960s, sociologist Arthur Stinchcombe did tabulate the conditions of rebellion and alienation for both girls and boys. His working hypothesis was that rebellion was an active expression of alienation caused by students' recognition that nothing they did in school would improve their future. This hypothesis panned out with regard to boys, but while alienation was common among girls, rebellion was almost nonexistent. In the end, Stinchcombe described and explained two kinds of alienated high school girls. The first didn't take classes seriously but they did pour energy into other high school activities. They had simply realized, he concluded, that the "good jobs allocated by the school" were "not for them" and set their sights on a vocational option that didn't depend upon academic success—becoming a housewife and mother. This move, in Stinchcombe's view, protected self-esteem and avoided total alienation. The second group suffered a double alienation—from academic work and from organized high school sociality. But although they were almost totally cut off from high school life, they didn't act out their alienation. They weren't rebellious. They didn't even play hooky, or not so you'd notice. They just walked through high school life like the living dead. Stinchcombe explained their confounding passivity in terms of a lack of expectation. Neither education nor social life held any promise for them, he hypothesized, because they didn't expect to have careers *or* get married. With nothing to look forward to, they were too depressed to rebel.[2]

Stinchcombe's theory-making is almost feminist in its insistence on including girls as the subject of analysis and its recognition of girls' vocational stalemate. But he could neither locate all the girls who embodied his subject nor fully understand those he did locate, because his emphasis on the future and education blinded him to critical adolescent disparities and realities. First, most girls were too well socialized by what Joanna Russ once called "the vanity training, the obedience training, the self-effacement training, the passivity training, the rivalry training, the stupidity training, the placation training" to rebel.[3] In addition, rebellion cost girls of the '50s and '60s much more than it cost boys. Not only was one mistake enough to redefine a nice girl as a slut but minor transgressions like staying out late at night were sufficient to label her as "incorrigible," a designation that could have very serious legal consequences. (Boys were judged incorrigible too, but usually for much more serious infractions, say, robbery and assault.)

Some girls responded with camouflage. By day, when adults were watching, they were zombies; by night, when they could elude their keepers, they came alive in the backseats of Chevys, down by the lake where girls fought each other with knives, out by the highway where the rebellious boys they desired played chicken. Others walked a very careful, precarious line between good-girlship and incorrigibility. A few threw caution to the winds, but they could rarely be found in high school, at least not for long, since they were soon restricted to the local home for wayward girls, where some girls spent all their teenage years because the behaviors summed up by the term "incorrigibility" were status offenses—that is, acts adults could perform with impunity but adolescents and children could not, meaning a girl could be sentenced to an institution for such an offense for as long as the status itself lasted.[4] Had he only looked there, Stinchcombe would have found plenty of rebellious girls—prostitutes, gang girls, shoplifters, truants, vagabonds, girls who had been reported to have had sex or an abortion or a baby or stayed out at night or run away for a few days or just talked back a lot . . .

When Gisela Konopka studied institutionalized girls in the '50s and '60s, she concluded that loneliness per se rather than concern about their marital prospects was primarily what caused girls to get into trouble. (Of course, lonely girls may not have had such great marriage prospects.) Both boys and girls suffered from loneliness, Konopka observed in her extraordinarily moving book *The Adolescent Girl in Conflict,* but loneliness wasn't "the central core" of boys' problems, because they didn't share girls' need for interdependence. If girls didn't have family and friends they could really depend on and be dependable for, Konopka thought, they would risk almost anything for a boy who gave any indication he would perform that role.[5] As the 1960s turned into the '70s, the U.S. Supreme Court determined that treating girls differently from boys in juvenile proceedings was unconstitutional, in effect leaving girls free to be as incorrigible as boys. At the same time, the ranks of alienated and rebellious adolescents were beginning to grow. A large number of students, many of whom had excellent academic records, were becoming disenchanted not so much with their professional futures as with the rules of the society they were scheduled to join. Specifically, they weren't interested in confining desire to marriage or going to a war they didn't believe in.[6] They resisted on both fronts and, in the course of their resistance, created new social forms and identities—becoming radicals, freaks, and hippies for whom hallucinogens and unconstrained sexuality were part of a general rejection of "appropriate" behavior. When they went truant, they hitchhiked to Chicago for the Democratic convention or stormed the Pentagon. When they felt desire, they had sex. And when their reproductive and sexual freedoms were challenged, they created whole movements to safeguard them.[7]

By the late 1970s, sex had become so acceptable that it barely constituted rebellion at all, and radical grass-roots activists were largely dispersed from the scene. In their place were second-generation freaks, punks, and Deadheads whose contrarian stances seemed motivated by reasons far more personal than political. In effect, alienation seemed to have gone passive. Now downers and self-consciousness were the diversions that absorbed suburban youth. Considering the shift in values and chemicals, sociologist Ralph Larkin observed that students no longer considered their teachers, ministers, or parents credible at all. The self was the one thing they could "believe in." School offered almost nothing. They found meaning only in "a radically present-oriented subjectivism" that played itself out in "partying, drinking, and smoking pot."[8]

Analyzing teenage subculture in a suburb plagued with adolescent suicides in the mid-1980s, Donna Gaines came down as hard as Larkin did on school and agreed that the idealism of '60s radicals had burned out of the subcults that inherited their images and attitudes. In place of political engagement, being wasted was the "nuclear core of teenage America. . . . Wired in the free world, wasted, rusting, going nowhere in overdrive." But where Larkin located the self as the core of the freak belief system, Gaines gave pride of place to music and the party. Kids understand "the right to party," she says, "as their right to create, express, and commune." Of course, the party also took teen minds off now dim employment prospects, humiliating school experiences, and depressing home lives.[9]

Girls don't get much more airtime in these studies than they did in those of the 1950s, and neither does sex. Larkin was oblivious to the role of gender. As to sex, his research was school-based and that often precludes sexual inquiry. Gaines's work didn't suffer from the same problems: she talked to kids far off school grounds and her gender vision was 20/20. But she found girls too time-consuming to get to know. "You have to be a best friend to get really close."[10] Even then they always had "a mission pending: some shopping, an errand, a planned chance meeting with 'him' which meant they had to travel light." And as to sex, she took it as such a given that it hardly merited mention.

By the time of my study, a motley assortment of punks, freaks, and Deadheads were such a standard feature of the high school landscape that they constituted a social group almost as established and recognized as popular cliques. These groups had some of popular cliques' unity as well: a certain expectation that their members look and think alike. But within the general similarity, there was also a considerable degree of variation: Outcasts came in ones and twos as well as groups. For some, costume was the most important feature of identity: leather vs. tie dye vs. a button-down collar. For others, the costumes were mere signifiers of a profound alienation from school, which frequently expressed itself through truancy as well. A few almost seemed to be waiting around to join the next wave of suicides.

This chapter looks at the accounts of a subset of this larger group: those girls who had experienced a hell or freedom year

—an isolated year of truancy and partying, even a year without any school at all—and said it helped them clarify their own perspectives on sex and romance. Most narrators of hell years were white, none were extremely poor. (The alienation of poverty is another matter, as the reports of teenage mothers began to reveal.) Some had two heterosexual parents, some a single parent (gay or straight). But if their backgrounds were fairly diverse, they had alienation in common. Was loneliness the cause, as Konopka suggested earlier? Was the future at issue, as Stinchcombe believed? And what about sex? And love? Did girls who hung out as equals with punks and Deadheads have the same negative relationship to "sanguine and alluring thoughts about marriage" that social historian John Modell found in their male counterparts? Or were their hearts as breakable as other girls'?

Bleak prospects for the future were almost never mentioned as a source of depression. No one, it seemed, had even considered vocation, and while they all thought global apocalypse was a real possibility, it didn't strike them as noteworthy. What they did mention was an intense dissatisfaction with the present—with school, loneliness, and almost all the people around them—and a fear that if they didn't make a break for it, tedium and melancholy might well set the tenor of their entire lives.

If teenage mothers indicated they didn't know what adolescence was for and the fast-track narrators saw it as their best chance for a head start, these saw it as a space between childhood and adulthood they could decide what to do with. Some were determined to use the time to cure themselves of the ravages of childhood by means of drugs, friendship, and sex. Others just wanted to have fun—not the tepid fun of popular girls but the fun of a wild adolescence, the fun of living on the edge, of hot, passionate sex with boys whose daring went far beyond costume, of drugs that put the body in deep freeze or sent it hurtling faster than the speed of light to the stars, the fun of the road. All placed their experiences in the past. Now, their line went, they were back at school, hard at work. They still had sex, but they didn't cut school and they didn't do drugs. But last year . . .

FIRST, SOMETHING happened to make a hell year necessary, these narrators were all sure, but they were a little sketchy and only mildly curious as to what. The first time Harmony began to cut school—early in junior high—she didn't have any idea why. Looking back, she thought she started cutting because she had skipped a grade and "it was difficult to be in physically" with kids who were older than she was once puberty divided them from her, but also because:

> Everything was made as boring as possible. In junior high school, it's just basically all those things you've already learned. So it's like re-gurgitating all this old stuff and it's just boring. Real boring. Espe-cially since I knew they were telling me a crock of lies. Christopher Columbus. You know, bullshit. Christopher Columbus discovered America. The Indians were *here*. You know, they weren't even Indi-ans. We call them Indians because *he* made a mistake. He thought he was in India, and we're supposed to be talking about how wonderful he was.

Like Harmony, Audrey, who took just about every risk in the book short of running away, associated her hell year first and foremost with becoming physically out of synch with her peers. Audrey had her first period at age eight. I asked if she had known what was happening when she started to menstruate. "Yeah," she nearly growled. I asked how. She snapped that her sister had told her. I asked what her sister had said. Her voice grew louder.

> She just told me the facts. She didn't make any story out of it, and I understood. I wasn't stupid. I didn't want to understand but I did.

It wasn't puberty itself that was the problem, she explained, but that she took the opportunity her body offered to pass herself off as older. By age twelve, she was five feet seven, she said, pull-ing out a photograph of herself then. Standing beside a pool in a bikini smiling at the camera alongside her best friend, she looked like a completely different person than the one I was interviewing. The Audrey talking with me had shoe-polish black hair styled punk and she was all angles in black leather pants and a black leather jacket weighed down with spikes and chains. The Audrey in the photograph was blond, curly-headed, and voluptuous—a teenage Marilyn Monroe. At first I thought she was pulling my leg, showing me a photograph of an altogether different girl, but then, much as one catches a glimpse of the child in an adult, I recognized the essence of her features underneath the blond curls. At the time she had been happy she looked "older," she said, because other girls her age were so "awkward," but she regretted it now: if she hadn't looked so mature, she couldn't have partied as much.

> That was the worst thing. I started partying when I was too young. I was like in sixth grade. . . . God knows how many boyfriends I had and I said, Wait a second. I can't do that.

When I asked what she meant by boyfriends, her anger flared again. "I was screwing them." She didn't "understand" at all, she said in a rare moment of vulnerability, and she was "taken advantage of."

Pam blamed the fights her parents had just before they got a divorce for driving her off course:

> I told myself it didn't really bother me, but I think it must have deep down inside. . . . I think that's why I went so wild.

And then, she and her friend Linda explained, life was so boring where they lived, you almost had to go wild to stay awake. I could see that. All flatland and split-levels, the inland suburb where they grew up didn't have much going for it. Same-size houses all built around the same time—circa 1949, 1950. A relatively small, unexciting mall you had to drive to. Not even a 7-Eleven within walking distance. No park, no art, no nothing. Well, there was one thing. The neighborhood was known as "the capital of crank" (a local brand of speed).

Other narrators pointed to simple loneliness as the cause of their unhappiness, as Konopka had understood decades earlier. Sherry said she'd been lonely ever since her parents moved from a very friendly town to one where social flux and anomie made people more likely to say "Wait on the porch" than "Come on in," and her loneliness grew too painful to tolerate as she entered adolescence. Carol said she got lonely when she started junior high, because the new school's mores were alien to her.

> I had been wearing long skirts and denim jackets my whole life and when I got to junior high school that was unacceptable. . . . It was

not acceptable to not wear a bra when you were starting to get breasts. Even if you didn't have breasts, you had to wear a bra. Finally, my friends forced me to buy a bra. They said, "We're never going to speak to you again if you don't wear a bra." So I went out and bought one and I wore it for one week. It was so uncomfortable. And I had really a lot of hair and I usually wore it in a braid or two braids and it was very long and I wore my long skirt and I had cowboy boots that I bought five years before that that had big holes in them. I was comfortable in what I wore. I liked my skirts and I liked my tee shirts. I wasn't a slob or anything but I was comfortable and now all of a sudden I had to wear tight jeans and sneakers and also I was very chubby, so I felt very uncomfortable that I was being put in this position that I had to wear tight jeans and I felt really fat.

Some girls said they'd always lacked close friendships with peers. Sally:

Like I said, I had always basically stayed to myself, and I didn't have any really close friends.

But somehow it hadn't bothered them as much in grade school, in part perhaps because they'd often had such close families. But now family wasn't enough.

Others added that they'd been in school for so long that they felt completely dulled out by the routine and exhausted by the continuous competition. They were entirely capable of keeping up but six more years of lonely drudgery—two years of high school, four years of college—just didn't seem bearable without a break.

Finally, well into their accounts, a number of hell-year narrators mentioned sexual abuse as a factor. That's why they'd always been so shy, they haltingly proposed—and why, eventually, they needed to take this time off. Confusion about sexual identity, in contrast, was never narrated as a cause of a hell year but some accounts culminated with bisexual experience, suggesting that sexual identity may have been an underlying concern.

FREQUENTLY, a hell year started small—with cutting a class or a day of school here and there to stay home or hang out—but gradually days turned into weeks and just hanging out into having sex and doing drugs. In junior high Harmony cut with a new friend, Lila. They had "a lot of fun," she said, warming to the memory:

> We'd get up every day and make everyone think we were going to school and then we'd go to school and then we'd go out to breakfast. We'd have this wonderful breakfast. And we'd leisurely, you know, just spend hours.

Eventually the administration contacted her mother.

> They would send home these little yellow slips to my mother. "Your daughter has been absent for forty days." You know. And I lied to her! For the first time in my life! "How was school today?" I'd say, "Oh, you know," and make up a story about what happened in school. So when she found out I hadn't been to school, she was really upset. It hurt her a lot personally. It insulted her.

Harmony didn't want her mother to feel she had done a bad job of mothering, because she hadn't. She'd been great and it had been hard, Harmony knew. Harmony's father hadn't been around for years and he'd never been much help. Her mother had supported Harmony alone; always been there when Harmony needed her; yet never put too much pressure on the mother-daughter relationship: kept up a life of her own.

Largely to spare her mother's feelings but also with a sense of relief, Harmony went back to school for the time being. She and her mother were both pleased that she made it through junior high and the first year of high school.

Second year, Harmony met Jerry in the class she hated most —math.

> By some twist of fate, the teacher told him to sit next to me. That was like a godsend, right? Because I was, I mean, you know, I was too shy. I would never have talked to him.

For a while she saw him whenever he showed up for class—every other week or so.

> Finally he took me to this really fancy Chinese restaurant. And I didn't like him very much. I was really attracted to him, the thing of

chemistry was there. But he was—you know, there was nothing good about him.

He was "obnoxious." He made a habit of saying things that made the other person feel bad.

And he was into drugs. A lot. He was selling cocaine to the dean of the school. He was selling cocaine to the police in that neighborhood, and he was very popular in the school because he was a drug dealer. So when he was hanging out, you know, all the real swingies would come up to him. I didn't like that at all, but for some reason, I really wanted to know him, and I felt that there was something worth knowing.

Together they cut school in earnest, going to the movies, getting high, and going back to her house after her mother went to work. Despite Jerry's entrepreneurial activities, their real romance wasn't with drugs but with each other.

Although they put a lot of time into it, their sexual relationship proceeded slowly. At first, they just made out for hours; then they began "sleeping together" through the long truant afternoons; finally, they had sex. I asked what the first time was like. "That wasn't with him," she said quickly.

It was horrible. I was fourteen, and I was real friendly with this guy who was like twenty-five. He might have been older. And, you know, he basically told me he didn't want any sex with me. He just wanted to be my friend. I liked hanging out with him because we could talk about, you know, politics and religion and all kinds of stuff I couldn't talk about with anybody else.

So then one day he just all of a sudden started coming on to me. It was a big surprise, you know, because he'd promised me he wouldn't. And then I told him I didn't want to. And he wouldn't take no for an answer. So he raped me but he—he wouldn't call it —I mean, I know, if someone sat down and said, "Do you remember Harmony, what happened?" He would never say, "I raped her." But that's what happened.

Because she'd been raped, Harmony worried that she wouldn't be able to have the kind of pleasurable sexual life she knew her mother and her mother's friends had had. She felt as if she'd been looking forward to the kinds of escapades, romances, and pleasures they confided to each other around the kitchen table since before she had any idea what they were talking about, and she wasn't going to let one brutal creep ruin it all for her. If anything was a birthright, sexuality was. What she had to do, in her own view, to overcome the trauma she had suffered and salvage her ability to experience passion was to arrange a pleasurable sexual reinitiation. This goal struck her as more than sufficient justification for cutting school.

She had told Jerry about what had happened even before they made out so that he would understand that sex might be difficult for her. "So he was like very, he was real sweet about how he handled me. Because he knew, he didn't want to, you know, freak me out or anything like that." She didn't want to freak out either. After several weeks:

> He suggested we take a bath together. We had never been naked in front of each other or anything. We had only been kissing. So we got in the bathtub and he had a hard-on and he started getting on me and he told me that you couldn't get pregnant in water. I was like, "Are you serious? Are you going to try to pull a stupid one like that on me? I can't believe it." So anyway, um, but he like, you know, he put his fingers inside of me.

That night Harmony had the apartment to herself. Her mother had a meeting.

> We slept together that evening and he was touching me a lot. But no oral sex or anything like that for a while. But I kind of figured that if I let him put his fingers in me and we took a bath together, you know, eventually we were going to end up having sex.

She got a diaphragm without telling him. He found it inside her when they were making out and took it as a signal that she was ready.

> He put his fingers in there and he felt it. And he was like, "What's this?" And you should have seen how happy he was. He was just amazed. That I did that. But I knew that once he found out that I had it, he'd start putting pressure on me. Up to that point, you know, he wasn't trying really to have sex with me, so we could play and get

hot and then he would be like, "Well, I can't do anything else because, you know, you don't have anything."
    And I'd be like, "Right."
    I was right. The second he knew that I had something in there,
he started pressuring me. I had it in me because I was just trying to
see if it was the right size. I wasn't asking for pressure.

Other girls might just have given in. But as long as she had any
choice at all in the matter, Harmony was never going to have sex
again unless she "was totally ready"; her mother had stressed the
importance of not having sex unless you wanted to.

Finally, she did feel she was ready. They set a date to have
breakfast together on a school day and then go back to her apartment after her mother left for work. As they approached her
building, they saw her mother rushing out late to work.

I was like, "Oh no!" I was so nervous and we started running. It was
icy and we started slipping. And I was so nervous.

Perhaps as a result, despite all her care and preparation:

I was a little disappointed. You know. I thought it was going to feel
a lot better.

After a while, however, she started to like sex.

It was like all those initial expectations were gone and I was learning
to really enjoy what we could have.

They started cutting school practically every day and going to her
house to have sex. Now her truancy began to frighten her:

It got to a point where we got in trouble and then we'd just go back
to school for a week and then we'd leave and then we'd get in trouble. So we were constantly in trouble. For like the whole year. It was
pretty horrible living with that over your head. You know, it's just
this feeling of losing all self-control, and you're like, "What's going
to happen to us?" And the more you stay out of school and the more
trouble you get in, the harder it is to get out of that. I felt like I was
lost in this bad cycle. But at the same time, I knew no one could
drive me back to school. No matter what.

At her wits' end, her mother agreed to let her transfer to an alternative program with flexible hours. Jerry transferred as well. Almost anything could have happened at that point. They could have cut so much they'd never have made it through alternative school. But as if she really had accomplished what she needed to and could turn her attention back to work, Harmony began to make up for lost time.

THOSE WHO SAID that loneliness motivated their hell year spoke more eloquently about the friends they made when they hung out than about anything else. That they had sex with some of those friends seemed almost incidental. Carol started cutting school at the end of freshman year, but the year was effectively over and her truancy didn't show up as a problem until Labor Day, when she told her mother that she wasn't going back to the top-tier school she had competed intensely to enter.

> And she said, "What do you mean?" Because I'd never mentioned that I hated it, and I really did hate it.

Instead of saying that she didn't have friends, she rationalized that school "wasn't letting me grow and experience myself." Her mother, an extremely savvy woman and a teacher herself, wasn't having any of that old line, and Carol did go back to school but began cutting immediately. Even when her mother drove her to school, she would just turn around and go home.

> At first, I would make excuses to my teachers. Oh, I was home sick. And then I just—I would go to half the classes and not go to half. I mean, it got to a point where I didn't care about cutting. I knew this was a hell year, and I couldn't do anything about it. I just really didn't want to go to school.

Part of her problem, Carol thought, in concert with a number of hell-year narrators, was timing. She was a member of the wrong cohort. As one girl said:

> I was kind of one of those kids who was really pissed off they missed the '60s.

If she'd come of age then, she thought, she would have had friends like herself: other people who understood the importance of social action and self-exploration. If you were gay or black or poor or fat or friendless or at the bottom of the fast track or simply a teenager who hated "the system" in the 1960s, you could get together with others who were like you, say that you were proud, and watch others step back and change their views. If you wanted meaning, you could create it or join it and others would join you. Of course, the '60s cohort was also her mother's generation.

For the first few months Carol cut, she did mainly just go home and lay around, but when the weather started to improve, she made for the park with an old friend and that friend's boyfriend. There they met more classmates who went to the park more often than to school.

> We sat in the park and just talked and read. But it was much nicer to be in the park than in school. That's what we did. I didn't go to school for a whole year. That's what I did.

It was April, perfect weather for hanging out. Her mother knew, but she couldn't stop her.

Her new circle wasn't exactly a bastion of progressive 1960s-style sentiments but, like her, they hated school.

> They were really wonderful people who were experiencing the same things that I was, and this was when I started experiencing really hating being in the fast track. Not just that I didn't have friends.

They "sort of got together and out of school dealt with the fact" that they weren't going to school:

> We very thoroughly dealt with all the things that we really hated about school and we came to the conclusion that it didn't matter. We had to go anyway. The only way to get out of it was to go and be over with it. It seems like little but that took us three months.

I asked how they dealt with it. They "really talked."

Annette spoke of the wonderful "wild girls" she hung out with in the park across from school who would, similarly, talk about anything. Sherry recalled the conversations she had with the kids she got high with:

> We'd sit around and we'd talk—just—and all of our deeper feelings would come out. . . . You really learn a lot about yourself because you can talk more freely with people who get high. They're more open. They're like the '80s hippie generation. . . . And they are wonderful people. They really are, and they helped me. They really listen because they're really interested in what you have to say. And that, that really opened me up. I can—I can talk to people now. It's no big deal now for me to talk to anybody about anything.

She used to be really scared to talk personally, Sherry said, because she had a bad experience with a cousin one vacation when her family was visiting his folks. She had willingly experimented with kissing with him on previous vacations. But when she was about ten and he tried to rape her, she kicked him "in the groin" and locked herself in the bathroom until her parents came home. The only person she told at the time, a friend from school, responded by scolding her about the kissing. The experience had made her afraid to talk about things that really bothered her with anyone—until she met her new friends.

For some girls, meaningful conversations and fledgling friendships were sufficiently miraculous to warrant making the park the center of their life. Annette grew up in a mixed neighborhood. She had one brother, much younger. Her African-American family had belonged to the middle class for two generations. Her grandparents owned their farm in the South, and she was very proud that she had come from people sharp enough to hold on to something in a place where everything made that even harder than it was in the North. But her father walked out on his family after losing his job and after that they didn't have much money. They had to move from a nice apartment to a ghetto tenement.

Annette dated her isolation to the move. The atmosphere was different in her new school, and Annette felt uneasy there—"on the outskirts, on the outside," a feeling that all the hell-year narrators had in common. She and her mother grew even closer than they had been.

> Basically, it was just her and me.

Annette's mother focused intensely on how Annette did in school—better in reading and writing than in math. When a teacher said that if Annette could get her math scores up she could go to a special school, Annette's mother really pushed her, saying she'd be "set for life." But she just couldn't do it, Annette told me ruefully, and she remained in her neighborhood school for tenth grade.

The failure threw her off track, as Stinchcombe would have predicted. Her mother's disappointment may have made Annette want to put some distance between them, but it's common for daughters to want space under the best of circumstances. In any case, in tenth grade, she began to hang in the park across from school. At first, she was equally friendly with everyone in the group. Then she began to become close with Dawn. Initially she referred to Dawn with the genderless noun "person" and pronoun "they."

> This one person decided that I was going to be their project, so to speak. They were going to bring me out of my shell and make me over.

From the outset, her mother opposed the friendship. In her view, there was something "not normal" about it, perhaps about any intense female friendship. But gradually Dawn and Annette became close friends.

> I mean, if you saw one without the other, we had missed each other.

At the same time, Annette began to have "dates." One boy was "real sensitive and quiet," an "artist." Sex didn't come up with him. The other was older, "a fun guy to be with," a "party type but he was very into his schoolwork as well as supersmart." He was in college, an electrical engineering major, and she said they got along "great" but didn't have sex. There was even a guy who, she told her mother, was the person she was most likely to have intercourse with. When I asked her to say more about him, she told me about his parents' impressive house and then about a famous female tennis star whom she had once pursued to a disco, where she got an autograph and a phone number (which turned out to be the number of the star's press agent). She talked about this crush all the time at home, she said.

IF ANNETTE had barely started to approach sexual activity by the time we talked, Carol and Sherry had gone well beyond sexual initiation. By the end of the spring semester, which she cut almost entirely, Carol had established a primary sexual relationship with one boy and had sex with her best friend and her best friend's lover. Sherry had had adventures too: half proud, half abashed, she said that she had had nine lovers in the year before we talked. The first time she had a crush on a boy, she said, she cried for hours and hours and hours just because he loaned his jacket to another girl, but she soon came to see that kind of sensitivity as immature. In fact, at present she didn't "see any problem in having a sexual relationship with somebody if there's feelings even if it's just a friendship." When I asked if she found sex pleasurable, she giggled and said, "Oh yeah," adding, "It's kind of funny actually because I don't think I've ever loved anybody that I've had sex with. Oh, except for my boyfriend now, who's very, very dear to me." So dear, in fact, that she even enjoyed being with him when they didn't have sex, which struck her as amazing:

> We have a really good time together and he's very open. . . . He's, he's the type who when you walk in the door, he'll come and hold you forever. I mean it's like he won't let go.

She really needed that "right now," she said. (But would she love him tomorrow?)

Both girls used contraception. Carol obtained a prescription for the pill before she had intercourse. Sherry didn't get one for months after she had intercourse, and the story of how she came to go on the pill was long and convoluted. She had been using drugs and having sex for months before her parents realized it and kicked her out of the house. She stayed with a string of friends for several weeks. During that time, her parents calmed down enough to get their bearings and set conditions for her return even as she came to understand how much she needed a home. One of these conditions was that she go with them to family counseling. In counseling, she argued that she could give up drugs but not sex: that she needed its pleasure and comfort to survive. Ultimately, the counselor convinced Sherry's parents that she should be on the pill.

As Sherry was telling me about the decision-making process, her mother came in with several bags of groceries, and they carried on a testy exchange about how the decision for Sherry to go on the pill was made, which ended with Sherry's mother saying, "Well, we won't get into it," and heading on to the kitchen. Sherry and I continued talking, but Sherry was on edge, and I changed the subject, asking what advice she'd give a little sister if she had one. "Don't ever lose her virginity," Sherry said, eyeing her mother. "Really?" I said, a little more amazed than I should have been given that the about-face was clearly meant to appease her mother. "Never," Sherry said. "Not until you really, really think it's time. Not unless you're absolutely positive. If you have a doubt, don't. 'Cause I kind of regret it, in a way. It's a kind of a thing that I wish I hadn't." "I think I've heard that advice from someone else before," her mother shouted from the kitchen. We all laughed nervously. At length, Sherry's mother finished putting away the groceries and left, saying ominously, "I shall return." Sherry noticed my eyes on the door. "She's very intimidating," she said. "She's a brown belt in karate. When she walks into a room, you can literally see people shrink." I nodded and Sherry said she had to leave. She was late for work.

IN THE END, the hell years these girls took didn't really involve particularly great risks for themselves or for others. Sherry smoked too much pot maybe and hung out with hippies. Carol took acid once and hung out with hippies. Harmony just stayed home and had sex. Annette didn't even have sex. Sure, they missed somewhere between some and a lot of school, but not so much they couldn't make it up, which they were well on their way to doing when we talked. They'd never get into Ivies, but with the exception perhaps of Carol, they never would have, and anyway it was water over the dam. Not all hell years were so temperate, however. Other narrators recounted far more serious transgressions: some that put them at grave risk, a few that violated the rights of others. In retrospect, some saw and regretted the damage they had done themselves. Others continued to celebrate their own nerve, narrating their hell years as great adventure stories.

That's what Pam's was. With flawless skin, ginger hair that hit her shoulders and flipped up, and guileless clear blue eyes, Pam looked like a butter-wouldn't-melt-in-her-mouth, drugs-have-never-entered-her-body, she-couldn't-have-ever-had-sex *Seventeen* cover girl. In the story she told me, however, she was, rather, a kind of 1980s Moll Flanders who more than once courted disaster but somehow always escaped. I interviewed Pam and her best friend, Linda, together, but Pam's story soon took over.

For excitement, Pam and Linda used to thumb rides together.

> Linda: Just to meet guys and stuff because we didn't have a car . . .
> Pam: Guys would pick us up and they would say, "Do you want to party?" and we would say, "Yeah."

They had some very close calls in those days:

> One time we were hitchhiking and this older guy picked us up. He wanted to take us out to dinner and have like a threesome. He kept on trying to touch us and stuff so we had him let us off at this parking lot. It was this big ordeal. . . . I used to carry around a pocketknife, and I pulled that out and started to scream and curse at him.

Another time they hitched a ride home with a guy in a van who dropped Pam off first. On the way to Linda's, he started saying "strange things." Just before he reached the corner she had named as her destination (she never told rides her real address), he asked her to talk to him while he jerked off. She refused and started to get out of the van.

> He reached over to grab my arm. I tried getting the door open and it wouldn't open. I don't know how I did it but I jumped through the window.

Their parents didn't have any idea what they were up to. On the nights they hitched, each just said she was sleeping over at the other's house. Other parents might have checked, even if only casually, but for a number of reasons, theirs did not, at least not in the beginning. Pam's parents had split up. They hadn't gotten along for years but "toward the end they started fighting out loud." Since the divorce, she had lived with her mom, who was having a hard time making a living. (Pam's dad taught at a major university, but her mom hadn't worked since she got married and secretarial was all she could get when she had to go back to work. The only way she could really make enough money to support them was by putting in extra hours. By the time she got her footing, her daughter was well beyond spending a night or two away from home.) Linda's parents were in the habit of worrying about Linda's sister, who had hit adolescence first. They took Linda's reliability for granted, not that big a mistake as it turns out. At least, she didn't go anywhere near as wild as Pam, who had been the quieter friend in the beginning. But even if they had checked, they probably wouldn't have gotten the picture, since the girls really were staying over at each other's houses, albeit later rather than sooner—that is, until they turned sixteen.

"The summer of sixteen," Pam recalled, a friend of theirs, Beth, moved to a trailer park in a nearby state. Because the trailer park was near the shore and there was always a party going, they used to visit her a lot. This was the beginning of what Pam called her "wild period," the time when she tried "to be free" and "live the way I wanted to, without any authority." Linda called it the "I-Don't-Care Stage." But ultimately Pam didn't care a lot more than Linda didn't care.

Freedom, at that point, she thought, was "the right to party" and the whole summer was a party. Friends led to friends led to friends. Everybody had something to offer, some kind of good time: drugs, sex, drugs, sex. One night Pam and Beth left a party and went to a bar, where they met a friend who gave them their pick of speed or magic mushrooms. Pam went for the speed as always; Beth tried the mushrooms.

She kept on eating them like they were candy. She did like at least four of them. We walked around with this guy and his friend. Then we were cruising in the car, and all of a sudden she started seeing all these colors flying at her and stuff. I go, "Oh, my God, are you all right?" So they had the idea, they wanted to take us to some motel. We didn't want that, so she got out of the car and she just ran. I tried going after her but I lost her, and I was really out of it. I just went back and I went to sleep in this motel. The guy left me alone because I just told him to stay away from me and he did. He was a decent guy.

So then I woke up the next day, and I took the bus back home, and I'm wondering, What happened to her? She had got picked up by the cops—the township police—and she had a bad trip. She was seeing demons and monsters and stuff. And the next day in the paper, there was a big write-up about her. The headline read: TEEN-AGE GIRL SEES DEMONS AND MONSTERS.

The memory still cracked her up.

The first time Pam had sex, it was with John, a guy from the trailer park. She and John were outside in a tent.

And Gary was mad because I wouldn't go with him and he was going to run down the tent with his motorcycle.

He kept roaring up to the tent and cutting the motor, making the experience with John much more exciting than it would have been in its own right.

With school due to start in a couple of days, Linda headed home. Her own sister had started messing up in school when she began to get involved with boys, and she had sworn she wasn't going to make the same mistake. She'd have fun, she'd take chances, but she wouldn't let school go down the drain for love or adventure. Pam, on the other hand, hadn't made any resolutions, and she didn't want to go back home or back to school. Picking up where her father had left off, she'd had a terrible fight with her mom before she headed down to the shore, and the idea of going back just stuck in her throat. In addition, although she didn't mention any particular academic difficulties, she hated school, as common a reason for rebellion as any. And then there was Gary. She'd always liked "the wild type," and Gary was wild all right. "The life of the party," "crazy into drugs and all that."

And oh, he was famous for his house robberies.

One night she actually helped him rob a house. "That particular night" Quaaludes quieted her conscience and nerves, but what she really liked was speed. And Gary.

At first sex hurt but then it was "great" because she loved him. For Pam, however, love wasn't a particularly heavy matter, and she was up-front about her ability to justify an action by "telling" herself she loved someone. She *really* loved Gary, though, she differentiated. They didn't use birth control because Gary's mother confirmed his claim that he was sterile and maybe he was. In any event, she didn't get pregnant. Just like her parents, she and Gary fought a lot. One time:

> We got in a fight and I was all drunk and walking across the road and I got hit. . . . The guy, he took me back to his house and fed me. He must have thought I was going to sue him or something!

She told the story comically, but it probably wasn't so funny at the time.

Then there were other stories she didn't tell until she was asked. When she'd finished talking and I asked if anyone had ever tried to force her to have sex, for example, she mentioned the time a friend of Gary's had offered her to a friend of his; despite the fact that it was pretty evident that everyone was too stoned to act on the offer, she'd been terrified. Then there was the day she hitched to a motel to answer an ad for a modeling job and found herself at the mercy of a guy who wouldn't take no for an answer. "Scared to death," she protested that she was in love with her boyfriend and offered to jerk the guy off. He settled for a blow job. Afterward she ran out to the road cursing and crying. For the first time in her life, she was afraid to hitch, but finally she did. Fortunately, she said, the glint coming back into her eyes, "this really nice guy" picked her up and took her out to dinner.

She and Gary really weren't getting along very well by then. One night he was "so rotten" to her:

> He wouldn't even let me sleep in the bed next to him. . . . He wanted me to give him a blow job or nothing. He actually just kept on pushing me out of the bed.

Wild with rage, she ran into the kitchen and got a knife.

> I knew I wasn't going to try to kill him. I just wanted some attention.

He grabbed the knife and threw it into the wall.

Nevertheless, Pam still wasn't ready to give it all up when the police intervened. "We were getting along so good the last couple of nights," she remembered wistfully. She'd been in the car when the police got him.

> We were all on [these Valiums] . . . and he just had this bright idea to try to rob a 7-Eleven. He was so stupid! I guess his mind was affected by these drugs. He actually took the whole cash register out, and he expected to get away with it.

The police responded to the alarm in a matter of minutes.

> We were hiding in the van, and the next thing I know there was this gun pointed straight at my head, telling me to stick my hands up.

They sent her back home, and her mom—finally realizing what she was dealing with—tried to get her under control.

> She used to do stuff like take my blow dryer away from me. . . . She used to hide the curling iron.

For Pam these weren't jokes. They were "real punishments." Her mother also tried to keep her from going out all the time, but Pam used to "just run out the door and not come back."

> This one time, she actually put the chair and the lamp right in front of the door and sat there all night long just to keep me there.

Pam was incensed. No way was she going to spend the coming winter boredom in lockup. She made herself "believe" she fell in love with a guy named Jim; went to the local family-planning clinic for the pill; made an arrangement that Linda should notify the police if she didn't hear from Pam every couple of weeks; and then ran away with Jim to Florida. They "conned" their way south.

We used to go to churches and stuff, and he'd say, "Oh, we just got married and we're trying to start out and we don't have no money." He'd make it sound really good, and the churches would, like, give us money.

As good as they were at conning, it was a hard trip. Most nights they slept on the road until they got to Florida, where they mainly stayed in a runaway shelter.

It didn't take many weeks of traipsing around homeless for Pam to begin to appreciate the virtues of her mother's apartment and in a few weeks she and Jim headed back north.

When I came back, I really appreciated having a place to live. Now I would never think of running away again. I really think I'm too old for that stuff. . . . You can get away with it when you're young.

She wasn't sorry for her days on the run, though. "They were experiences," and she treasured the memory of "the shore, the way that it was." Besides, for all the risks Pam had taken, Linda was the one who had had the most traumatic experience: a friend's boyfriend had raped her when she was too drunk to stop him, right there in their hometown.

Pam still spoke enthusiastically about crank. She had given up drugs for aerobics, but although she now saw speed as a health risk, she didn't narrate any sense that perhaps it had impaired her ability to think or remember. She still had a taste for "the wild type" as well, and at the end of her account she started to fill me in on her plans to seduce and reform a guy she had recently met who had a fatal weakness for crank.

Unlike Pam, Audrey had many regrets. If Pam's was an adventure story, Audrey's was a morality tale. She thought she'd given her parents too hard a time, especially her mother, about whom she felt very protective. She also believed that all the drugs she'd taken had damaged her mind, and she wasn't sure it would ever recover. Audrey's first real trouble started the summer she was twelve. She had talked her parents into sending her to camp in California, and it was there, over two thousand miles away from everyone who knew her real age, that she really began to drink, do drugs, and generally act out her idea of being teenaged. Still no sex, though, until one afternoon when she and some other campers were taking a walk and she saw a guy.

> I was just walking, and I turned around and saw him, and I started talking to him. He was really tall with blond hair and muscles and tan. California bullshit. I remember, I walked away with him . . .

"Out in California," she explained, guys were always saying, " 'Oh, live and be free,' you know. 'Go around screwing everybody as long as they don't have a social disease.' You know, that's how they are out there." At the time, however, she took his interest to mean that he was serious about her.

> I thought, Wow, he really loves me.

The first time she went off with him, they had sex, which she liked "a lot." When she got back to camp, she was in big trouble.

> I almost got sent home. I was like pleading, "No. Don't tell my mother. She'll kill me. . . . Give me another chance." So they did.

She managed to see him a few more times.

> I saw him for about a week. Then he left.

No moaning and groaning, no melodrama for her.

> I said, Oh. Fine. I can have the same attitude.

In the end she was sent home for drinking.

> My parents had poured in all their money for me to go out there, and I got sent home. . . . Now I'd never do anything like that. I wouldn't fuck it up. But then, I had no guilt. I didn't care. I was so fucked up on drugs, I didn't care about anybody.

Back in school, on and off, she started to identify as punk, and she did drugs every chance she got—mainly ludes but also heroin. Then tragedy struck. She and her best friend spent New Year's Eve "eating ludes." By morning, her friend was dead. Au-

drey grieved by repeatedly getting "into trouble" over the course
of the next year. She was in fight after fight in school and doing
more and more drugs. Her parents grounded her "for life."

> I just laughed at them and went on anyway.

Ultimately, her behavior landed her in juvenile court, where a
judge threatened her with institutionalization. She said to herself, " 'Wait a second, wait a second. I'm not that tough.' I
straightened my ass out. I was just turning thirteen."

It wasn't easy. She'd missed a lot of school and when she'd
been there, she hadn't really been there. In addition, the people
she had hung with resented her change of heart.

> I said, Well, fuck it. I said, You're not going to be anything when
> you get out of school . . . if you live.

Although she no longer did drugs and she tried to avoid fights,
she continued to wear leather, spikes, and chains to school. Punk
was her identity, her stance toward the world. What she liked
most about punk was its romantic detachment. She thought the
world was "so fucked up, it's just like boiling," and this made
her scornful of hippie attitudes:

> Somebody's going to go, "Peace, man," and a neutron bomb is go-
> ing to fall on them.

She also detested "all that rock bullshit."

> Oh, you're in love forever, and you find somebody, and you live in
> your white house with the picket fence, and the garden, and the four
> kids, the 4.3 kids, whatever the hell it is.

She wasn't sure it was an improvement, but that dream was over.
Everybody was "wiser" now.

> It's probably worse in a way. People probably should be a little more
> naive, so they wouldn't get so fucked up. But it's too late now.
> Q: It's too late?
> Audrey: It's too late.

She believed in having sex anytime she felt like it. It didn't have any meaning in the scale of things. In fact, given the disastrous state of the world and most human relationships, it seemed important not to increase strife by being sexually possessive.

Because she continued to dress punk, teachers and other students continued to treat her like trouble:

> Even if I was just walking through the halls, they'd say, "You stupid heroin addict. You dumb punk." I'd always get into fights. I'd sit there and say to myself, "It's not worth getting into a fight. It's just not worth it." But I did it anyway, because that was the only way to shut somebody up. Then I'd come home, and my mother would look at me, and she couldn't believe it. I'd start fights with teachers. That was so stupid. I got into so much trouble—just starting fights. People are so much bigger than me. I'm not that big. I used to get killed.

Her punk identity wasn't her only problem.

> My mind was so burnt out, and I was so stupid. I'm still not back to what I should be. My brains were rotted.

Despite it all, she managed to graduate from junior high, but the school administration wouldn't let her take part in graduation because her hair "was all different colors," and she was dressed "all in black." She and a friend sat in the auditorium in "chains and leather and sneered at everyone." They felt "like shit afterward anyway" because nobody had even noticed.

Her fighting continued in high school until she began to slamdance, which she felt let her exorcize her aggressions without getting in trouble. Her first and only pregnancy to date occurred early in high school—the 3 percent risk with the mini pill (possibly a bi- or triphasic combination pill) "hit" her, she explained—and it gave her second thoughts about her approach to sex. For one thing, Audrey felt she had to let her mother know she was having an abortion, in case she "died on the operating table," but she had hated destroying her mother's "romantic illusions." For another, the abortion itself was a pain, and she didn't want to go through another one, so:

I don't go out just to meet somebody to fuck around with. I'm not like that at all anymore. It's stupid. I'm the one that's going to get pregnant.

Besides she had met a guy she was "compatible with." Between them, "everything was pretty rational" (her highest praise). Neither of them ever got jealous, for example. It was fine by him that she had a lot of friends who were guys—most punks *were* guys, she noted. For the most part, sex wasn't an issue with her "guy friends." Like the boys popular girls went with in between boyfriends, they didn't expect her "to fuck around with them."

They just consider me one of the guys. And I get along with them unless I'm really attracted to them. I can talk to them like I could talk to a girl. It doesn't matter.

She wouldn't have sex with a girl. She drew the line at lesbianism. Her boyfriend didn't have to worry about that.

If somebody likes another girl, that's fine. That's just the way they are. It just doesn't fit me personally.

But occasionally she was really attracted to one of the guys and it was all right with her boyfriend if she went ahead and had sex, she said. The previous summer she had practically lived with someone else, a guy who went to bed with his spikes on. She described their relationship as "violent but equal."[11]

He'd never like beat the hell out of me, and say, "You better do this because I'm a guy and I'm stronger."

Because they were "the same" sexually, the violence was like "fighting fire with fire." In general, violence was "sexually exciting" but only to a certain point.

If there's a gun to your head, I don't think that's sexually exciting. Or if he beats the hell out of you with a lead pipe.

However, she didn't have to have violent sex, she said. "I'm not always like that. It just depends." In fact, she was beginning to be able to imagine being with someone and "doing nothing," not even having sex, "and being just as happy, depending on the person, depending on the situation."

How ON EARTH, one might fairly ask, did these girls ever manage to go so far afield? They all had at least one parent, and most of the time, someone at least was paying attention. In fact, these very reports indicate that most of the narrators' parents were actually very close to their children, and they were acting as parents as well as friends, trying some combination of protectionism, counseling, and tough love. Pam and Linda did escape their parents' vigilance in the beginning, it's true, but think of Pam's mother sleeping in a chair in front of the apartment door in a desperate effort to keep her daughter under control; Sherry's parents locking her out and then taking her back and going into counseling; Annette's mother trying to protect her daughter by making their small family her only social world. It's hard to think of what else they could have done. Teenagers can't be controlled like children: they're too big and too resourceful. Institutionalization might have kept Audrey and Pam from taking as many drugs as they did, but then again it might not have, and it certainly wouldn't have improved their prospects in life.

To their credit, none of these narrators took the easy adolescent route of blaming their parents for their condition, not even when they had strong grounds to do so. They didn't chastise themselves severely either. These weren't confessions. They were reports. In effect, these narrators accepted responsibility but not blame. If they needed to combine sex and danger, they assumed, or to forget about work for a year to concentrate on sex and love, or just sex, it was their life: they had a right; they knew better than anyone else what they needed.

Whatever one may think of these accounts, this vantage point seems radically new. Girls of the past may well have played hooky, shot heroin, taken speed, robbed houses, run away, conned ministers, gotten in fights, or preferred dangerous, promiscuous sex over true love, but it's hard to imagine any girl framing her transgressions as those above did before the late twentieth century, assuming not just the right to sex (with or without love) but the right to risk their health, even their lives, not to mention their education, in pursuit of whatever goals they set themselves. The goals alone are surely artifacts of the time: salvaging the capacity to enjoy sex in the wake of a rape, having a thrilling adventure while the heart is still young enough to take the heat of speed, crime, and desire; finding releases for a residual anger so overpowering that only violence will even begin to reduce it to tolerable levels.

The most obvious way to read these stories is melodramatically—as further proof, if we needed it, that Western civilization really has hit a new low or that girls desperately need help—but they can also be read as signs of progress in the struggle for gender equality. To be equal, it's reasonable to hold, girls have to be free to be as bad as boys: as resistant, as rebellious, as potentially politicized. If at last they are, perhaps gender is nearly undone. Indisputably these hell-year accounts display some remarkable shuffles. In addition to taking responsibility for their own actions, these narrators were sexually accountable, insisting—to the extent circumstances allowed—that sex be an even exchange, virtually always using contraception and handling abortion in a serious way. There are even a few signs of a greater awareness: a sense that they are living within a bigger, albeit dangerously fucked-up world, a notion of gender equality, and a recognition of the importance of reproductive rights. In another period, perhaps these narrators could have forged serious political commitment out of their anger, their realism, and their pain, but, finally, that's not what was happening here.

To the extent that these narrators had to rebel to wrest their lives and their bodies away from their parents' control, overcome the damage of childhood, and join their generation, it was probably better, as they themselves said, to rebel than to remain quiescent, traumatized, and subjugated. But virtually all of these narrators, it's critical to recall, feared for themselves during their days of hell and freedom, even those who barely put themselves in any danger at all. Harmony was unsure she'd ever get back to school and scared of falling off the edge of the earth altogether. Annette was afraid too, even though she didn't miss much school at all or even have sex. Audrey was getting the shit beaten out of her at school, and she'd soon spent enough time on the street to know the importance of keeping an edge instead of burning your bridges. Carol lost her chance at an Ivy League education.

As for Pam, she may have made a joke out of bargaining the guy in the motel room down to a blow job, but she knew she was lucky to get out of there alive. And Sherry? She struck me as scared even as we talked. For the whole previous year, she'd been "oblivious" to school, she said. "It was just in one ear and out the other," she was so stoned. Now she was two years from graduation at the mercy of a mother and father who had thrown her out already.

Some have argued that girls like these go wild because feminism has both given them the mistaken idea that they can transgress as freely as boys and destroyed the very family that traditionally kept them ladylike and safe.[12] In many of these cases, however, familial control was the problem. Annette's relationship with her mother, for example, was so intense it seemed to keep her from establishing relationships with her own peers. In other instances, a parent's double binds and cruelties were straight-out destructive. Sherry's brown-belt mother wouldn't even give her daughter a break while I was present, for example, and then there was Audrey's father, who—after insisting that I allow him to drive me home late one afternoon that I'd spent talking with his daughter—took me instead to a major highway nowhere near my home. "This is where you get out," he said, leaving me standing, confused, in the driving sleet. By the time I finally hiked to a bus stop and made it home, I was furious enough to do a lot more than just stay out all night dancing in spikes and leather.

Of course, not all parents were responsible for their daughter's condition or behavior. Something else was at work: undisclosed sexual abuse, confusion about sexual identity, or something else altogether, something that might not emerge for years or might never emerge. In any case, as Audrey said about true love, it was "too late now." What was done was done. It was reality. If there was a price to pay, well, then they would pay it. Both Audrey and Sherry, for example, believed they had burned their minds out with drugs. That was the past. Now they had to bear the humiliation and work their way back as best they could.

As it happened, all in all, they were unbelievably lucky. Pam came home in one piece and enrolled in a GED program. She was almost finished when we talked. Next term she planned to enroll in a local college, where, she figured, the atmosphere would be looser than in high school. She even had a plan to get a job that would satisfy her wanderlust: flight attendant. Harmony graduated from alternative school with flying colors and got a scholarship to a good progressive college. Carol transferred to a less rigorous high school, finished, and got into college. Ditto Annette. As for Sherry, I don't know what became of her but, for my money, a lot depended on what her mother did. Audrey was still behind academically when we last talked, and I wasn't sure she'd make it through a regular college. She still seemed burnt out, but she was writing poems at an extraordinary rate and she was managing a punk store with an iron fist.

What would sex be for these girls? Love?

Even as we talked, their views and desires were in flux, and it seemed unlikely they'd become simple and clear anytime soon, if they ever would. Annette went back and forth, talking one minute as if she would make a life with a man, another as if she expected to run off with a woman any second, and there's no telling whether Audrey or Sherry would ever choose the monogamy they were just now beginning to be able to imagine. It seemed unlikely there'd be many more hell years in any of their futures, however. As boys are so often said to have done, they'd gotten most of the hell out of their systems.

WITH ALL THE RULES the hell-year narrators were prepared to break, they upheld one: the rule against truly loving another girl. Carol had sex with her best friend a few times but she put her male lovers first, and although Annette fantasized about driving off into the sunset in Martina Navratilova's Jaguar, it was a boy she considered having sex with. Audrey dismissed the idea altogether. "If a girl ever went after me," she said, "I think I'd be like yech." Not all teenage girls said they felt this way, however. On the contrary.

6

Passionate Friends

Narratives of Lesbian Desire

> Denied access to an accurate historical record, we
> knew only that our foresisters wore neckties, and
> committed suicide all over the last pages of the
> novel.
>
> —Blanche Wiesen Cook
> on coming out in the 1950s

Well into the early 1980s, to name was to organize, and
sexual identities were declared and politicized with remarkable speed. The process destabilized a long-standing consensus regarding which sexualities were acceptable and which
were aberrant as a discourse of "liberation" set new terms for
gay identity. Within feminism, lesbianism came to represent var-
iously a choice, a deeper reality, or a political imperative—a
chance to have romance without oppression in some views, to
wrest free of romance in others. Relying heavily on developmental theory, some sex educators supported the concept of sexual
pluralism but positioned *adolescent* homosexuality as a phase.
Neutralized, homosexuality became innocuous in liberal circles
and popular in some feminist adolescent cliques. "Why do you
want to be on the lesbian radio show?" one Socratic but nervous
mother asked a daughter who belonged to a clique that came
out en masse in ninth grade. "You haven't gone that far with a

girl yet." Unfazed, her daughter retorted, "Well, I haven't gone that far with a guy yet. Why assume I'm straight?"[1] This extraordinary moment in the history of sex in the United States passed quickly as a homophobic and antifeminist backlash arose. By the mid-'80s, the worst epithet in teenage lingo was "faggot," and the emergence of HIV/AIDS in the gay community had become an excuse for increased prejudice and violence. In one survey, teenagers repudiated racial and ethnic prejudice but viewed lesbians and gay men as "legitimate targets" of attack.[2]

The narrators here are the heirs of both the struggle and the backlash. They were born during the heyday of lesbian feminism; entered adolescence just as the tide turned. The heterocentrism they faced as they came of age (remember the studied heterosexuality of popular, fast-track, and even hell-year narrators) turned into homophobia as they came out. The stigma against them increased before their opened eyes, and feminism, which had provided a wider social context and a sense of meaning for the previous generation of lesbians, virtually disappeared. But despite all these changes, somehow a sense of a collective consciousness remained, perhaps because, unlike so many of their forebears, these girls at least knew that there were others like them. In some places, teenage lesbians had established not just their own cliques but their own locales—adolescent lesbian nations.

> These girls were all lesbians from when they were like fourteen. . . . It wasn't even like they had older lesbian friends. It was like they created their own young lesbian world. It was amazing. It was incredible. I don't know where they found the strength.

And:

> And we finally went there and we were in the parking lot and there was like a swarm of women around us—like all these athletic women there, like "Come on inside, guys . . ." And I was like, Oh my god, what is happening to me? And they were like, Oh, she's so cute. And I was like, Help me, God help me. And I was like, God, I love this.

If the neighborhoods these girls lived in didn't have any visible lesbians, at least everyone knew about places where there were

—New York, San Francisco. They knew of lesbian rock stars and tennis players and politicians. As soon as they were old enough, they'd go "looking for lesbians," and find both the love and the community of their daydreams.

The experiences of these narrators are uncommon; it's still rare, although increasingly less so, for girls to be "out" or identify as lesbians in high school. It can take years to discover or develop a sexual identity, and it's hard enough to survive the pressure toward conformity in such relatively straightforward matters as dress or speech in high school. During the course of the general interviews I conducted, only eight teenagers told about sexual experiences with other girls. Since that was a much smaller fraction than most studies would have predicted at the time, I made additional efforts to locate teenagers with lesbian experience, interviewing participants in two lesbian and gay teenage discussion groups. The resulting sample was as demographically diverse as the general sample, but it does include some narrators who were out of high school.[3]

It's very likely that had I followed all of the girls in this book through their twenties or thirties, a number of narrators who thought of themselves as heterosexual would have come to define themselves as lesbian and vice versa. Sexual inclinations can change and change again. A popular girl or fast-track narrator may come out someday. A lesbian may decide to go straight or bi. (It's not just adolescent development at work in such shifts: it's adult development as well. It's *life*. Repression may lift. Experience may sour one toward one gender or lead one to notice another.) These narrators assumed, however, that their lesbianism would last and to tell their story as it was told to me, I'm going to refer to them as they referred to themselves, accepting their lesbian presumption in the same way that I have accepted the heterosexual presumption of other accounts.

KNOWING THAT other lesbians existed, these narrators didn't drift into lesbianism unconsciously, as earlier studies report previous generations of lesbians had.[4] Rather, they said they saw it coming, often as early as childhood, through their feelings for others or those of others for them. "What made me a lesbian," traditionally a highlight of coming-out stories, was of little or no interest. They didn't think that lesbianism needed an explanation. It wasn't a problem. It was an identity, a source of pleasure and love, fantasy and hope. Somehow it seemed to come naturally. What *was* interesting to these narrators was the process of coming to or upon that identity or practice; experimenting with it, making lesbianism visible, dealing with the fallout; and then, sex itself—the great pleasure of sexual experience.

Jean "had an idea" that she would become involved with a woman. She "knew that would happen." Shannon "always wanted it to happen."

It was a matter of desire.

Kendra said she was:

> one of those people who always knew I was a lesbian. I knew that girls my own age weren't interested in girls . . . and so I had really made up in my mind when I was pretty young that I would have to play this game of, you know, boyfriends and that kind of stuff until I was a certain age and then I would be able to go out and find all the lesbians.

Kelly claimed it began in kindergarten.

> Okay, back in preschool, I had my little girlfriends.

When she and her friends played house, Kelly added, she played "the male." In fourth grade she became fascinated with her dad's *Playboy* magazines:

> There was one centerfold that I really remember. I would look at it every day and think, Oh my god, you know. What I would give to be with this girl! As time progressed, so did my fantasies, and you know, I'm exploding with fantasies.

She fantasized "about almost every woman" she saw.

> And then sometimes I would think, Nah, not her.

Julie began to think about "homosexuality or whatever" when a friend "suddenly walked up and started making these offers to me, throwing me into an abyss of confusion."

Eileen didn't even begin to think about herself sexually until "around fifth or sixth grade" when her friends "started playing spin the bottle seriously." None of the boys wanted to kiss her, "which was okay because most of them I really didn't like."

> But it sort of hurt in a way. Because I really felt odd. But I could never explain to myself either why I felt odd.

As fast-track girls recounted getting contact lenses, putting on makeup, losing weight, and acquiring trendier wardrobes, and some hell-year narrators described going punk or '60s, lesbian narrators, too, placed importance on changing physical appearance as part of the greater project of self-transformation, often detailing a series of haircuts as a prelude to coming out.

> Every week I would go and get my hair cut just a little shorter until it was finally down to a crew cut, and the girls' dean called me into her office and told me if I got my hair cut any shorter I'd be kicked out.

Julie didn't discuss her appearance until near the end of her interview, when she remarked that her short hair often caused people to mistake her for a boy. (I thought her carriage, the set of her jaw, and the insinuation of her gaze probably had more to do with it.) She had cut her hair, she said, sophomore year, right about the time when classmates reported that she began to send romantic gifts to girlfriends. As to her current minimalist haircut, her girlfriend had "cut it much shorter than she was supposed to."

> All I wanted was a trim.

Her girlfriend, Lauren, spent a good half hour describing her own physical transformation. Lauren's initial haircut gave her "real pangs." Then she "tried a whole bunch of different styles" until she ended up with an "asymmetrical" haircut which, she declared, "I like and I'm going to keep." Very short, straight, and boyish on one side, longer and perm-curly on the other, it was as ambiguous as she.

COMING OUT can have several stages. Just realizing lesbian desire may take a long time, and because it's sometimes a painful realization, there's a tendency to forget, to start over. Then, revealing desire to others—saying to another girl, "I'm attracted to you," saying to a parent, "I'm attracted to other girls or women"—frequently takes longer still. While feeling lesbian desires seemed natural, these narrators said, other stages were difficult and confusing.[5]

> I knew I was, but I didn't want to come out. I wasn't sure, you know. It was a bad time.

The body acted up:

> Seriously, like my whole body changed. . . . I was having headaches all the time and I couldn't talk to my parents and I just couldn't eat at all. I'd eat cereal and drink some milk but I couldn't eat and I couldn't function and I couldn't see myself as a lesbian at all. I couldn't say "lesbian," I couldn't say "gay," I couldn't say "queer," I couldn't—I just couldn't deal with it at all, but I knew what I was feeling. It was *very* hard. It was very strange.

Unexpected, vehement dislikes surfaced. Susan:

> It was painful and I hated my father. I just remember hating him then, and just thinking he was the most incompetent stupid person in the world.

Susan thought this sudden dislike had been provoked by his disapproving comments about her relationship with a friend from school.

> He had said a couple times like, "I don't like this friendship with Anne at all." And I was like, "Leave me alone. Just don't talk to me about it. I don't want to hear it from you."

But she despised him.

> I was like, What a jerk. I hate him. I hated him. I didn't know why.
> I just hated him.

Others noted that as they began to think of themselves as different, they began to isolate themselves.

> I sort of, like, quietly withdrew from everyone—my family, my friends, everyone. And I just became friends with Gerri.

Above all, girls did not want to make a mistake.

> If it is not what I was, then I don't want to be it.

To make sure, they read everything they could find.

In earlier decades, those who wanted to read up on lesbianism first had to find what little literature was available and then survive the poisonous homophobia it purveyed. At the beginning of the twentieth century, the adolescent female intimacy that had been of enormous importance to nineteenth-century women became suspect and it stayed that way. Advice books for girls warned against affectionate friendships. "And don't kiss other girls!" William Lee Howard's *Confidential Chats with Girls* exclaimed in 1911. A few years later Irving David Steinhardt warned sharply against "overaffectionate girlfriends," sleepovers, even pointed compliments from girls. Counting on girls' vanity to keep them straight, Lois Pemberton's 1948 *The Stork Didn't Bring You!* advanced the argument that only those who were "physically unattractive" or had "grotesque disabilities" would have "unnatural sexual relations with their own sex."[6]

The enterprising few who looked to more adult texts either found psychological studies that viewed lesbianism as a mental disorder, one more sign of female masochism, or the midnight underworlds of Radclyffe Hall's *The Well of Loneliness*, Djuna Barnes's *Nightwood*, and Ann Bannon's *Women in the Shadows* and *Odd Girl Out*, where women were allowed to fall in love with each other but only at a very high price. As readers of true romances are trained to expect a lifetime of devotion and wealth for a first kiss, lesbian readers learned to anticipate cut wrists and nights of lamentation from this body of work. Science fiction writer Joanna Russ tells of having written a story on the basis of this kind of reading in which "a tall, strong, masculine, dark-haired girl" throws herself off a bridge after she falls in love with another girl. "I couldn't imagine anything else for the two of them to do," Russ cracked.[7]

Second-wave feminism and the lesbian and gay movement gave young lesbians a lot more to read and a lot more to feel good about. Teenagers who went to stores and libraries and looked for information on lesbianism now found, alongside the old fear-mongering standards, feminist works like *Sappho Was a Right On Woman*; *Our Bodies, Ourselves*; *Lesbian/Woman*; and *The Joy of Lesbian Sex*; antic, erotic classics like *Ladies Almanack* and *A Woman Appeared to Me*; the poetry of Audre Lorde, Adrienne Rich, and many others; a growing shelf of lesbian biographies and histories; new novelists like Blanche McCrary Boyd, Bertha Harris, Kate Millett, Valerie Miner, and Jane Rule. There were also books on coming of age as a lesbian, including Catherine Stimpson's *Class Notes*, Rita Mae Brown's *Rubyfruit Jungle*, Nancy Garden's *Annie on My Mind*, and Sandra Scoppetone's *Happy Endings Are All Alike*, as well as Ann Heron's collection of teenage writing, *One Teenager in Ten*. The problem became how to read it all. Every narrator I spoke to had read some lesbian-feminist work—at least *Rubyfruit Jungle*—and become convinced that lesbianism should be an acceptable identity. They also knew a good deal about the possibilities and problems of lesbian life and something of how to talk and think through the objections they would meet.

Uncertainty ended where the body began—usually with revelatory first kisses. Hally was rapturous about her first kiss, which brought her out:

> And finally we went outside and we held hands and it was like butter. It just felt different than anything I had ever felt. And then we kissed and it was the most incredible—I knew I was gay at that minute because I had made out before and it never felt like that. And it was just so incredible. It was like the rockets, the fireworks, the feelings. And I felt stoned and I felt happy and I felt—it was just incredible. It was just amazing.

And Claire:

> Every bone in my body was tingling.

Both women and girls who fall in love or lust with one another often also "fall in love with being a lesbian," as Joyce Hunter, who has long counseled lesbian and gay youth, has observed. Fear and shame vanish. Confidence and happiness prevail.[8] For a moment—a month? a year?—everything is simple and clear.

It sort of like solved all my problems in a way—until I went home.

"No one is more romantic than a lesbian in love," social scientist Deborah Goleman Wolf commented, and these stories support her observation—to a point.[9] These *are* very romantic histories. But they are also very hot. And comic. Picturing themselves as suitors and seductresses excited these girls and struck them as funny. When they found themselves taking sexual initiative and acting on passion, they were impressed, amused, and aroused:

It turned me on incredibly.

Eager but inexperienced lovers, they found their misperceptions and mistakes—even their most successful seductions—hilarious. One recalled how she and her girlfriend categorized "the levels of disgustingness" in preparation for becoming sexually involved:

The mostly disgusting is like a hand job, and exceedingly disgusting is like oral sex. . . . We had decided next time one of us spent the night over at the other's, we were going to be on the next level of disgusting, and then the week after that we were going to be mostly disgusting, and then we were going to be exceedingly disgusting. And so then, um—somehow we didn't do that in stages at all. We sort of managed it all in one night and felt very much satisfied with ourselves in the morning.

Orgasms—as rare as hen's teeth in the heterosexual narratives—were reported in every lesbian account. Only girls who had been with men initially saw orgasm as a feat.[10]

Ruth was experienced. She knew what she was doing. It shocked me because I didn't think it would be like that. I didn't know really what to expect, but I didn't know it was going to be like that.

Q: But, specifically, in what ways was it different? What surprised you?

A: I reached my climax.

Everyone else saw them as great but hardly rare. "You just kissed me," one girl remarked to her lover, "and I had one." It's not very hard to explain this orgasmic difference between lesbian and heterosexual histories. Once they got past the stigma, the narrators of lesbian sex had less to worry about. Sex and reproduction are "naturally" separated in lesbian sex, and force is rarely an issue.[11]

So FAR I've been telling only the beginning of the story about lesbian adolescence—the part about coming out and experiencing pleasure. When these narrators began to talk in more detail about their lives—about home, family, school—their histories became more complicated, difficult, and divided. The original plot of twentieth-century lesbian fiction, literary critic Catherine R. Stimpson has remarked and others have amplified, assumed damnation as the lesbian fate. The more contemporary has proposed an "enabling escape" from family and local restrictions. These histories indicate that while both damnation and escape remain relevant themes, there's a new possibility—one that the lesbian and gay movement has long fought for: integrating a lesbian identity or relationship into everyday life.[12]

THIS IS a story a couple tells.

Well, to a few people, yeah.

They know each other's renditions by heart. They aren't tired of telling their love story yet or of listening to each other. The story is about coming out and becoming sexually involved. There are two loving families, a few embarrassing moments, and a happy ending. If it weren't a lesbian story, it would be a perfect summer movie.

Tall and willowy, with fluent hands, light skin, an infectious laugh, and a boyfriend, Jean began hanging out with a lesbian

clique in high school when a good friend of hers came out.[13] A
little after, Shannon caught her eye in chorus. An ace tennis
player, Shannon had a muscular rangy body, marble blue eyes,
light wheat hair chopped in a circle above her ears, and a head-
on way of talking. She looked gay but so did a lot of the jocks.
Shannon wasn't in the lesbian clique, Jean knew, but she did
hang out sometimes with a girl in the clique whom Jean knew
slightly. Jean didn't want to "ask" about her but she was "just
so curious."

> I just had to find out.

Finally, Jean passed Shannon a note asking "if she had something in common" with a "mutual acquaintance" who was out.
Shannon:

> I never actually said "yes."

Shannon didn't say "no" either. She had not actually answered
the question for herself, although she had confided her suspi-
cions to her best friend, Sue, who insisted it wasn't so and tried
to get Shannon to wear makeup and get a boyfriend. Shannon
and Sue were very close.

> I mean, it was almost as if we were lovers but there was not—nothing
> sexual.

Coming out is hard on friendships like that.[14]
Shannon consulted a therapist who "more or less" told her
that she was a lesbian: "That's where I am and that's what I'll be
and I should, you know, there's nothing wrong with it." But
Shannon had not acted on her desires before she met Jean. The
two began to get to know each other "because," Shannon explained, "we had this class together and we had a project we had
to do together." Actually, Jean had engineered the project when
Shannon was out of the classroom. Shannon had ideas too:

> Hopefully that something would happen.
> Q: And feeling how about that?

Shannon: That I wasn't going to make the first move, but I wouldn't discourage her from doing so.

Jean, on the other hand, had given up her sexual expectations, persuaded by their earlier conversation that Shannon was a long way from coming out.

No one was home "except the dog who was in between everything." Jean tried to focus on the play they had to write.

But I had a hard time looking at her . . . and—and she kept pushing: "What's the matter? What's wrong? What's wrong? Why is it that you can't look at me?" And so I told her, "I just have a hard time looking at you because . . ."

Shannon: I knew what she was thinking.

Jean: You know, I just . . . I had little feelings. You know, I didn't know Shannon that well.

Shannon: She thought I was strange.

Jean: Strange, yes. . . . Well, she used to be very, very quiet all the time and never spoke, and she was not like that in her house at all. Well, she was very pushy.

Finally, Jean told Shannon what was on her mind and they started talking about becoming lovers. Shannon's main concern was her mother or best friend "finding out about anything."

" 'Well, why do they have to find out about anything?' " Jean responded. Shannon was silent. Jean "touched her hair," then kissed her.

And then she grabbed me and she threw me . . . !

Shannon: She always says that. I didn't throw her.

Jean: Well, you know, she responded.

Jean started to take Shannon's clothes off, but Shannon stopped her.

Jean: I don't know why!

Shannon: I was scared. It was not that I didn't want to but I was scared. Things were moving too fast, I thought.

They scheduled another meeting the next day to work on the play. Jean:

I thought we'd get a little work done this time.

They met after school. It was raining heavily. When they got to Shannon's house, Shannon gave Jean "something to change into." From then on, sex bollixed up chronology. It wasn't easy to recall the sequence of events. They went back over their steps like detectives.

> Shannon: And, uh—I don't know, some way or another, we ended up in my bedroom. I don't—I don't even remember exactly what happened, do you?
> Jean: No. No. I don't remember—I know we were in the bedroom, but I don't remember how we got in there or what led to that.

Shannon:

> I think my—did my mother come home? Or did we . . . ? I think we thought my mother was coming and so we both jumped up and got dressed—I don't know how long. Well, it started in the living room and we went into my room because it was in the back of the house and I figured if my mother walked in we wouldn't be caught, you know, right there.

Shannon's mother was "pretty open-minded," but Shannon didn't think she would appreciate walking in on a lesbian sex scene. They thought they heard something. "My dog barking probably," Shannon said wryly.

> Shannon: So we both jumped up and got dressed.
> Q: Which means you had gotten undressed?
> Shannon: Oh yeah, oh yeah.
> Jean: We skipped that part, didn't we? We got undressed in the living room. I don't remember everything that went on but, um—I don't know. And, um, well, we were half undressed. I have to say that I remember that my jeans were not completely off because I had to hop into the bedroom.

It was "a little awkward" for her, Jean said:

> I mean, the most that I had ever done was—kiss, you know, and I don't know. It was—it was just—different—from, you know, what I

had been used to and—and what I had been taught. And—I don't know—I did feel comfortable. Things were a lot softer and—I don't know.

Both Jean and Shannon seemed to feel their discomfort required an explanation. (Heterosexual girls expect to be discomfited; lesbian girls, that everything will go "naturally.") Shannon acknowledged feeling "a little uncomfortable," because "I didn't know her that well." She also felt "a little uncomfortable" when she "thought about" what she was doing.

But—but it was nice, you know. It was something that I always wanted to do and now I could.

I asked how they knew what to do. Jean said she'd had a little more sexual experience than she had previously indicated and she'd "had friends." She asked Shannon if she had known about the kinds of things they did together before.

Shannon: I don't know. It was just—I don't know. It was just natural.

They finished the project that day. School ended. Jean was scheduled to go away to a camp, where she was a counselor. The day before:

Jean: Okay, that Wednesday was a hot day, right!
 Shannon: I'm embarrassed.
 Jean: It was a wild one.
 Shannon: Go on.
 Jean: Thanks! Oh god, I know—we went out with a group of my friends.

They went to a gay bar.

Shannon and I had to go to the bathroom. So we got the key and, well, we started kissing in the bathroom. I thought I had the only key but . . . well, you need it explicit? Okay, this is really embarrassing. Well—well, I took Shannon's sweater off and she was wearing walking shorts. The weather was warm. It was during the summer.
 Shannon: Right before the summer.
 Jean: Right before the summer.

Shannon: You were going away.

Jean: Yeah, I was—this was the last day I was home. Well, yeah. . . . I sat Shannon up on the sink! And—I proceeded to, whatever —I'm very uncomfortable—and—she—you know, she had an or- gasm, and right after that the door opened and someone came into the bathroom. There were two men coming into the bathroom.

Luckily, Jean had just walked into one of the bathroom stalls.

The next morning Jean left for camp. All the counselors were lesbian, Jean said. They used to have "shower parties," Shannon interjected. Put on the spot, Jean explained:

It was just nice for all of us to get together in the shower house, where we weren't scrutinized by everyone else at the camp—the straight girls. Well, we had a radio. It was an open shower, you know. And we'd soap each other, we'd lather each other up—just friendly stuff. Nothing, nothing sexual, though. (*She* thinks something went on.) Nothing went on. Nothing went on the whole summer.

There were "straight campers" and "gay campers." The "straight campers" were comfortable with the presence of les- bians, Jean thought.

They really liked it, I think. It gave them something to talk about, and I'm sure a lot of them had crushes. Some even lied and said they were lesbians too, so they could hang out with us.

Shannon missed Jean.

I would wait for her phone calls at night. . . . I was suffering.

Shannon was trying to get her best friend Sue to understand about her and Jean, but "she wouldn't listen, she wouldn't un- derstand." Finally, she took a day off from teaching tennis to see Jean, who had the campers in her cabin carry in an extra bed. They put it right next to Jean's bed. Shannon moved over to Jean's bed during the night.

And, uh, well, Shannon slept with me. You know, we made love that evening and we were a little noisy. . . . Then right after we finished a camper came walking out of the bathroom.

In the morning, they had "a late breakfast" and Shannon went back home. She didn't feel "unsure" about herself anymore but she was worried about "losing, you know, people that I cared about." She didn't tell anyone "for a long time." Finally, in the autumn, she went over to Sue's house and told her that she had kissed Jean. Sue slapped her and told her to call Jean and say she wouldn't see her anymore. Shannon made the call, but tried to convey something more.

> An unsaid message, you know, like something strange is going on and I can't talk now.

Sue then told Shannon to get out. Shannon bicycled to a phone booth and called Jean to explain.

> And I was crying . . . I didn't want to lose this—this person but, you know, there was something about myself I knew that I had to have that she couldn't accept.

Then she bicycled for a long time to calm down. When she finally got home, "all relaxed," Sue called.

> She said, "Well, okay, we'll work things out," which I thought was, you know, going to be something positive. But, of course, that was just the initial thing and then she went back into the same thing— you know, "I don't want you to ever see her," and all this stuff.

Racism compounded homophobia.

> She . . . made comments even about how disgusting it is and comments about her being black.

Jean had had a boyfriend before she became involved with Shannon. She wanted to break up but:

> I felt like, Well, Shannon is still putting me second to Sue and here I am throwing Charles out. . . . I just felt like, Am I—am I being fair to myself? It was very confusing for me because it seemed like she was so under Sue's control.

Finally:

I just decided to take my chances. I kind of, I got into myself. And I just tried to wait to see what would go on.

She waited for Shannon "to make the decision on where to draw the line with Sue." For Jean the question was:

Which one of us was going to be most important to her in her life.

Shannon told her mother that she was a lesbian, and she and Jean began spending nights together on the living-room pullout couch.

She once or twice, you know, hinted that it made her a little uncomfortable but she never said, "You can't sleep together. Don't sleep together." So.

Jean confided to her sister that her friendship with Shannon was sexual. Her sister told her mother.

Now I'm glad that she did it, because it would have been a lot harder to go to my mother myself. But my mother asked me and I started to lie. So I said, "No, no, *no*, ma," but then I said "yes," that it is true.

When Shannon met Jean's grandmother.

My grandmother asked me, "Oh, is that your girlfriend?" And I said, "Oh, yesssss," and she said, "No, no. Is that the girl you're going with?" You know, she wanted to make sure I knew what she was talking about. So I was very happy, and I heard her say, "Oh, there's nothing wrong with it. They're not doing anything bad."

Shannon finally told Sue the truth. End of friendship.

THE OPENNESS that Shannon and Jean eventually achieved was not possible in all parts of the country or in all families. Maria's family was both conservative and religious, but together with Stevie, she faced them down, rejecting the solution of enabling escape, insisting instead that her parents change their views. Full of the stuff of melodrama (a traitorous cousin, malicious aunts, a murderous father), this tale is nevertheless, finally, a romantic comedy.

Boasting with pleasure that they'd been together four years, Stevie and Maria proposed themselves enthusiastically as "good" interview subjects when I met them at a lesbian and gay youth group. They got along famously, aiding and abetting each other's self-presentations—funny, lovable seriocomic heroines making up a zany love affair as they went along, filling in details for each other with gusto. With the comforting distance of hindsight, even violent family scenes struck them as riotously funny. Since they didn't have homes in which they could speak comfortably, I met them at a friend's apartment. As we began to talk, they nestled cozily on the sofa, Stevie—a chunky young woman with wiry black hair—leaning back and putting her arm around figurine Maria, who held Stevie's other hand in her lap. They remained in each other's arms for over three hours.

Like Shannon and Jean's, theirs was a match of differences— Anglo vs. Hispanic; art vs. business; masculine vs. feminine; voluble vs. reserved—yet they never talked about oppositions or differences per se. Throughout the interview, Maria took the first turn at most questions, looked surprised when I asked Stevie a question (as if she thought Stevie was there simply for moral support), and often interrupted when Stevie spoke.

Stevie took Maria's preemptive strikes in stride and seemed to relish everything Maria said without giving up on her side of the story. Stevie told stories—adventures, episodes—though emotions did show through in her gestures. Maria spoke about feelings directly. Stevie's mother, a secretary, and stepfather, a salesman, were Anglo. Maria's extended working-class family emigrated to the United States from Cuba when she was about three years old. She and her cousin Louise, both only children, were raised almost as sisters.

Stevie and Maria attended a Catholic girls' high school, where there were other lesbians. Of the two, Maria was the conventionally "pretty" one, but in Maria's view, it was Stevie who was "beautiful."

> I just saw her and said, "Oh god, she is so beautiful." You know, it was just like love at first sight, for me, for *me*, not for her.
> Stevie: Well.

After a pause, Stevie picked up the thread.

> I thought she was cute and she laughed at everything I said. I liked
> her cousin a little bit then, coming on to me. At that time, I was sort
> of looking for someone and wanting to get out of my other relation-
> ship. So I was like—anybody who came along.

From the beginning, Maria was "feeling things" for Stevie:

> But I really didn't think I was feeling them. It was a strange thing
> of, like, How can I be feeling these things for another woman, you
> know. I just put it out of my mind, and then it grew and it grew, and
> I didn't know why. I couldn't believe it.

They got into the habit of playing "tricks" to "get a little closer
together." Kid stuff. Playing Eskimos "just to rub our noses together." Racing to the movies just so they could "bump together." Soon Stevie liked Maria better than Maria's chic cousin.

> I mean, I was feeling things for Louise, plus I liked Maria a lot. I
> thought she was so cute, and she was just always laughing and smil-
> ing, and I swore I saw a little twinkle in her eyes. I was like—ha-ha.

Often she brought Maria mementos. A little dog with a fire
hydrant for the time they saw *The Jerk*. A Miss Piggy. A framed
baby picture. All the Mr. Men books: "Mr. Happy. Mr. Silly. Mr.
Everything." Jealous, Louise—who had a reputation for lying
and had been caught in a "lesbian incident" herself a year
earlier—went to Maria's parents, saying that Stevie, profferer of
trinkets and Mr. Silly books, was a lesbian sex fiend drug dealer.

Maybe Maria's Cuban parents feared that the sweetness growing between their daughter and this stolid chivalrous Anglo girl
would lead to more than friendship. In any case, they began
telling Maria tabloid horror stories about lesbian love. Maria was
still child enough to take these stories literally.

> I actually thought that Stevie was going to kill me, because my par-
> ents said, "You know what they do? They even get married and then
> they have jealous fights, and then they kill each other." They said,
> "There was once this lady, who was a lesbian, and she brought her
> lover home one day and her father didn't want them doing some-

thing sexual or something, and then one of the lesbians got mad and killed the father." This is what my parents told me.

One afternoon Maria came home from school and found her mementos from Stevie piled in a heap on her bed. Her mother said, "I want you to throw everything away." Maria said, "No, I'm not going to throw everything away." The heap remained for a few days. Then her mother put it all in the garbage.

"You know," Maria mused, "it was so obvious from the letters and the little notes that we loved each other. We had feelings for each other." But they didn't understand themselves. One day Maria's mother found a strip of dime-store photos of Maria and Stevie together in Maria's wallet.

And when I came out of the bathtub, I found her crying, and I said, "What's wrong? What's wrong with you?" And she said, "Nothing, nothing, nothing." And I knew something was wrong because my mother, she was hysterical. I thought she was going to have a nervous breakdown. And then I found the pictures in her pocket.

Maria begged her mother not to tell her father, but he too heard her mother crying and came in saying, "What's wrong? What's wrong?"

And then, oh, he was mad at me and he wanted to slap me around and hit me, but my mother stopped him.

If Maria had to engage in a decadent, stigmatized activity, her father pleaded, let it be something less reprehensible:

I'd rather you be a prostitute than be a lesbian. You could be a murderer. You could be a prostitute, and that would be fine. We'd still love you.

Because her mother said, "I am going to *try* to stop loving you," not "I *am* going to stop loving you," Maria believed that her mother would come around if she held her ground. She was right. Because of her mother, her father didn't kick her out. For months they lived like strangers.

When he came home from work, I went into my room and didn't come out until the next day. We couldn't face each other. I felt ashamed for betraying the family like that, and I guess he was ashamed of me too.

Like straight girls who prove their innocence by not planning ahead and not using contraception, Maria invoked the rule of spontaneity. Nothing was premeditated, she argued.

I wasn't looking to find, I wasn't looking to have a relationship. I just had it. It was innocent really.

Stevie supported Maria's point with another example:

I remember holding her hand from time to time, you know. But we didn't say, Oh, what are people going to think? *Now* we think that way.

Maria added:

She used to toss me around in the air. We used to have fun. And I never thought that it was anything wrong.
  Stevie: It was wonderful. I was always making her laugh.

Maria's parents insisted she see a priest.

They figured that a priest would change me.

But she replied to the priest with the same logic of love she had used with her own conscience.

I said, "There's no way I'm going to stop loving her."

Perhaps it was a sign of how Americanized Maria was that she saw love as the irrefutable answer to religion, but she was also using an argument that had been used successfully on her by Stevie, who had spent hours in gay bookstores looking for arguments that would advance their courtship:

Stevie: I would always say: If there's love, it's just love. It's not something horrible. I could understand if you were hurting somebody.

The "love" that Maria bravely defended in the face of considerable intimidation had so far consisted of Eskimo kisses, hand holding, and the occasional deliberate jostle. Maria thought:

> This is going too slow. I have to do something here. So I said to Stevie, "Well, let's become hickey sisters." She wanted to give me a hickey on my arm. I said, "That's not going to work, on my arm."

Finally, the first kiss:

> Stevie: This was in the train station. It was bad. I don't know how many people were around. I kissed her lips and then she said, "Nooooo." And then she just walked away. I thought, Well, should I just ignore that she said no? Because in my mind I thought, That's not no.

That night Stevie wrote Maria a note. "It just said, 'I love you.' "

The next weekend they went to a movie at a central city theater. The illusion of privacy that movie theaters create drew them in.

> Stevie: We missed the whole entire movie.
>   Maria: I don't even know what it was about.
>   Q: You mean you made out through the whole movie?
>   Maria: Yes!
>   Stevie: Isn't that crazy? And it was so slimy!
>   Maria: It was eerie because everybody was around and you wonder—these people were sleazeballs.
>   Stevie: All these slimy men were behind us, and we didn't even realize it. We were just desperate for any movie.

To go further, they needed privacy. Stevie didn't have her own room. Maria's parents wouldn't let Stevie in the door. Just in time, Stevie got a house-sitting job. The first time she and Maria went there they had Stevie's little sister in tow:

> Stevie: We just went into this little room and we were kissing and lying next to each other, and I touched her through, um—were you wearing your nightie that time?
>   Maria: Mm-hmm.

Stevie: I bought her this little yellow nightie. This was the first time we ever did anything besides kiss. And I just put her down and then I touched her through her little yellow panties. She was soaked. [Hoots.] And I didn't realize. I didn't do anything else because my sister was banging on the door.

Maria continued the story:

They had a piano in the other room and her little sister would be playing the piano and then we'd hear her little footsteps and she'd knock on the door: "Stevie, Stevie, are we leaving? What are you doing in there?"

Then Stevie:

The next day . . . I had brought some wine and I put it in the refrigerator and then I pulled out this couch and put all the air conditioning on and we were there for six hours, but it was just mainly hugging and kissing.
Q: And you still had all your clothes on?
Stevie: No.
Q: You took all your clothes off?
Maria: She didn't.
Stevie: I didn't.
Maria: She never did and I had this little lace, what was it?
Stevie: I don't know.
Maria: I don't know what it was. It was strange.
Stevie: And somehow I was kissing her all over, and then—I knew I wanted to . . .
Maria: Remember, you used to ask me: May I do this?
Stevie: May I do that? So our word for oral sex was kiss-kiss. So eventually I asked her may I kiss? Kiss? You know, kiss-kiss. But anyway that first day I was just kissing her legs, you know, and the inside of her thighs, back and forth, and I just would sort of rush over that little area there, you know. I was too scared, you know. And meanwhile her little panties were on. And she goes, "Wouldn't it be better if my panties were off?"
So then, I was like, "WOW!"

This continued for a while until:

Stevie: It was a red-hot day. I turned on all the air conditioners. I opened the bed. And then we didn't wind up going there.

When the woman called Stevie for her messages that night, she said, "By the way, Stevie, did you turn on the air conditioners?" Stevie said, "You mean someone was in your house?"

After Stevie lost her house-sitting job, Maria started staying home "sick" when her mother and father went to church. Stevie would arrive "like ten minutes after they left" and depart just before they were due home.

Maria: And that was so scary.
Stevie: It was like a railroad apartment. The only way to get out was through the kitchen and there were bars on the windows.

Giggling hysterically, they mimed how they had to hurriedly take off their clothes, make love, and rush out.

We had it all figured out. They had to wait ten minutes for the bus.

Both of Maria's aunts lived in that building. "We could have gotten caught so many times," Maria realized. Once they rented a room:

It was the fear, the fear. I remember one very cold winter day we were downtown and we went to the YWCA for an hour, just to be together. And it was like—we paid thirteen dollars and told them we were going to stay there. And then we made love and meanwhile every time, while Maria was getting undressed or something, I kept stomping on roaches, and saying, "Oh, it's nothing."

Eventually Maria talked her mother into letting Stevie visit. Stevie was so nervous the first day she came to the house, she turned around and left.

I ran up the street to the flower shop and bought a rose for your mother. And I just gave it to you to give to your mother and I started crying. I was all upset. . . . Your father was at work.
Maria: My father didn't know. My mother never told my father that Stevie had been in the house.

Mother and daughter kept the secret of Stevie's visits for months.

I used to be always hiding. I'd hide in the basement. I went out the back door when he'd come home.

Gradually even Maria's father accepted Stevie into the house:

Stevie: All the time before we were even in a physical relationship, I used to say, Well, why don't they want . . . ? She wouldn't tell me. Why? Why? Why don't they like me? What is it? You know. Anyway, so, I thought I'll show them. I'll learn how to speak Spanish and I'll show them that I'm a good person. Well, I haven't really learned how to speak Spanish, but they know I'm a good person. So eventually I was brave enough and her mother said I didn't have to leave when her father came home provided I was very quiet and subservient to her father. And he came home and he didn't really care.

Eventually Stevie "spoke to him a little in English, because he speaks a little bit. Not very well. But we've gotten close." More and more, Stevie became a part of the family. Maria's mother even started cooking with her in mind.

"She's not coming tonight?" That's what my mother says. She goes, "After I made this chicken dish?" (It's like a stew, and Stevie loves that.) She doesn't leave food out for me. She leaves it out for her.

Stevie's extraordinary determination in courting Maria's family had saved the day, but there was a catch. Once Stevie was welcome in Maria's house, even allowed to sleep over, the lovers didn't feel right about having sex there. For that, they started leaving school early and going to Stevie's family's apartment. They kept their clothes on because Stevie's sister frequently barged in. When that happened, Stevie would say: "Shhhhh. Maria's sleeping," and Maria would whimper that she was sick.

They thought it would get easier after graduation, but between part-time jobs and college, they hardly had a spare moment. Things couldn't go on as they were. When we talked, they had already started collecting household goods for the day when they could afford their own place. Cuban girls rarely leave home until they marry, Maria said, but she had made up her mind, and she had even thought of a way to bring her parents around: having a child by alternative insemination. Although Maria planned to teach, Stevie foresaw taking major financial responsibility for the family she and Maria were planning, and Maria's parents were beginning to appreciate the promise of Stevie's devotion, perhaps finally realizing they weren't losing a daughter, after all, but gaining a butch.

IN THE PELL-MELL of comedy and romance, it's easy to lose sight of the extent to which this group of funny love stories represents a radical departure, not just from previous lesbian experience but from much of teenage heterosexual experience as well. Love was requited and triumphant as well as balanced by work, friendship, and family. Sex was great. Color and ethnic differences were immaterial and everywhere they went, these narrators encountered—if not "out" lesbians and tolerant heterosexuals—at least people who ultimately proved ready to open their hearts. How did this wholly new plot come about?

Patient, stubborn, loving, and resilient, these narrators never took rejection for an answer. They insisted upon their right to be lesbians and stay in the families and friendships and schools that nurtured them. But the success they had in persuading their families to keep on loving them was not just a function of their wit, determination, and compassion. True, they were diplomats and strategists of the first order, but they were also fortunate in their families' flexibility, which ultimately enabled love to become tolerance and tolerance to become love. To a large extent, this was a result of the lesbian and gay movements, but other changes were at play as well. As families have gotten smaller, for example, children have become far less expendable, even more precious. The desire to hold on to them may well lead parents to temporize and work at tolerance until they have gotten beyond the initial jolt of homophobia. Then they begin to watch their daughters' relationships—to evaluate what's going on. With phobia out of the way, it's hard to complain. These families were faced not with murderous lesbian fiends, but with young women who had a profound interest in becoming a part of the family and seemed ideal daughters-in-law. As determined to "institutionalize" their relationships as many boys seemed determined to stay free, they came through and through and through.[15]

There are some reasons to think twice about happy endings

like these, however. As we have seen, it's crucial not to lose the
self in love; essential, especially in adolescence, to keep growing,
reaching out, questioning as well as affirming the self. When
women love each other, the vaunted female tendency to forge
intimate connections in case-hardened steel can choke not just
autonomy but also growth, individual identity, love, and desire.[16]
But at the same time, fusion—bonding so tightly that individual
identities are submerged either one into the other or both into
the couple—is a survival mechanism for lesbians, a necessary an-
tidote to hatred and alienation and invisibility. In a less sexist,
less fragmented world, girls would not need love so much. In a
less homophobic world, teenage lesbians would not hold each
other so tightly.

WITHOUT the persistent support and love the narrators above
enjoyed, coming of age as a lesbian was a much more confusing
and disorienting experience, one that sent many teenage girls
into a tumult that few escaped from unscathed and some didn't
live through. A second group of lesbian narrators recounted this
experience. Mainly from the middle of the country, they seem
kin to the hell-year narrators in their sense of isolation, but while
the hell-year narrators believed they just needed a little time to
find or heal their sexuality or cure their loneliness, these girls
believed they had to get through adolescence as quickly and un-
obtrusively as possible. They planned to lie low until they were
old enough to leave home when they could search out other
lesbians and live as outlaws, continuing the traditions forged in
the absinthe- and opium-saturated Paris nights and beery American afternoons of the literature—Djuna Barnes, Radclyffe Hall,
and Beebo Brinker.

Back in the days when almost all teenagers waited out adolescence in a sexual limbo, this kind of hiding wasn't so hard. You
just did what everyone else did. Went to football games. Kissed
good night after dances. But when intercourse became the adolescent rule, sex became an inescapable problem. These narrators didn't want to have sex with boys and they couldn't risk
the truancy that freaks practiced. Having to repeat a year of high
school's agony might well, given the ever-present possibility of
suicide, be the death of them.[17]

At once the most daring of the lesbian narrators and the most old-fashioned, the most alienated and the most vulnerable, both Kelly and Eileen described growing up with a sense that they would never be able to be themselves among the people they grew up with. Kelly dreamed of going to California to "start a new life," maybe playing guitar. Eileen wanted the big city— perhaps the club world or film. While they waited, they made do. They increasingly withdrew from those around them and bided their time until they could leave.

Eileen was from a small southwestern city. She had a crew cut, a pale elfin face. In a 1940s-style man's overcoat, with wide smudgy eyes, gaunt cheeks, and a narrow chin, she could have been the daughter of William Burroughs and Shirley MacLaine. Her hometown was a forcing pit of conservative sexual politics. We talked about that for a while before she settled into what she later told a counselor at the group home she lived in was "the story of my life." In five and a half hours, she said fewer words than many girls say in two and she was hard to hear as well. She had a hesitant way of talking about her life as if she were telling a story she had made up or heard or couldn't bear.

Her father, an engineer, died when she was nine. After his death, her mother went to work as a night nurse, leaving Eileen in the care of brothers too young or too traumatized themselves to behave responsibly. They tormented her regularly, she said. Then when Eileen was fifteen, her mother died, and Eileen was handed first to one family and then to another. She retreated further. In mourning, disoriented, she must have been a disturbing presence. She often locked herself in her room to work on a pornographic novel she imagined would net her enough money to get away.

> The first scene would be male and female. Then the next scene would be the female masturbating. Then it would be two women and a man. Then a woman and two men. Then a lesbian scene. Then another male-female. Then I'd throw in some bestiality or S&M, something like that. That was the plot: who was going to have sex with who in each chapter.

Her aunt found the draft in Eileen's drawer and shipped Eileen off to her other aunt's, where Eileen started stealing liquor from her uncle's cabinet.

This was probably the worst period in my life because I was really suicidal at this time. I had decided if I was going to do it, I was going to take a bottle of sleeping pills and drink some whiskey, you know, right before I went to sleep at night so that I would have all night to die before anyone found me.

She wanted to kill herself because she felt "awkward around everybody."

I just felt something was completely different about me.

But each time she came near to taking her own life, she put it off.

And then I started thinking, Well, when I turn eighteen and leave home, then I'll be okay.

Her second aunt's husband attributed her condition to drugs, despite Eileen's insistence that she had never used any (she was even "antimarijuana" at that point, she said), and enrolled her in a boarding school. Eileen "was really mad at being kicked out" of her aunt's.

And about this time I was beginning to think, you know, Well, I don't fit in anyplace.

At least boarding school was full of kids whose families, like Eileen's, couldn't handle them, but were rich enough to pay for a roof over their heads rather than just kicking them out onto the streets, as many teenage mothers' and hell-year narrators' parents had. Weekends she and a friend drove around and drank and smoked and took acid and met guys.

I don't think I ever made out with them. I saw them more as just a nuisance. I wasn't attracted to this friend of mine. She was just my friend but we got along really well, which was strange since she listened to all this disco music. Driving down the street, disco on the radio!

It was fun, but she still felt out of it. She looked up "lesbian" in the encyclopedia but didn't find anything. She thought "women's lib was dead and all that."

> I felt completely alone. If I thought about what a lesbian would look like, it was like a truck driver. Completely stereotyped. A really ugly homely girl. I couldn't imagine myself being that.

Yet she also keenly suspected she was. And she "was really getting disenchanted with these guys." Finally, she decided,

> I wanted to try it with a woman at some point.

She began to call herself bisexual.

Eileen's was the longest search for a female lover of any in the lesbian stories. She didn't meet anyone that summer, as far as she remembered, and when she went back to school, all her friends from the year before were gone. The friend she used to go disco driving with had gotten engaged.

> I was like kind of jealous in a way because she liked him better than me, even though I wasn't really attracted to her, you know. It was like he had intruded on the time between us.

She looked around for a new friend and noticed Connie.

> She was really into punk rock. She had all these chains and stuff. I think this was the first time I actually fell in love. We used to get drunk a lot together.

One night Eileen was "really drunk."

> And I told Connie I was bisexual. It was very hard for me to do. And she said she was too. And I was really surprised. And really happy. I just like kept thinking about her more and more.

But she couldn't bring herself to "kiss her or anything."

> So one day we were in her room and I finally said to her that I felt more about her than a friend. It took me a really long time to get

that out. I think she knew what I meant but she didn't really react to it or anything. She just played it off.

Connie told Eileen that she had slept with her best friend back home. From then on Eileen kept thinking:

If I hung around for long enough that maybe I'd get to sleep with her.

Connie and Eileen used to hang out in the art room at night listening to "morbid electronic music" while Connie was painting.

One night we turned out the lights. We were sitting on the floor, and I put my head in her lap, and I had really long hair, and she started braiding it. It was really nice. And that was about all we did. We really didn't touch each other or anything. You know, but that was the first feeling I ever had of really being in love with somebody.

Later a guy Connie liked came in.

We were on different sides of the room. We were just listening to the music. I don't think we were really talking or anything. And he came in, and he made some sort of innuendo about what we were doing. That really disturbed me because I didn't want anyone to know I felt that way, because it was such a small campus. And it was really homophobic.

They never had sex. They drank more and more.

Eileen never got caught bringing in alcohol or using drugs, but Connie got expelled. Eileen started to feel "really rebellious." She and Connie made a plan to meet in "a cheap hotel" over Christmas vacation.

The actual plan was that we were going to do a lot of drugs for a couple years and then kill ourselves.

To finance the plan, Eileen was going to sell acid on campus. She gave Connie two hundred dollars to buy their supply. The acid didn't arrive.

All through that Christmas, I was really depressed. At night I would stay up and cry.

Of course, she couldn't tell her brothers what was wrong.

When she got back to school, half the acid was there with a note saying that the rest of it had been sold already and the money was in a bank account.

And so I had fifty-three hits of acid and they were gone in like two days. I felt really bad because that Saturday night everybody on campus was on acid except me.

At the end of the next semester, she and Connie finally took a trip together to the West Coast, but Connie spent the whole time with guys.

Somehow Eileen had kept her work up and she decided to go East to college. There, surely, she thought, she'd meet some lesbians. As if this resolve liberated her, she started telling everyone in school—including some reputed dykes, all of whom she found too bland—that she was either bisexual or gay. She saw this as an oblique invitation to seduce her but no one took her up on it.

That summer she read in her local newspaper that 11 percent of her town was gay. There had to be a lesbian community that she had missed. But even knowing it was there, Eileen—who was crafty enough to smuggle and sell cigarettes on campus, who could turn a whole school on to finance a trip to San Francisco —couldn't find any lesbians. Utterly at a loss as to how to realize her fantasy, she started experimenting with every drug and lover that came her way—participating in a ménage à trois and having intercourse with both her brother and his friend. Trying to tell about this, she lost track of the chronology; trying to live it, it seemed, she lost what sense of self she had had.

Eileen did make it East to college, but by the time she got there she was in serious trouble. Still, she tried to live out her dream. She put up her Patti Smith posters, told everyone she was gay, and began to follow up on the lesbian ads in the alternative papers. She went by the gay students' union but didn't like it any better than she had liked the jock clique at boarding school. At last she met a woman in a bar.

And I was really nervous, and I did not get like this with men.

They went home together and:

It was really exciting. It was really nice. It wasn't like you were waiting for the big thing, you know, where the guy sticks it in you. She made breakfast the next morning.

One night she and her roommate decided to go out together to some clubs. At the first club, a girls' band came on, and Eileen fell in love.

Actually, I fell in lust.

She arranged to do a video project on the band. The first taping took place at a rehearsal, and the lead singer and the guitarist drove her back into the city.

These were both women and they were both gay, but they did not identify with being gay. They just slept with women.

A couple of weeks later, they came to the studio to watch her edit the video. When they left, they asked if she wanted to hang out with them and she said, "Sure."

And, so we were driving around and we smoked a joint. And I had quit smoking pot at this point. I had really decided I didn't like it. So anyway we smoked a joint. I got really high off it, and then they asked me if I wanted to get *really* high, and I said, "What are you talking about? I'm already high." And they said, "No, we mean *really* high." And what they were talking about was heroin. You know. And I didn't—really say yes or no. Because heroin was something I had always wanted to try, but I had never been offered it.
  Finally the lead singer ran into this one building and came back with these little bags of heroin. And we drove over by the river and parked there. And I still had not said yes or no if I was going to try it. But I felt kind of stupid to be sitting there.

These were the days before everyone knew about the hazards of sharing needles.

So it came right down to it, and they had the needle ready and everything, you know, and they asked me if I wanted to snort it instead. So I said, "Well, as long as I'm going to do it, I may as well do it right." So this girl, the really cute one, went ahead and hit me. I got a rush, but there was nothing really that great about it, and mainly, I just liked being with her, you know. I figured if I was going to hang out with her, I was going to have to do this.

The next time Eileen saw the lead singer, the band was going to play at a well-known punk club and Eileen had arranged to shoot the gig.

It seemed like I was really Somebody.

After the show, Eileen, the woman she had a crush on, and a few others went to Eileen's dorm room.

And I really wanted to sleep with this woman. So when we got back—you know, we needed a place to get off—I asked my roommate to go sleep in another room. I really felt bad asking her to do that, you know, but at that time I had one thing on my mind, which was to sleep with this woman. I had never been so attracted to a woman in my life.

Gradually, everybody left but Eileen and the lead singer and the lead guitarist and two other girls. They turned out the lights and lit candles.

And I leaned back in this one corner. And this lead singer started moving closer, and she was really afraid to make a move on me. So she moved a little closer to me, and finally I just reached over, you know, and kissed her. And we started making out. And then when the other two girls saw what was going on, they started making out. We ended up having sex on the floor. I have to say, that was about my most exciting sexual experience. Because here was this girl that a few months ago I'd seen on an album cover.

She felt she had "finally achieved" what she "wanted."

I had this great-looking girl. I was shooting heroin, which was really so uncool that it was cool. I wasn't doing too well in school, but I wasn't doing too badly. I had B's and stuff. And I was in New York.

It was late. She stopped talking. There was more to her story but she didn't have to tell it. When I asked if she needed a ride home, she had me drop her off at a halfway house for addicts.

KELLY HAD the vocal rhythms of a hard drinker: the pauses between words, the slow emphatic tone, the slur. She wore heavy stiff Levi's; her starched white shirt opened to reveal a stretched-out white tee. She grew up in an agricultural center but her sultry farmhand way owed as much to the movies as it did to local mores. Her dad was in and out of jail. When he came home, he beat the shit out of everyone he knew well enough to recognize. Her mom worked wherever she could—the supermarket, the mall.

Kelly kept her distance from her peers. Her life had been a lot harder than theirs; she had enough to do keeping up her nerve, surviving. And it wasn't as if she needed friends to help her get a fix on how to live. She knew what she had to do. Get out on her own. Get away from her father. Find some lesbians. She and a slightly older girl, Marcy, became friends when she was thirteen.

I liked her a lot and I thought of her sexually when her and I started hanging around together. And then I heard that she was gay.

Marcy had shoulder-length blond hair and "she was just built" and she was old enough to buy liquor.

Something about her attracted me, and we were friends for an awful long time. And then one night we went out and got drunk and I said, "Well, Marcy, I heard that you were gay."

And she says, "Where did you hear that from?" And I said, "From so-and-so."

And she goes, "Well, if I get drunk enough, I think I could be."

And I said, "Heh, heh." We were pretty drunk that night.

They were in a car. Kelly asked Marcy to kiss her.

> And she just kind of looked at me, and she says, "Sure." And I was kind of turned on by that, you know. And it just kind of went from there.

I asked how she felt that first night:

> Very excited. You know, I had never felt anything like that before. I was really turned on, and I wanted to just grab her and take her to bed then.

Kelly had watched the Playboy channel avidly.

> So I basically knew how to do it. It's just that I didn't KNOW how to do it, you know. I'd seen it done but I didn't know how to do it.

"Practice was exciting," Kelly found. "You know, it lasted for a long time. Until she'd pass out on me." Soon Kelly was spending "almost every night" with Marcy. Soon after that they broke up.

The breakup was Kelly's doing. In telling what happened, she complained that Marcy wouldn't leave her alone *and* wouldn't say she was gay *and* was sleeping with a guy. Under the circumstances, Marcy's fixation on her made Kelly violently angry.

> She would follow me everywhere, and it got to the point where I'd say, "Bitch, get off my back," you know. "Leave me alone. Give me some space." And she wouldn't. So I finally told her, "I can't see you anymore." She goes, "Well, I'll never be able to love anybody again." And I said, "Yes, you will."

Kelly told her parents she was gay. Her mother went right on talking about something else. Her father said to keep away from his girlfriend's daughter.

She began going to the bars looking for lovers. Underage, hard-drinking, and belligerent, she probably was a scary figure. She said she'd accumulated nine lovers by the time we talked. All had broken it off. She talked about them the way girls with multiple heartbreaks talk about boys and men:

> They lead you to believe that they love you and then all of a sudden [clicks her fingers]—out the door.

Still, she loved the bars, she said. They were the only gay community she knew.

For all their concentration on difference, finally, this second group of stories had one theme: Where I came out, these narrators all said, there was no lesbian community. My family was cold and narrow-minded. There was no true lover in sight for me. I did what there was to do. I drank. I did drugs. The next thing I knew I was an addict or an alcoholic. Now I have trouble with my memory, and I don't believe in love. None of this would have happened had there been others like me who were visible and approachable (and attractive) so I didn't have to feel like such a freak.

This reading fits well with the notion that the self-destructive elements present in lesbian culture—alcoholism, drug addiction, slashed wrists—are wholly products of internalized stigma. But the relationship between sexual identity and feelings of alienation may not be so clear-cut. Eileen's inability to find lesbians despite her cleverness and their numbers raises the question of whether her lesbianism constituted a cause of her alienation or simply a pat explanation for it, a specific name she gave to a more nebulous condition of overwhelming isolation. Similarly, claiming a lesbian identity can be a rationale—a cover story—for heavy drinking, drugging, and isolation that have very different causes. But if the lesbian desire of these narrators was a rationale, perhaps it would also ultimately be a saving grace.[18]

In the media, stories like Kelly's and Eileen's end with addiction and death, but both still had reason to believe they would ultimately make an enabling escape. Eileen was near enough to completing drug treatment to feel pretty good about her chances when we last spoke, although she was clearly also terrified that the needles she had shared might yet condemn her to death. Kelly had just decided she had to stop drinking. She was losing memory, and after what she'd been through, the idea of losing anything else was not acceptable to her. Both were striving to become artists—one a musician, one a writer.

READ FOR the future, these histories prophesy domesticity and integration on the one hand, separation and rebellion on the other. Feminists will wonder what has happened to the articles of faith that seemed part and parcel of lesbian identity during the second wave. Where is the push against the boundaries of gender; the critique of heterosexuality; the urge to smash romance; to take over the government? What to make of lesbians for whom "we" means simply "she and I"—rather than my sisters, my lovers, my kind?

Unlike their predecessors, the narrators of this chapter exhibit little inclination to use their personal lives as a political tool, nor do they seem to have much to say about how heterosexuals should live. To some that may seem irresponsible. But in the end, heterosexuality is best reconstructed by those with a personal interest in it. And in their refusal to acknowledge any contradiction between maternity and power, lesbian identity and family continuity, rebellion and femininity, these narrators are surely continuing their predecessors' efforts to push history forward. Moreover, the evidence of the recent past—the burgeoning of lesbian and gay high school groups, for example—indicates that the political is not about to be forgotten for the personal.

The real problem is how to get lesbian teenagers through adolescence in one piece. There's still so little support available, especially in the middle of the country, that almost any development helps to counter anti-gay discrimination and stigmatization.[19] Those who narrated this chapter have already survived. Those who managed to remain a part of their families are transforming lesbianism from something alien and frightening into something understandable—familiar; those who had to escape are keeping the tradition of rebellion alive. How those lives will go—what the rebellion will be about, how far these girls will manage to integrate desire and domesticity—depends on history.

So FAR all the narrators of this book have recounted experiences with peers. Frequently, one teenage lover was two or even three years older than the other, but when such a difference placed one lover in high school and the other out, that kind of age discrepancy wasn't treated as significant by the girls who experienced it. Teenage girls who had relationships with adults, however, believed that they were telling a very different and much more exciting and dangerous story.

7

Precarious Time and Fugitive Passage

═══════════════

On Getting an Adult Lover

I simply did not know a thing about my darling's
mind.

—Humbert Humbert in
Vladimir Nabokov's *Lolita*

There's nothing new about sex between adult men and
teenage girls. It's an old, old story, but as views about gender and sexuality have changed, so has the reading of the tale.
In the early nineteenth century, it was thought to be about bad
girls—sluts and temptresses, wrongdoers not victims—and the
weak men who could not resist them. Even if a girl said no, it
was all her fault. The late nineteenth century reversed the formula, enacting age-of-consent laws that defined girls as inno-
cents, incapable of consent, and men who had sex with them as
criminals. From a girl's perspective, the result was approximately
the same: In the first instance, she was detained in order to protect innocent men; in the second, she was detained for her own
protection.[1]

Age-of-consent laws remain in force to this day. Reasonably,
the Supreme Court should have invalidated at least those that
held minor boys criminal for having sex with minor girls after

finding differential treatment in juvenile proceedings unconstitutional. (If girls were as willing as boys, why were only the boys criminal?) But, rather, the Court has responded to the issue of age of consent as if it belongs to an altogether different realm of logic. As recently as 1981, it agreed that a seventeen-and-a-half-year-old boy who had had sex with a sixteen-and-a-half-year-old girl was guilty of statutory rape, not because she was an unwilling participant (though that much was clear from the trial), but because she was under eighteen. Given this decision, the many state laws that still criminalize intercourse not just between adults and girls but between peers are evidently still enforceable.[2]

Although feminism played a major role in the enactment of age-of-consent laws, feminists heatedly disagree as to whether the statutes are beneficial. No contemporary feminist has supported criminalizing sex between minors, but many have supported laws against adult intercourse with minors on a variety of grounds. As a movement for gender equality, feminism opposes practices that can tutor the young in inequality, and sex between adults and teenage girls strikes some feminists as a clear instance of this. Others simply believe that the young don't have the strength or maturity to know their own minds or hold their ground in the face of adult pressure or suasion and need additional legal protection. But many feminists don't agree. These call for strict, well-enforced statutes against the crime of rape and the abolition of age-of-consent laws, which make no distinction, as anthropologist Gayle Rubin puts it, "between abusive situations and loving ones."[3]

What do girls think? There's virtually no testimony. Some propositions on the subject appear, of course, in melodramas about girls forced by their families to marry old men or seduced into having sex with somewhat younger ones or raped by one or the other. In addition, romances, with their consistent pairing of virginal heroine and fatherly hero, provide endless encouragement for girls to see men as the most appropriate erotic choice. But as much reason as there may be to suspect that these engrossing fictions shape girls' desire, they don't directly convey girls' own point of view. A few contemporary novels by women —Marguerite Duras's *The Lover* is one fine and provocative example—begin to explore the terrain of girls' desire for men more credibly, but still, by and large, it's uncharted territory, and girls' desire for mature women is more uncharted still.[4]

Yet girls' relationships with adults not only have a long history; they have remained very common despite the laws against them. A mid-1960s British study found that just over a quarter of all girls had an older partner at first intercourse, and *most* girls say their first lovers are about three years their senior.[5] (There are no figures on teenage girls' sexual relationships with women.) Some of these experiences are not voluntary: they are rape. But just over 10 percent of the narrators I encountered told about actively choosing sexual experiences with men or women five or more years older than they. This chapter focuses on these accounts to seek answers to questions too rarely asked: How do such experiences affect girls? What are the expectations of girls who seek sexual experiences with adults? How much power do they feel they have vis-à-vis an adult? How do *they* feel about age-of-consent laws?

MOST NARRATORS of affairs with adults were stunned to hear that there is such a thing as an age of consent. They didn't think of sex with an adult as anything to be ashamed of or to hide or worry over. On the contrary, they took pride in these conquests. Catching a man (or a woman, for that matter) was treated as a big step up the ladder toward adulthood, and narrators who succeeded in the enterprise represented themselves as the Horatio Algers of teenage girls' romance. They had no doubt that they could differentiate between abuse, coercion, and consent. Often they supported the claim that they consented by narrating having initiated the experience: "It was just so much my idea," said a nineteen-year-old looking back on an affair she had with her mother's colleague at age seventeen. "I was all over him. I would never leave him alone." Even when the interest was mutual, the timing was completely theirs. "Nothing happened" until they said, yes, now, I'm ready.

In fact, for these girls the distance that the men or women initially maintained was a large part of what was so attractive, so adult. For an adult to have successfully initiated a relationship with a girl, he or she had probably indicated astonishment that the narrator was really so young.

He was talking to me. He was asking me different questions.

"Do you know how old I am?"

He goes, "You're probably about seventeen, eighteen."

I said, "Do I look that old?"

He said, "Yeah, bodywise you do."

I said, "I'm only fourteen."

He's like, "Oh my god. What do I do now?"

I knew he was like kind of funny about saying anything else to me. After a while I told him, "Okay. I'll give you a try. It's no problem."

Otherwise, he or she was out for now:

When I was visiting my dad, a magical thing happened. I was at the roller rink with my dad and his girlfriend. And I was sitting down on the floor. Resting. And this guy kept coming around and he kept looking at me, and he was pretty cute. And after a while, he asked me to skate with him. And it turned out he was Hungarian. So I skated with him and he asked me out. So the next day we spent the day together. And, um, I didn't—I didn't like him much at all. First of all, he was twenty-three and he didn't seem to mind after he found out that I was seventeen. When I said to him, "You don't mind that I'm so young?" He said, "No"—in his lovely Hungarian accent— "no, I like to go out with little girls." That was terrible.

That was the end of the story of the Hungarian, but some men didn't give up so easily. On the contrary, men who didn't have professional reputations at stake could demonstrate incredible patience. Maggie was thirteen when Darnell started coming around.

Right then and there I was busy climbing trees. Fighting with boys. I wasn't thinking about that stuff. So I told him, "I'm not really into that, so I don't think we can have a relationship like you're looking for." Because he was much older than I was. He was a man. See, being that I was a child, you know, I wasn't interested in kissing and carrying on.

He was prepared to court and wait. At first she was contemptuous of the way he showed off for her and repeated his invitations. "He acted so stupid." But she seemed to revel in the power of saying no. It made her like him. A year passed. Finally, they talked:

So he goes, "What are you doing tonight?"

They began to see each other, but it was two more years before they went to bed. He wasn't in a high school hurry. He had other women, and he had had sex before. His wasn't an emergency desire.

AGE WAS the first thing that the heterosexual accounts revealed, and narrators stressed it repeatedly. Jacquelyn:

And, you know, I met him, and he treated us out to dinner. He was an older guy, I would say about ten years older than us.

Ruth Ann:

That was the year my mother came back, so I was about thirteen. Something like that. But anyway, he was old. He was twenty-nine. I know, I know.

Along with a lover's age, heterosexual narrators also emphasized the physical attributes that proved he was a man, not a boy:

The thing was, he was a man. He was an adult man. He wasn't these nineteen-year-old boys who were clearly boys. He had a full beard, which he shaved off later, in the summer. He had a hairy chest. He has a barrel chest and he's very strongly built. It was just nothing like boys.

Two kinds of men were most commonly described as the objects of attraction. The first kind embodied the archetypes of peer glamour: rock musician, athlete, dealer, artist, or someone who spent a lot of money in romantic and exciting ways.

He came and he met me at my door and he kissed me on my cheek and we got into the limousine and we were going! And I was like— I was—I don't know. I was drugged or something. I was just real impressed about it.

Liza went after a guy who managed a band. Melody pursued a man with a convertible. Typically, such men were five or six years older than the girl—older but not old enough to be her father.

The second kind of man represented the generation of the narrator's parents. He had a job. He had a paycheck. He was capable and solid—the kind of man her father could have been if he'd lived, or stayed, or not been an addict or an alcoholic or a workaholic. The kind of man her mother might get to date. Often he was, in fact, a colleague of a parent or a friend of Mom's boyfriend or of an in-law.

Both kinds of men were thought to have something special to offer—something of value to give or teach. But it was enough that they were men and that they knew about sex:

> I figured, I got somebody older. He's going to teach me something. You know, he knows a little more than I do about sex. So I know I'm learning from him. Which I did, you know, I really learned.

While most teenage girls' narratives about romance began with *being* wanted, these most frequently began with being excited by someone and going after them:

> It was always sort of a slightly hysterical excitement. I just felt so like [sings] destiny, like [sings again] this person is great. Like, okay, go very slowly.

Or:

> And then my father said, "I have a working associate. She's coming here. Can she use your bedroom?" I said, "Sure. I don't mind sleeping in the living room." I met her and my heart went, Pitter-patter, pitter-patter, jump jump jump.

Desire is not necessarily expressly sexual, but in these accounts it was. What all the girls who went after adults said they wanted was sex. And while a few accounts ended in marriage or living together as well as with pregnancy, those were not the narrated goals. Sex was.

The most common heterosexual story was that of the one-night stand that was also a sexual initiation. Narrated as comic and light, these events began with curiosity and pleasure and had experience as their only goal. They are among the few heterosexual initiation stories that did not include precoital negotiations for lasting commitment or despair when none emerged. Two accounts of one-night stands follow. The first is wholly comic. The second includes a briefly broken heart.

Sixteen-year-old Jen was on vacation with her father, stepmother, and younger brother:

> We went to Alaska and northern Canada this past summer. And we were in a different hotel practically every night. We'd drive all day, then look at some sight, then get a hotel and sleep and drive off again the next morning. And we drove and drove and drove and drove and it was terribly boring. And Dad would stop and look at steam engine museums and—I hate steam engines.
>
> And I started looking around, you know. So in the hotels, I'd look at the desk clerk. I'd look at the porter. I'd look at the waiters and the bartenders. And—I'd sort of watch them all. Just sort of like— hmmm, he's not bad.

She and her brother "looked" together and teased each other about who was interested in whom. "You know, I sit there looking at all the guys and he sits there looking desperately for some girls. There weren't very many. He was really out of luck on that trip." The bartender caught her eye.

> He had on a long-sleeved white shirt with rolled-up sleeves. Underneath he had a white tee shirt with something written on it? And I was wondering what it was, and . . . he had dark curly hair tied up in a ponytail. A dark ponytail.

She liked his hands.

> You know, strong, fine-boned hands. And I thought, Hmm, this is nice. And I kept looking at his shirt, thinking, What does it say?

She also noted favorably that he was older.

> I estimated he was between the age of twenty and twenty-five. . . . And that was ha-ha! You know, older man.

After dinner, her father and stepmother went for a walk:

I wasn't supposed to smoke. My dad didn't know about it. So I thought this was my chance to have a cigarette. And . . . there was a motorcycle with a sidecar. And a trailer behind it—a matching set. And—like the motorcycle had gloves to put your hands in, you know, attached to the handlebars. It was such a beautiful thing. I was standing outside looking at it and I noticed that Wayne was inside in the lobby looking out at me. I'm like, "Eeek. Embarrassing," so I thought, Should I go in and talk to him? Maybe I should, maybe I shouldn't. So I finally decided, Okay, I'm going to go in and talk to him. Just as I'm about to get there, he opens the door. It turns out he was coming out to talk to me. He'd been standing there going, Should I go out and talk to her or not? So just as I got there, he opened the door to go out and I'm like, "Oook."

They hung out for a while together and talked about rock and MTV. Then she and her brother went upstairs to the lounge to play a game of billiards, but the machine broke.

So Billy said, "Go find your bartender friend and ask him how to work the machine."

She felt "really stupid," but she went. Wayne fixed the machine so they could play for free. Later he asked her to go for a walk.

So I said, "Okay, sure." Then he said he had to go back to his room to change out of his clothes because he didn't want to get them messed up. So I went off with him through this pitch-blackness at eleven o'clock at night. He had this one little room with everything that he owned practically in there and the bathroom down at the end of the hallway. I'm like, "You live here?" Yeah. He had his skis sticking up in one corner, towels and sheets and everything in piles, clean clothes in that pile, dirty clothes in this pile. All of the tapes that he ever owned in another pile next to his bed. Total mess.

He cleared off a space for me and I was sitting there looking through his record collection while he changed his clothes. He stood behind me and changed from the black pants he'd been wearing into jeans. I was very careful not to turn around and look. I was like, Why is he doing this? I thought, Don't look, Jen.

Finally they went out for a walk.

We walked through this big dark forest. . . . We talked about horror movies, and all of a sudden, he said, "You know, all night I've been looking at you and thinking that I want to kiss you."

And I'm like, "Oh, my god." I don't know, I don't know what I said. Something that now embarrasses me about what a coincidence because I've wanted to too. I was like, What am I supposed to say? Um, so he walked over and there was this huge height difference. I'm like, "Ooh." So I was like up on my tippytoes and he was like bending his knees a little bit. And we kissed and the difference between kissing him and kissing Martin, my boyfriend back home, was just mind-blowing. Maybe it was the difference in my age and my feelings about the whole matter, but whew! He kissed good.

And for a while we just kissed and then he put his hand on my back. Then he put his hand on my back under my shirt, and his hand was freezing! I'm like, "Aaack." He said, "I'm sorry, my hands are cold." And I said, "Your hands are freezing." Then he said, "Do you want to go back to my room?" And my mind stopped. I'm like, Jen, this is one of those lines that gets handed out. You know what's going to happen if you go back to his room. You know he's expecting to have sex with you and you're not going to.

And, uh, then I thought, Jen, this is the only chance in your high school years. . . . And it's too cold to stand here and make out, so go to his room.

Her mother walked through the room Jen and I were sitting in, and Jen changed the subject for a few minutes. When she was sure her mother was gone, Jen took up her story again.

Anyway, so I finally decided, All right, go back to his room and continue making out. See what happens but don't let it go too far, because I hadn't done anything except a couple of kisses with Martin, so there was no way I was going to let him go too far. Then as we were walking back, I said, "You do know I'm sixteen." And he was like, "You are? I didn't know that."

And I said, "And I've never done anything with a guy except make out, so don't expect me to do too much. I mean don't expect that I'm going to have sex with you, because I'm not."

And he said, "That's fine."

I'm like, He said that a little too fast. I don't know that I trust it. So I was going through this whole thing of I shouldn't be doing this. And then in the back of my mind, Go ahead. There's nothing wrong with it. Nothing's going to happen. . . . Ooooo, I couldn't stop shaking.

So we went back to his room. I'm not going to go through all the details—it's going to take much too long and I don't want to tell all the details of this—but I ended up having sex with him. Having met him about seven hours earlier, I had sex with him. I let him persuade me, you know, to go each step further because I wanted to. And I thought, I shouldn't be doing this. I don't even know the guy and what's everyone going to say, and what am I doing, and all this sort of stuff. But also, not only did it feel good, and not only was I enjoying myself, but I thought, you know, this is this huge big chance thrown in my lap to actually experience all these things that I'd been dreaming about for centuries.

And when it came to—you know, he asked, "Do you want to have sex?" Actually he said "make love." Which I thought—I've never considered it making love. I always thought of it as having sex because to me that was what it really was. And I said, "Well, you know, I refuse to do anything idiotic and get myself pregnant. Do you happen to have any birth control lying around the room?"

And he said, "No, I don't." And I said, "Well, forget it then because I'm not going to take the chance of getting pregnant." And in the back of my mind I suddenly thought, But, Jen, your period is due in about three days, so you couldn't get pregnant anyway. And I thought, Ah-ha-ha! This is good, but I was still thinking, You shouldn't do it. I mean, I don't know this guy. I mean, what am I doing? I'm crazy. I'm insane. But at the same time I thought, This is so fun. This is good. . . .

He's twenty-one, right? I'm sixteen. Um, he took it very slow. Very relaxed about everything. He didn't hassle me or push me or, you know, say, well, Do this, do that. He took it very slowly . . . and it was very easy. He came on the sheets and afterwards he said, "I've come once. I'm not likely to come again too soon. So, you know, if you want to just see what it's like to have, you know, a man's penis inside you, we can do that. And, you know, there's no danger of you getting pregnant." I'd been warned so many times that when a guy says, "That's all right. I'll pull out in time," ten to one he's lying or he'll lose control and forget all about that and just enjoy himself. And so I thought, Jen, he's handing you the biggest line in the book. And then I thought, It doesn't matter because I couldn't get pregnant because my period's due in three days. You know, so I thought, Yeah! All right! Okay.

And so, we did have sex. Well, actually, I've been very unsure whether to call it "having sex" or "fooling around" because he didn't come inside me and I didn't have an orgasm. He tried very hard actually to give me an orgasm. And after a while I said, "Well, don't worry about it, because I'm enjoying myself anyway. It doesn't really matter to me. Don't wear yourself out." So, although his penis was inside my vagina, there was no actual ejaculation inside me. So I want to call it that anyway—who cares about the details? So I've decided that we had sex.

Q: It's definitely intercourse.

J: Yes? Oh, good! So I'm right. I'm justified here. Good.

When we went back over the details, her behavior didn't sound as "free" as it had the first time. She had insisted they keep the lights off:

And I didn't touch him. I was perfectly happy to rub my hands across his chest and across his back but I did not go down below his waist. Because—I was scared. You know. I mean, what am I supposed to do? No idea. And you know, he didn't ask me to do anything and so I didn't. And I've thought about it since then and I thought, Idiot! Think of how many more things you should have experimented with while you had the chance, while you had a guinea pig there. So I'm sort of mad at myself now about it that I didn't get up the courage to—touch the male organ. But at the time I simply didn't have the nerve.

She went back to her room early in the morning:

And I got woken up at nine o'clock in the morning. For breakfast. Oh, it was terrible.

The entire next day she slept in the car.

While I was in the car, though, I could remember every single touch, every single minute of that night. For about a month, I could remember every—I mean, like, you know, his touch, I could almost imagine that he was right there again.

Remembering was sexually stimulating.

I could lie on my bed at night and I could almost feel him lying on top of me and I could almost feel him breathing in my ear and oh god, when he breathed in my ear, I went crazy. I loved that. That was my favorite part out of the entire evening.

Back home in high school, she had vague plans to see Wayne again. Maybe she'd go back to Alaska. Maybe he'd come to the city where she lived with her mother. It didn't seem likely, though, and she didn't seem to count on it. She had made sexual initiation special by removing it from conventional expectations and connections and from her everyday life. For her, first sex had nothing to do with true love or permanence or making a baby. It was a preface, at most a first chapter, in her sexual life.

MARLINA WAS eighteen and had two babies when we met, not from her relationship with Hugh, the man whom she first had sex with, but from relationships with two different, much younger, men. A program for teenage mothers directed me to her. We talked in her tiny bungalow on the edge of town where back yards met cornfields. Toys were strewn on the front yard like lawn ornaments, but inside, the bungalow was spotless—not a pillow out of place, not a trace of dust. Marlina had wispy light hair and pale watercolor-blue eyes. She wore pressed jeans and a cotton knit top. She was pretty without working at it. Her toddler, Peter, took an active part in our conversation.

The first time Marlina "laid eyes on" Hugh—a friend of her mother's boyfriend, Tony—she thought he was "really good-looking." Paging through her diary, she found the entry from right after they met.

Okay, it says, "I am really serious about this diet. I want to be pretty for Hugh. Not only for him but for myself."

She recalled she "wanted to act more responsible and sensible," and to stop being "such a tomboy." Hugh was in his mid-twenties. Marlina was thirteen. In the beginning, it was just flirtation.

I'd catch him making eyes at me, and I'd make eyes at him.

She read from her diary:

I gotta have him! I gotta keep him! I want to marry him! I want to have his children!

One night her dad was visiting. He let her taste his wine. She had two glasses while he was there. He left the bottles behind when he went home.

And I guzzled the bottle of red. Then I guzzled the bottle of white. Yes, I did.

When Hugh came over later:

The way he was looking at me, I knew, from that night on . . .

She turned the diary pages. "Some time passes," she said.

Hugh came over one night after work. It was late, and Tony was tired. So Tony talked to him for a while and went to bed with my mom. And so me and Hugh stayed up playing chess. And, um, since he was working *and* going to school and he had to get up early, he said, "Why don't you give me some of your diet pills, and I'll give you a Valium and you could take it sometime, and you could probably get high off of it." And I said, "Yeah, okay." You know, "Anything for you."

She went into her room to get the pills. He followed her.

It wasn't really unusual for him to be in my room because . . . my whole family . . . we used to all sit in my room sometimes so we could listen to the stereo or whatever.

They "made a dope deal," she said, laughing, and "sat in there talking." At first, he was sitting on her dresser. He worked his way over to the bed.

He sat down on my bed and we talked. And I remember it made me nervous, him sitting on my bed while we were alone and it was late at night and my mom and Tony were asleep. I was nervous. I had a feeling.

She got up a couple of times to do some things.

And when I came back he was lying on my bed, falling asleep! And I shook him and I said, "Hugh." And he was still conscious, you know. He could hear me. He knew what was going on. He—he was like, "Yeah . . . ?" And I was like, "I know you're tired, but if you're going to go to sleep, you should move to the couch."

And he said all right, he would. But he kind of was dozing off again. You know. And I—he looked so comfortable and he looked like such a babe. So I watched him for a while. I don't know if he knew I was or not. I don't think he could see me. I wanted to let him sleep there, but I knew I couldn't. And so I watched him for a while and after I'd had my fill, I decided to wake him up.

And I was shaking him, saying, "Hugh, you got to move. You've got to wake up and move."

And so he was like, "Okay."

And I said, "All right, I'll help you up."

He lifted up his hand and I went to pull him up and he pulled me down. And he just kind of breathed on me and kissed me and I was like, "All right!"

Quickly she thought it over. Like Jen, she decided that she would take advantage of the sexual opportunity Hugh presented.

In my mind, I was thinking, I am not going to pass this up.

They slept together.

And I was really relaxed. I mean, I was trying to be. I was nervous but I was just so much in love with him it was like this was what I always dreamed of. I wanted it to happen, and when it did . . . it didn't hurt as bad as I thought it would. You know, it wasn't that bad. It was nice, and I felt really good in his arms, and it was like a fantasy.

When he left that morning—he left at eight—there was hardly any blood on the sheets. When I went to the bathroom there was some blood and that's when I tried a tampon. I said, If this is ever gonna work, it's gonna work now. . . .

In the morning, Tony knocked on my door. . . . Something about, "When'd Hugh go home?"

And I said, "Eight-thirty." Or "Eight," or something like that. Yeah, I said, "Eight."

He goes, "This morning?"

I said, "Yeah."

He says, "Really?"
I said, "Yeah."
"You're kidding?"
"No."
He said, "Well?"
And as I walked by him, he said, "Well. Well, well." And all day
Tony was smiling at me like he was going to crack up. He was amazed
because he thought of me as, like, The Little Virgin, you know.

Hugh never had sex with her or made out with her again, but
he didn't cut her off. He treated her partly as an adult, partly as
a child—chiding and worrying about her. Marlina was broken-
hearted for a while, she said, but soon lost interest. A few months
later, her mother gave her the choice of moving back to her old
neighborhood or staying in the neighborhood where Hugh lived.
She chose to move. They saw each other a few years later, but
her teenage sexual dealings with him never went beyond their
one-night stand.

WHAT ABOUT romances that last longer than a night or an
afternoon? Did girls lose the advantage over men that youth,
beauty, and relative indifference appeared to give them at the
outset? Or did men lose relative power as girls grew more knowing and independent? All the narrators who told about extended
relationships with men stressed the power of youth in relation to
adulthood. They did not share the adult belief that age differences imply inequality. It was not obvious to them that adults
were one-up on the young. Just as their lovers drew on the advantages of adulthood, they drew on those of youth, they said. If
he was more experienced, she was a faster learner. If he knew
more about life, she knew more about the future. If he made
her feel grown, she made him feel young.

These narrators enjoyed the advantage that the ambiguity of
adolescence gave them. When they wanted autonomy, they argued that they were "adults." But they defended their claim to
freedom and pleasure on the grounds that they were still "kids."
They declared themselves fully conscious of playing off pubertal
ambiguity to seem knowing or gullible, young or mature, strong
or weak, depending on the situation.

Men assume young women are naive. These narrators delighted in using this presumption like a poker face. Being half child, half adult was to control two languages:

> Sometimes I would go beyond my level, and I'd talk to him like I was up there with him. I'm saying to him . . . when I'm talking serious, I can talk to you like I was a grown woman myself. Then again, I can talk to you like I was a child.

Sometimes the narrators left realism behind in their claims to power. Reversing the proposition that the young need to be protected from the old, Belle hypothesized that young women pulled energy from older men, speeding the aging process.

> They can be young and then they can look very old. Because I remember before, when I met him? He was perfect. I mean, he looked like he could pass for sixteen or seventeen years old. Look at him now, you'd be like . . .

Suzette perceived something akin to Belle's purposefully destructive energy, and given her family history, it worried her. Her stepfather had died in her mother's bed, she said. "She gave him a heart attack."

> To this day, I don't know how she gave him that heart attack. What exactly they did when they were making love, for him to have a heart attack like that, and now at times when I have sex with this thirty-eight-year-old, he starts to breathe too heavy and I get kind of scared. I don't want him to die on me. I swear I don't. I don't want him to catch nothing, no heart attack, no nothing. And like by me being so nasty, I figure I might be giving this man a heart attack. He's trying so hard to give me this sensation, and he ain't doing it. So sometimes I stop and I wonder. I say, I better take it light on this old man.

The fear probably had an element of curiosity in it. Knowing how to kill a man in sex might come in handy one day. But Suzette didn't talk about anger. None of these narrators did.

Of course, not everyone's sense of power involved control over life and death, but all these narrators indicated they had some cards in their hands. Their lovers could be ruined professionally, those with middle-class lovers knew, if their affairs were made public. No narrator reported using or even threatening to use this power (although Linda did leave her lover's letters where her mother could—and did—find them, setting off an enormous brouhaha), but even unused, that power operated as a safeguard and a leveler.

PERHAPS BECAUSE they had professions to protect, middle-class men typically tried to avoid the trouble girls represented. As a result, while poor teenage girls often told of a thrilling period of time during which they were able to pick, choose, stall, and refuse men, middle-class teenagers told of laborious efforts to get a man to have an affair with them. In these accounts, the adult was indifferent and otherwise occupied; the girl interested. Once attracted, girls became hunters and seducers: they plotted, they angled, they chased. Men resisted. Wily trout, they were incredibly hard to catch. (Reluctant women, in contrast, were not presented as wily but as closeted, homophobic, and afraid.) A girl had to persist, demonstrating patience, rigor, and cunning. In sexual debates that lasted for months or even years, she tried to persuade him to be with her. He, in turn, tried to talk her, and himself, out of it. She was too young; it wasn't right; her mother wouldn't like it. The girls uniformly hated these arguments, and they resented being reminded of their youth and dependency. But they could be just as patronizing. Prudence:

> He really had internalized a lot of the moral codes and he really did feel like there was something wrong with our sleeping together. At the time, I just felt he was really condescending and I'd get really furious. But now I believe he was sincere.

In their narrations, these girls showed themselves to be patiently Jesuitical. If they were also actively seductive, they did not describe that, and, in general, these narrators flaunted sexuality far less than the broken-heart narrators, whose appearance typically belied their purist stance. Perhaps these narrators were just mature enough to understand that their youth itself was seductive.

As they cajoled and persuaded, cons became pros and pros became cons. Carla, who went after a partner in her mother's law firm, read me a copy of a letter that she had sent him, adding some commentary (in parentheses) along the way.

> It would be nice if we could be casual lovers, but you say it's absolutely impossible. You say you see what will happen when I run into reality. And I can understand in one sense how you say you see better than I do, because my view is obscured by my desire, but I also know that I would like to sleep with you. (I mean I had had some sex at this point, but I really hadn't enjoyed it.) And I know you want to sleep with me, too, at least on one level.

While lesbian narrators all expected to ultimately get their woman, girls who went after men were less sure of victory.

> He was just so unattainable in my mind anyway.

But, in the end, every one of the narrators bagged her erotic prey.

To the extent that sex was the goal, both heterosexual and lesbian girls found it had all been worth it when they finally went to bed. But while heterosexual girls pretty much surrendered the active role once they had accomplished their purpose of getting a man to have sex with them, lesbian girls said they remained the active partner in bed that they had been in pursuit. Claire:

> I felt very much like I was the more aggressive. . . . She didn't know I hadn't done this before. And I think somewhere in my head I thought that *she* had done this before. But she hadn't either. I kind of, up to a point, maintained a ruse that I had all this experience, you know. I don't know why. I mean, I guess I was somewhat concerned that she'd be worried about corrupting a minor or something like that, so I had talked that up, you know, making references that this was no big deal.
>
> We had been doing this little hand-holding routine. And . . . I kind of pulled her into bed and you know sort of moved over until I was more like on top of her and started to kiss her and, you know, kissed her neck and started, you know, to undress her, kiss her breasts and, um, and . . . it just sort of went on, you know, stroking her thighs and all that kind of stuff. Finally I wound up going down on her and she was very into that. And that was pretty much it, you know.

Q: She didn't make love to you?

A: Well, yes and no. I mean, I was like at the point where I was going to have an orgasm regardless of what she did. But I think she actually did make love to me. I mean, she went down on me and stuff and, um, that's never been particularly satisfying to me. And she was like a little more tentative. You know, after I had gone down on her she kind of said how, you know, she had never done this before and . . . I was surprised because while it wasn't like totally the easiest thing in the world to—to get her into bed, it was also not that difficult. So I didn't think that this was like particularly new to her.

Um, and so then I didn't want to push her into doing something she didn't want to do. In a funny way I felt kind of protective or something. And I think I was more interested, in a funny way, in making love to her than having her make love to me.

I asked Claire how she had known what to do. She guessed she'd read about it.

I mean, it wasn't like I had read an introduction manual or something. But it didn't seem very difficult to know what to do. And she was also extremely responsive. Since then I've learned that she was probably more responsive than a lot of people, which was probably good. Good for my ego.

WHILE THE narrators emphasized the power of youth, their accounts did imply that age conferred power as well. Above all, narrators of experiences with men prized their lovers for erotic knowledge. The first time wasn't necessarily perfect, but soon enough, things were going great. Often these narrators talked about men in bed the same way they talked about men in the world. Men had more sexual resources. A place to go, things to use, tricks of the masculinity trade:

He used, you know, all kinds of things, coconut oil, massage oil, candles . . . he was very good at—he took a lot of care in having sex. And we tripped. I mean, I took acid with him. The first time I ever did. . . . And he was a very romantic figure.

Men did a wider range of things in bed than boys, these narrators said—pleasurable things. After the first time, which wasn't much, one narrator said:

> I started learning all these crazy positions, all these movements. I'm like a regular walking magazine.

Melody had "more different experiences" with her older lover, her father's best friend. They started up a flirtation when she was in high school. When she went away to college, she spent most weekends at his place. "You know, he's not like a straight missionary-type person. He likes to try different things. And I think that made me more at ease." I asked her to be a little more specific. "Oh, god," she said and laughed.

> He was very kinky. I mean, you know. He called me just about every night when I was in school and we'd talk for two or three hours on the phone and we'd plan out, you know, weeks in advance, what we were going to do the next weekend I was up there. And one weekend it was just total darkness. Everything was dark and he lit candles. And he always gave me a backrub with warm baby oil and he's a sex fiend. And that—that made me a sex fiend. I love sex. I'm a sex fiend. And, you know, I got a pair of black pumps—real thin heels with ankle straps—and, you know, the whole works and we were very, very kinky.

I asked what "the whole works" meant.

> Lace, lots of lace, and sexy nightgowns and underwear and bra and hose and the high-heel shoes and he tied me up once—no, he didn't tie—he used handcuffs. Not string but handcuffs. And then there are the different positions. We didn't just do the missionary position. . . . There was doggy style. Rear entry. Anal penetration once. Never again. I told him that. And I love oral sex. So there was a lot of oral sex.

Men could also keep going longer than boys, giving girls a better chance at orgasm:

> When is a man a man? When he can control himself, you know.

In addition to sex itself, girls also prized the way the affair made them feel even when they weren't actually having sex or even in the presence of their lovers. Liza:

> Sleeping with him always left me feeling very special the next day. It was really wonderful to get back home late at night and sleep and go to school the next morning, knowing that I had slept with somebody the night before.

Liza's permissive parents did not object to her staying out late or seeing Brian. Most girls had to see their older lovers secretly, but this only heightened the sexiness of the affair.

> I was just intoxicated. Part of it was, I was sneaking around. I would sneak into the house at three and four in the morning, five in the morning.

As much fun as it all was, it also had the very serious benefit of strengthening these girls' sense of themselves. The affairs took the pressure and bad feelings out of their peer relations, making it possible for them to get through high school. They felt recognized.[6]

> It was finally clear that I was different from other high school kids. All through high school, I had all kinds of revenge fantasies against my peers because I never felt like I was adequately recognized as special as I was. And this was proof—this *man.*

In addition, spending time with an adult, these narrators claimed, was like taking an advanced-placement course in life. Adulthood rubbed off on you, they thought. Being with older people, one said, "advanced" her mind. She didn't want it "playing back down." "Let's put it this way," another said, explaining what she liked about her lover. "He was a good teacher."

For some, the benefits were more psychologically complex. A number of girls spoke explicitly about being "fathered" by their lovers or finding in them "a substitute parent." Psychoanalysis has treated the wish to catch a father—or take a man away from a mother's sway—voluminously. When girls realize they cannot become their mothers' lovers, they are supposed to "take refuge," as Juliet Mitchell put it, "in the Oedipus complex"—that is, turn from their mothers to their fathers and then to outsiders who represent the father.[7] Most psychologists claim that girls follow this pattern symbolically and unconsciously whether or not they actually have fathers. These girls reported doing it consciously, expressly connecting the wish to catch a father to a previous lack of good parenting, or to indifferent or abusive parenting. They wanted a surrogate father, some explained point-blank, because they hadn't had a father or they hadn't had one for a long time or they'd had a bad one.

It's an idea that actually has a feminist tradition. In business and the academy, feminists praise the notion of "mentorship," and in feminist literature, literary critic Rachel DuPlessis notes, female heroes often turn "to parental figures" for "reparenting," forging "an alternative fictional resolution to the oedipal crisis that these parent figures evoke."[8] But feminist reparentings are specifically not supposed to involve a sexual exchange.

These narrators didn't see any problem at all in trading sex for fathering. In fact, they seemed to feel themselves fortunate in at last having something that *could* be traded for fathering, something that would lead a father figure to turn his warming, fertilizing, corrective attention on them. This attention didn't just make them feel good; it began to make them *be* good, they said. Like real fathers, their lover-fathers taught them to distinguish right from wrong and to respect their families. Suzette, for example, described the older man in her life as "a father figure"—half teacher, half dad. He was teaching her how to live, how to treat others well, how to be loving.

> I swear he's like a father to me. He can tell me right from wrong. "Don't do that to your mother. Don't say that. Do that for your mother. Be nice." He says a lot of things that I don't want to hear and I know a younger guy wouldn't tell me. A younger guy might agree with me. But he's really showing me the true facts.

Carla thought her "substitute parent" made up for the emotional losses she suffered when her parents divorced, an event she described in her life history as a fall from Eden.

Cast in these terms, girls' experiences with adult lovers sound almost perfect: the narrators claimed they got only and exactly what they hoped for, and they became more mature and responsible in the process. Yet surely these relationships were potentially damaging. Even accepting that the men who loved these girls were always supportive in the heat of these affairs, what about at the end? Were these girls left standing when the affair was over? How corrosive was the breakup?

In contrast to the happy accounts we've heard of love with peers, lesbian relationships with adults reportedly got rocky in a few weeks or months. Frequently, the women involved, who were often in pretty bad shape to begin with, tried to put as much distance as they could between themselves and the double shame of having gone to bed with someone who was both of their own gender and underage.[9] When this happened, the suave initiators rapidly lost their confidence. Claire sank so low that she was institutionalized for a while. Others told of months of alcohol and drugs before they got hold of themselves. To win an erotic mother and then have her treat her lover/daughter ambivalently was evidently one of the worst things that could happen to a girl.

By contrast, loss and jealousy were simply not issues for many heterosexual girls involved with adults. Perhaps the entire thing had always seemed so improbable no one really imagined it would last. Or perhaps having viewed the men instrumentally, the narrators actually were relieved that these relationships wouldn't be the final word in men's lives: after all, some of these men had wives and children. ("I was an extra," Darlene said complacently.) In the case of girls who had explicitly sought out father-substitute lovers, perhaps the experiences that had led them to seek a parent in a partner had already conditioned them to think of a father as a fleeting entity, much as some also assumed that it was natural to have boyfriends in addition to a surrogate father.

A few of the men initiated breakups. As with two-timing, so with these disruptions. They came with the territory. The breakups hurt, but so did dad's love for mom. Carla didn't shed a tear:

> It was the kind of thing that when it's very hurtful, you don't cry, you don't mope around depressed. It goes to a different level, somewhere else.

Liza also "didn't like to mope around about it." This was an adult affair. She didn't even think she cried. "I was kind of inside. Like at night I would sear." There was nothing to do. It was a fact of life.

Luckily, although a few of the girls had been pregnant before they got involved with men, none of them got pregnant in the first two years of their relationships. This wasn't an accident. Many girls are not sure "boys" can get them pregnant. Men, they know, can. If they were old enough to attract a man, these girls reasoned, they were probably old enough to get pregnant and to avoid doing so.[10]

> And that's when I got my first birth control, a diaphragm. When I was dealing with this older man, I thought it must be time for me to get birth control.

They all used birth control unless and until they had decided that they wanted this man to be the father of their children, a rare decision overall.

After a breakup they did not instigate, some girls went right out and got new lovers. Liza and Carla got "boys" from school, but Liza found boys too immature for her. The night Brian broke up with her, a boy from school asked her to a party. His name was Drew.

> So for about a month I saw this guy named Drew. It's very funny. He was the sexual opposite of Brian. He went to my school. Really inexperienced but very sweet. Unworldly. Really bright. Really nice and funny but so pure—like, really pure, and sexually too. He had never slept with anybody. I slept with him. It was terrible. For a month, it was terrible.

Both Liza and Carla reported the same thing about intercourse with the boys they took up with. Carla:

> We had sex a lot. It wasn't so great. I mean, not really. He was pretty inexperienced. Part of why we had intercourse a lot was because he would come very fast and then we could do it again. Lucky me.

Liza:

> He would come the minute it began.

The worst part wasn't the sex but the lack of challenge.

What can I say? For a month I was in love with Drew. It was like sacchariney. And of course flashback to eighth grade, one morning I woke up and like Drew was very sweet and nice but just not enough. There just wasn't any challenge in him. I don't want anything I can't have, but I want there to be more effort. I want some intellectual tension in the conversation. He was so inexperienced in so many different ways.

The men who had given them up soon summoned Liza and Carla back. Carla kept her young lover around just in case. Suzette secretly kept both young and old lovers on hand, appreciating each for different reasons. Liza had already resolved to break up with Drew when Brian called.

Like, "How are you? Do you want to have coffee? Are you still okay?" So, and then, pretty much ever since, there was Brian.

When Ruth Ann's mother became involved with Ruth Ann's first lover, Ruth Ann resolved on getting a new man. She didn't even consider a boy. After she got over, as she put it, losing "her first love" to her mother, she met her "son's father" in a bar.

I was sitting there, drinking soda, and he started playing the pinball machine, and he just turned around and we were looking in each other's eyes, and we just kissed. And it was the best kiss in my whole life. I'll never forget that kiss. Because it was like we barely touched, you know, but it sent shivers up and down my spine. I've never been kissed like that since either.

So then that night we wound up fooling around in a car. The next day, he wouldn't even talk to me because he was ashamed of himself. . . . That's how we started seeing each other.

If anything, teenage girls found it easier to be dumped than to extricate themselves from sexual relationships with men. In *The Use of Pleasure*, Foucault comments on the importance of timing in Greco-Roman "relationships with adolescent boys," particularly "the difficult question of precarious time and fugitive passage" that was expressed first "as a problem of 'limit' ":

> What was the age limit after which a boy ought to be considered too old to be an honorable partner in a love relation? At what age was it no longer good for him to accept this role nor for his lover to want to assign it to him?[11]

The majority of these narrators reached a point when they wanted to leave those who had reparented them. Then, frequently, the same men who had tried to hold them off, or who nurtured them through an alienated adolescence, tried to keep them in place, sometimes with violence, always with "love."

A few of the girls described themselves as "cold" and said it was easy for them to cut their adult lovers off. But the majority thought of themselves as warm and loving, and they found it hard to make the break. Love is a very hard argument for girls to reject, as we've heard again and again, even when intermixed with violence or condescension or paternalistic control, and it was especially hard for these girls, whose love was both that of a child and that of a lover. In addition, separation is virtually always hard for girls, and this separation was like none other because it compounded the difficulty of leaving childhood with that of leaving a first marriage. I interviewed several of these narrators over a period of years, and I held my breath for them as they approached this pass.

Liza's parents attempted to help her begin the break by giving her a trip to Europe for her sixteenth birthday. Liza didn't go:

> I just couldn't, I don't know why. Something was going on in me. I had to do my laundry before I could leave and I just didn't do it until the day before. . . . I just didn't go. . . . I hadn't even thought about my travel plans. It was amazing. I don't know how I did that. I can't explain it.

But finally, most of these men, like Humbert Humbert, lost the girls who used them to grow up. As other teenagers make the final pull away from parents toward college or adulthood, these girls pulled away from their "substitute" parents. They began to feel attracted to peers, who had, in the meantime, grown increasingly into "real" men and women. By the next year, Liza, for example, was champing at the bit. During the year, Brian pressed her to stay overnight at his place when she wasn't supposed to. She wouldn't do it, she said, for her own reasons.

I have to assert to him that if I had complete freedom, I wouldn't stay there every night. It is very important for me to have my own space.

She began cutting down on the frequency with which she saw him. The next summer she went to Cape Cod as a mother's helper. When she came back, she saw the age issue differently. He had had more chance for variation than she:

Lots of different kinds of relationships that I hadn't had.

She wanted the chance for variation and "more perspective." As if he were a parent she had left behind who had no business inquiring into her personal affairs, she fooled around with "a lot of people" and didn't tell him. "Is it betrayal," she asked rhetorically, "if you don't flash it in their face?" She answered her own question: If you need to see somebody else for your own individual growth or because you need a perspective on your primary relationship, it's not betrayal. It's an obligation to the self. But since a man would probably not understand that, better not to tell him.

I fooled around with somebody else because I needed our relationship to work. Right? You can't quite say that. Who would understand that? I certainly wouldn't.

Nevertheless, fooling around with other people did take some of the tension out of her relationship with Brian, and they got through the first half of the next school year okay. Second semester was a killer, though. Separation loomed.

I don't really want to see other people right now. That's not what it is. Somehow I can't accept the fact that I can enjoy him now but that when I go away, there well might be other people I want to see. That happened today, this realization, so you're getting a very hot-off-the-grill topic. . . . And if I don't spend much time with him in the next two years, it doesn't necessarily mean I'm not going to ten years from now. Because I have felt, since the first day I met him, that there is some long-term, weird future. I don't know what exactly. Friends? I just feel he's a kindred spirit. So.

So? So what? Her parents and their good friends worried over Liza's fate between her return from Cape Cod and her departure for college. Would college, like Europe, be a trip she would postpone for several years? Or would she be able to act in her own interest and go?

Liza went. She did well. She had many lovers.

Carla also got to college but that wasn't the end of her romance with her older lover. She ran to him at the semester break, and he did not treat her well. Nevertheless, instead of returning to school that year, she got a job and an apartment, some friends and lovers, and settled in to recover not so much from her relationship with him as from her childhood. It was years before she was ready to go back to school.

WHILE MANY GIRLS who told about loving boys narrated melodramas ending with their own romantic victimization, most who told about voluntary sexual relationships with adults cast the account as a story of development that proceeded from victory to knowledge and realism. (Those who narrated sexual relationships with adult women also reversed the story told about relations with peers but in a different direction. Lesbian peers made peerless lovers; adults were damaged and dangerous.) Few adults will take this rendition of these experiences at face value. Assuming that sex between children and adults is inherently bad, they are likely to castigate the adults involved as pederasts and dismiss girls' arguments that they chose such relationships as "false consciousness," but the narrators are too old to be properly framed as children and too pragmatic to be written off as merely deluded. Feminists will mention a less easily dismissed distinction between "free commitment and agreement by equals" and "domination, subordination, and inequality," as theorist Carole Pateman has phrased it. Sex educators will surely and reasonably worry whether girls' power is conceivably sufficient to successfully demand that men use protection against AIDS given the fact that women in general consistently fail to do so.[12]

But of all the supposedly consensual relationships I heard

about in almost a decade of interviewing, by far the most exploitive involved peers who based consent on the promise of an exchange—love or meaning for sex—that was not fulfilled.[13] In comparison, narrators of sexual relations with adults felt both satisfied with their experiences and powerful because they were able to realize the expectations of pleasure and learning on which their consent was based. And if the narrators occasionally skipped school to see their lovers, by and large their academic performance improved as love strengthened their self-esteem.

Not all the concerns that these narratives raise are resolved by this observation, however. Perhaps those girls who acknowledged that they looked to their relationships with adults for surrogate parenting were doing the best they could for themselves given their circumstances. Nevertheless, parenting is not an equal exchange, and certainly not a service performed in exchange for sex: it's by definition a gift of unconditional love, and that's important. The experience of receiving unconditional love confers a sense of self-worth that cannot be easily produced in any other way and is a talisman that the individual can hold on to throughout the life course. It makes the process of separation possible and protects against complicity in one's own exploitation. As clear-minded as these girls seem about their situation, their willingness to barter sex for parenting suggests a more unexamined, desperate need, one that might well make it extremely difficult for them to say no to a fatherly lover who asked them to have unprotected sex in the name of love. On the evidence, however, neither girls nor women have the wherewithal to induce men or boys to use protection when they don't want to, and this suggests that the problem of protection and AIDS has much more to do with gender than with age.

Not all these narrators claimed that they looked to adult lovers for parenting in any case. About half said they had had plenty of emotional preparation by the time they became involved with their first adults. They were precocious, they said. Their only concern was erotic. Reversing previous assertions that they held the most power in these relationships at the close of their accounts, they wondered how, as adults, they would ever re-create the wonderful experience of inequality—of, as Liza put it, feeling "like jelly" that being with someone so much more powerful and experienced than they produced? How would they find erotic prizes as spectacularly hard to get and worth the effort as their first men? Liza thought sex would be "worse" the older she became, because she would know more, have more experience, and expect more. The lesbian narrators, for their part, did not foresee this problem. Once they got over the shock of loss, they decided it was their own power that excited them, and that, they expected, would only increase.

POWER IS also at issue in the last group of narratives, but while girls who sought relationships with men ultimately acknowledge the erotic thrill of inequality, the narrators of the next chapter —like earlier lesbian narrators—found equality and their own power erotic.

8

The Game of Love

═══════════

Equality and Romantic Strategy

In the end, the changed life for women will be
marked . . . by laughter.

—Carolyn G. Heilbrun, *Writing a Woman's Life*

Like so many dreams that begin in theory and idealism,
romantic equality has usually read better than it has
played. After almost two decades of deferral and experimentation, most feminists have come to accept a compromise between
politics and eros in private life. On the day when women are no
more financially dependent on men than men are on women,
when sons and daughters long for the romance and power of
their mothers' as well as their fathers' lives and look to both
genders for nurturance and care, when boys play dolls as often
as girls collect baseball cards and half the U.S. senators are
women—on that day, we have consoled ourselves, the psychology
of love will change, and with it the world. Clearly, that time is
not yet at hand. Gender still loads the dice of difference: the
ERA is dead; Barbie lives on; working moms swoon more from
exhaustion than passion; sex is too often a danger, too seldom a
pleasure; and "balance, equality, mutual everything," Katharine

Hepburn's romantic objectives in *Adam's Rib* seem more like a fairy tale than *Cinderella.*[1]

But haven't expanded educational opportunities for girls and political intervention, new contraceptive options, the right to abortion, and the participation of women in the labor force changed the psychology of love at all for ordinary teenage girls? Haven't boys altered their ways at all in response to girls' increasing equality? Does a teenage girl have to be a genius or a completely disenchanted rebel to experience romantic power and enjoy sex with a teenage boy?

Out of four hundred teenage girls' accounts, I have only one describing a teenage boy as the mindful, sensuous, respectful dream lover of the feminist vision—Cindi's. When Cindi first met Scott, she had just changed schools. They eyed each other for a few weeks, then went to the movies one weekend. The whole movie, Cindi said, she just wanted to hold his hand.

> And he told me later he really wanted to just like hold my hand, and I said, "Well, why didn't you?" and he said, "Well, why didn't you?" And then we went back to his house and we were downstairs in his kitchen and all of a sudden he just pulled me over and we just started kissing, and he was like, "Wow!" And then he said, "Let's go upstairs."

Upstairs:

> He was like, "Did you mind when I kissed you before?" and I said, "No," and he said, "Well, can I do it again?" and "Yeah," and so we started kissing and we ended up sleeping together, but we didn't have sex or oral sex or anything. We were just kissing and holding each other the whole night.

From the first, she wanted to have sex with Scott.

> Not at that immediate time but at some time, just because everything was really right. I really liked him. We always had good times together. I was never turned off by him in any way. And he would always say, "Oh, I really want to have sex with you," but he didn't say it in the way that made me feel I had to. He'd just say it like I knew that he really wanted to. . . .
>
> And then we started to, we were always having sex, whenever we

got the chance, but we weren't having intercourse or oral sex. Then we had oral sex once and then we had it another time, but it wasn't all the time, and I wasn't uncomfortable about it. I think maybe he didn't want to just always do it all the time, because maybe he thought then the relationship would get too like sex-oriented, and he didn't want that to happen. He'd just talk to me and he'd say, "Just tell me what's wrong and tell me what you want," and then he would say, "Oh, I really want to have sex with you."

Finally after about a month, they had intercourse.

And it was really, really good. It was a day during school and he said, "Do you want to sleep over?" And I said, "Yeah." And he'd always say, "Do you want to have sex?" and I'd say, "Yeah, I really do, I want to have sex with you but when the time is right," and that night when we had sex, he said, "Do you want to?" And I said, "Yeah, I do, but just be really careful."

He was really, really good about it. Really nice. He made me feel really, really good and it didn't hurt a lot. I mean, of course, it hurt a little bit, but it didn't really hurt as much as I had expected. I had heard from my friends, "Oh, it killed, it killed. I really was going to tell him to stop but I just figured I'd go through with it." So I was surprised because he made me feel so comfortable. He would just say, "Relax. Don't worry about it. I won't hurt you. Tell me if I'm hurting you," and stuff like that. I wasn't even really nervous and it really didn't hurt that much and I was surprised. We didn't use any birth control. He just kind of pulled out.

The next day she told her mother she needed a diaphragm.

She said, "Why? Because you've had sex?" and I said, "Yeah," and she said, "Oh, okay." She didn't ask me, "Oh, did it hurt?" or anything, because she knows that I would tell her if I wanted to. So she made an appointment and I went to the gynecologist and she was really nice and I got a diaphragm and everything was fine. It kind of made me feel older.

After that Scott and I started having sex all the time, lots and lots and lots. Besides the fact that I would stay at his house almost every night, like in one night we would have sex like three or four times. That seemed like a lot to me. A lot. It was really tiring. He'd always say, "Are you having an orgasm?" and I'd say, "No," and he'd say, "But I want you to have an orgasm," and I'd say, "Well, maybe it just takes time, maybe it will happen," and I'd say, "But, you know, it's really okay. For now I'm really satisfied without having an orgasm, just being with you and everything. It's just fine. It's great for me." And he said, "Well, good. You know. That's good." And then about four months after we started having sex, I had one, and then it didn't happen for a while, and then it happened again once, and, you know, it's nice, it's a great feeling.

Then on field week we fell in love. I'd thought all along, You know, god, I wonder, could I fall in love with him? And I always thought, Yeah, I know I could. I know I could fall in love with him. I know that it will happen. And it was, I was going back to camp again, so I was really sad, and we were lying in the same tent one day, and we had just had sex, and I was really scared, and all of a sudden, I started to cry. I guess maybe it was like the first or second time I ever cried in front of him, and he was like, "Why are you crying?" and I was like, "I'm just sad because I'm going to leave, and I won't see you, and I'll really miss you," and he said, "But don't worry about it, because I'll come up and visit you at camp," and then he said, "I really love you." He said, "You're the first girl that I really loved the way I love you. I mean, I really feel like I'm in love with you," and I said, "Yeah, I feel that way too," and then that was like—I don't know. It seemed like it made things a lot better. We were much closer, and I was much more comfortable around him, and I was really happy, you know, really, really happy.

It takes two to fall in love like that. It wouldn't have happened if Cindi and Scott hadn't each had many childhood experiences that made them comfortable and patient with the body and the heart. But as lucky as Cindi was in Scott, hers wasn't, finally, an equality story, because Scott always had an edge over her: he knew more and he consistently took the lead.

Equality stories, by contrast, were on the cool and wild side of romance. Their narrators were strategists. They planned for their pleasures, and they took romantic payback as a rule. (If one guy hurt a narrator in this group, the next few guys she met had better watch out.) They represented themselves as assertively and conventionally feminine (long hair and lined lips, crushed velvet and striated spandex). Several called themselves "postfeminist." All the same, there's a lot of feminism in their stories, and despite the cool calculation, a lot of romance. These narrators were literally the daughters of feminism. All their mothers worked and exercised economic power within their families; many of their mothers were active members of the movement. In this respect, like 1930s movie heroines (whose invisible mothers were the suffragettes of the early twentieth century), these narrators came to equality as if to a birthright.[2] They refused masculine dominance, and they were never passive or subordinate. They displayed initiative and took responsibility in every sphere—including sex, romance, and the equally valued realm of friendship. They treated femininity as a style, not a destiny, and romance as a comic avocation for which they had a special flair. Take Anja's opening romantic vignette, for example. "There are some sort of funny moments," she began. At a concert she saw a boy standing nearby.

> And then I realized he was standing next to me. And so, in a really tightly packed crowd, I was sort of standing there and our hands sort of hit each other. And mostly when you do that you kind of, you know, pull your hand away. But I said, Well, I won't move it if he won't. He didn't. And so our hands were kind of touching and then we started holding hands. And we were standing there in the crowd and we didn't look at each other at all. We were just standing there holding hands and going like this. . . .

She stroked her palm:

> And it was really funny. It was really nice. And then the concert ended and the crowd started to disperse and I sort of looked at him. And I just couldn't bring myself to say anything to him, because I thought, No matter what I say, it'll just like shatter it, you know. So we kind of just let go of each other's hands and walked away.

Classic romance plots, as literary critic Rachel DuPlessis has observed, use "the developing heterosexual love relation" as the central—often the only—organizing element in narrative action.[3] Many of the stories we've heard so far follow that pattern: the engine that drives the story is the quest for love.[4] Romantic strategists had a cumulative rather than a dissociative approach to experience which they applied to romance as well as to learning and friendship. This cumulativeness decentered romance, kept it from taking over and quashing the self. It left room, as radical popularity did not, for public achievement, for being "smart," successful, sociable, and sexual. At the same time, it kept ambition from pushing out love and friendship, melodrama from pushing out comedy.

This group of narrators constitutes a very small sample—twelve girls—but they had a lot to say, and their stories have a great deal to offer all kinds of girls who want to find romance without becoming love's victims. Most talked very quickly, packed their accounts with incident and observation, took no time out for sighs or tears. The result is long on insight, although perhaps inevitably somewhat short on historical context. There's some Jane Austen in their voices, some Alix Kates Shulman, some early Erica Jong, as well as some Katharine Hepburn. But these parallels take us only so far, because more than any other narrators, these girls were inventing a whole new approach to romance. They derived their ideas about how to conduct their love lives not from specific preexisting models, but from their own sense of equality.

Like so many other narrators, they began their tales *in medias res*—what happened yesterday, or the most recent boyfriend, or a first kiss—and looped backward and forward through time. But they assumed an unusual degree of continuity between preadolescent and adolescent romantic experience, locating the roots of their teenage relations in very different childhood behaviors than did other peers. Teenage mothers, for example, tended to emphasize their role as little women in preadolescent games like Marriage and House; fast-track friends spoke of their image as little scholars on the proving ground of academic precocity. Romantic strategists, instead, focused on the continuity between the chase games and gender rivalries of preadolescence and teen romance.

"THE BOYS always chased the girls," Andrea Dworkin wrote in *Ice and Fire*, "and it was a hard chase and we ran places we had never seen before and hid in places we were afraid of." This rendition of the chase game fits Dworkin's view of a sexual world in which women are the victims and men the victimizers, but not all renditions of the game are so grim—or so simple. Barrie Thorne's careful ethnography of children's chase games reveals that they have a "gendered structure," but roles are not fixed:

chasers and chased alternate. Children's own descriptions of the games reflect this, Thorne found, with girls tending to say "boys chase the girls" while boys said "girls chase the boys." In this way, each claimed "a kind of innocence," albeit of a different tenor than the innocence Dworkin's account claims for girls and women.[5]

The girls I talked with never told it Dworkin's way. Maybe it was because they were born after feminism's second wave, but even the most traditional girls told of girls chasing boys, not the other way around. Stealing kisses was the goal, and bold, nervy girls filched them anytime, anyplace:

> She'd walk up to him when he's like at the sink cleaning out paints . . . and just go kiss him.

When they succeeded in enchanting that most resistant of romantic quarry—the preadolescent boy—they became legends among their friends, who felt humble in comparison:

> He'd just follow her around forever, you know. And I was just like, "How did you do that? That's so incredible." And she would just like do that all the time. And I was so shy around—I couldn't do anything.

Frequently, the bold ones even teamed up to get their kisses, turning kissing into the chase game—Run, Catch, Kiss—which girls reported playing as tirelessly and cooperatively as boys played ball.[6]

Carol Gilligan has observed that girls typically put the initiatives and skills they learned in preadolescence behind them as they head toward adolescence and glimpse what's been called "the wall," the many obstacles that keep girls from full equality. Depressed by their recognition that they will be subordinate as adults, they begin to sit back and wait instead of doing their fair share of chasing. As a result, they lose moral clarity and academic force.[7] Gilligan's solution is to elongate preadolescence. It sounds reasonable. A longer preadolescence would give girls more time to develop their identity in the context of friendship and play before entering the lists of love. But it's hard to imagine preadolescents agreeing to the proposal. For most kids, preadolescence is like being a colonial subject. You're not autonomous. You have almost no inalienable rights, and you're a sitting duck for abuse. A teenager, in contrast, is halfway to independence, gradually accumulating rights, and in a position to spend at least some time in the liberated zone outside of home and school where teenage sex—like most of the quasi-rebellions of adolescence—usually takes place: the automobile, the time between school letting out and dinner, Saturday night, the 7-Eleven parking lot. It would be some fight to take all this away or even just postpone it until, say, high school graduation.

Impractically and rather dangerously, a few commentators have suggested physically delaying puberty (an enormous amount of exercise has been proposed). Among other obvious flaws, this tack would decrease the time that girls have to practice balancing love and work.[8] Yet they need more practice not less. As the fast-track friends realized, they have so much to learn. But if neither approach seems workable, there is another option and some narrators described it: taking preadolescent skills along into adolescence and into romance, adding love to the mix of life, an approach that clearly served those who managed it very, very well.

ANJA AND GINGER were best friends. Their parents were professors and artists. Anja's mother virtually supported her family, and Ginger's mother carried her share of her family's finances. Neither Anja nor Ginger grew up with a great deal of money, but by adolescence they were so familiar with their city's museums that the Met's Rembrandts and MOMA's Warhols might as well have been family heirlooms. Half middle-class, half bohemian, they enjoyed a sense of being both financially secure and set apart. Unlike the fast-track friends, they were completely at home with their own intellectual gifts. Early on, they won places in one of the best public school programs in the country. Since then academic success hadn't been so much a goal as a given. They worked at learning but they didn't worry about being smart enough.

Anja had a smoky kind of beauty, like Bacall's; she specialized in sidelong glances. Ginger had radiance; energy seemed to fly off her like gold shavings. They were self-consciously feminine and sexual. Anja spoke slowly and continuously; Ginger, so fast that five minutes of her talk produced four times as many pages of transcription as five minutes of Anja's. Both knew just what kind of material I was after, and they stayed on point. Ginger had less sexual and romantic experience than Anja but she was a witty observer. In combination, their accounts described a path from preadolescence to adolescence that decentered romance and maintained gender parity.

Popular girls, as we've seen, take a sporting attitude. Anja and Ginger went a step further. They won the right to enter games by being sharp and aggressive, and they played more like boys than like most girls (who are far more apt than boys, studies indicate, to stop playing at the first sign of discord). With working parents who didn't have time to waste on tattletales and adjudication, they and their brothers and sisters had learned early to work things out among themselves, to keep games going by negotiating and strategizing.

Both Anja and Ginger related playing Run Catch Kiss avidly in elementary school. Anja even recounted a girls' revolt in the face of a school directive to give up the game.[9]

> It was one of those games that the older kids played. And so one day we were all kind of hanging out at lunch, like, "Oh, what should we do?" And someone thought that up and all the girls kind of agreed. And then we started playing every day and then the principal said, "Well, I don't think you should play that."

They argued that the principal was "crossing our rights by not letting us play." When she didn't back down, they retaliated:

> Maybe like thirty of us would go and sit on the back staircase and play spin the bottle.

In high school, Anja began to accumulate sexual and romantic experience earlier than Ginger. Sex was hard for Anja to talk about, but Ginger wanted her to. Like generations before them, the friends came up with a "code"—numbering sexual stages. Amazingly, they thought they had invented the scheme.

> #1 was kissing. #2 was torsional petting . . . you know what that means. And then #3—the a's were boys doing things to girls and the

b's were the other way around. And so a's—#3a—well, #3 is like manual stimulation. So #3a was like the boy to the girl and #3b was the other way. And then #4 was oral sex, #4a and then #4b. And #5—sex.

In that it classifies active and passive roles for each gender, their code is unusual and telegraphs the eye they had for power differentials.

Anja had reached #4b, and Ginger #2b by junior year when the boys started playing Doubles Killer—an action game of opposing pairs.[10] The pairs shot at one another with plastic tracer guns—inexpensive toys that shoot flat plastic disks ten to fifteen feet. A pair was out of the game when both members had been zapped.

Doubles Killer was already underway when the game's organizer, James, told Anja the boys were placing bets on fooling around with girls.

> He said, "This guy Lonnie has this bet about this girl that he's going to fool around with her by June and he'll get a hundred dollars for it."
> I said, "Oh, god, that's so tacky."
> And he said, "Oh, come on, it's one of those things guys do."
> And I said, "I'd like to make a bet about a guy."

He took her up on it.

> And he said, "Okay, I'll bet you about Sam. I'll bet you fifty bucks you can't sleep with Sam before March."
> And I said, "Okay, fine."

She bet she would sleep with Sam before March. About the same time, she and Ginger talked James into letting them play.

> All the other guys got on James's case. Why did you let a couple of girls in? Girls aren't going to take it seriously. It was a men's club. And Ginger and I got really mad and we were like, "Well, we're going to show them."

Now Anja and Ginger were in two games that previously only the boys in their class played—Killer and Chase. In the former, their first opponents were Sam and Artie, whom Ginger had her eyes on. Artie had a minor leg injury. The boys probably figured that would make the girls go easy on him, but instead they increased his handicap, removing the pins from his crutches when he wasn't paying attention. It was a wily move, but eventually Sam managed to "shoot" them both.

So we were dead. But Sam said, "I really have respect for you guys. That was a great plan. You guys were really aggressive." And we were like, "Cool, cool."

Impressed at the seriousness with which Anja and Ginger approached the game, James gave them another chance. The following morning they staked out one opponent's house before school and shot him. "Ah! Phew." The next morning they "staked out" the second boy.

And we went to his lobby and we were going to go up to his apartment but he came out just then, so we got him right there. And we were like, "Great! We won!" you know.

They had qualified for yet another round. For several days, they snuck out of their houses by back doors, got off buses a stop or two early, hid in bushes. These defensive maneuvers kept them in the game but they needed an offensive strategy to "kill" the boys:

Ginger and I had this plan: she'd come to my house, come in through the back door, and they'd be like waiting outside our house. And then we'd go out the back way and circle around and take them. It seemed like a good plan.

But the boys got Ginger when she was leaving her house for Anja's. At this point, Anja's play grew cautious.

I began to live my life by this game and like never go out of the house.

Meanwhile, her crush on Sam increased exponentially. To further her romantic aims, Anja made a bet on the outcome of the next round: Loser buys dinner.

I was trying to play it up like I was really confident even though I was pretty sure I was going to lose because there were two of them and only one of me. But everyone was telling me they were so stupid because it had been like a week and they hadn't gotten me and it was just me and two of them. They just looked so bad, you know. Which was really fun. There was supposed to be a Mixed Doubles Killer next, like boy-girl pairs, and everyone was asking me to be their partner. And I was like, "Well, you know, I don't know. I'll have to think about it."

So anyway I tricked them. One day Sam went to the bathroom for a minute and I said, "Artie, let's go for a walk." We walked outside the school block and then I was like, "Come on, Artie, come shoot." Because once we stepped off the block we could shoot.

And he was sort of scared to because Sam would be mad at him if he missed, so I just like backed across the street and then I turned and ran and I got away. And so they looked really bad because they had two of them and I just escaped.

Getting "so sick of the game," Anja challenged Sam to a shoot-out.

I got behind a car and we shot, and he got me. But it was honorable, you know, because I stayed in for a week and a half—just me against the two men. I was just so glad to have it over.

She began negotiating their dinner plans.

I said, "Well, I don't think I should have to take Artie out for dinner. He didn't even get me." And he said, "Well, I don't know."

She won. It was to be just Anja and Sam.

So I told him I'd take him out for dinner Saturday night. And I was really nervous. I didn't know where I should take him, what I should wear or anything. And I said, "He's probably going to forget and I'm going to have to call and confirm. And he's not going to know what I'm talking about." And Ginger said, "Oh, come on," you know.

She took him to a Mexican restaurant. "It was a very platonic evening." She "really didn't know what he was thinking" until the next week when he called to say, "Well, since you took me out last weekend, I can take you out next weekend."

At school they talked over possibilities. Appropriately, they decided to watch the finals of *Jeopardy!*

> And Artie was there. And he said, "Oh, you can go to my house if you want." And I like thought this is such a setup, you know. His best friend is offering the keys to his house. But I thought, Oh, who knows. Because Sam had never had a girlfriend before, so I figured it's wasn't too much of a setup.

While they were watching TV, he put his arm around her.

> And I was like, Okay, is he going to do anything or not? And he wasn't. And I was like, Oh no, this is terrible. And I thought, Well, maybe he's just scared. He's not sure if I want him to. So I was being cute and cuddling next to him and I thought he definitely knows.

In the end, she took some initiative and he took some.

> Finally I just sort of leaned over and when I leaned over, he kissed me. And then we were, uh, there for a while.

When Artie's mom came home, Sam and Anja went out to dinner, then back to Anja's house to "fool around some more."

> Q: Fooled around—1, 2, 3, 4—?
> A: Okay. Well, first, at Artie's house, it was just 1, you know. And then here it was uh—uh, kind of a lot—uh, like everything except 4a and 5 if you remember what that is. And if not, you're out of luck.

In joining Doubles Killer, Anja and Ginger had updated a little boys' game to include the challenges that gender difference entails—an impressive win in itself. And in the same clever play, the girls bridged preadolescent and adolescent romantic experience and entered the arena of teen romance with such preadolescent skills as gamesmanship, boldness, and initiative intact, drawing on the game itself for a way of understanding and responding to romantic experience.

The gamester perspective that these girls brought to gender relations made them unusually aware that in teen romance, as with any other game, it takes at least two to play. (It may seem like an obvious point, but very few narrators really understood this. To Tracy, for example, boys existed to fall in love with her; to the fast-track friends, they were almost guinea pigs.) In addition, they began with an advantage common among popular girls—many collegial friendships with boys, some based on athleticism and some on academic activities. Finally, their performance in the game, and their allure, probably moved the boys farther in a romantic direction than direct come-ons ever would have. Recall how badly clumsy assertiveness served the fast-track friends, and the sad plight of dressed-to-kill broken hearts. The boys responded to the new ripples in their world of boyish games with the idea of Mixed Doubles Killer.

GINGER WAS NOT as fast off the romantic mark as Anja, but she didn't get tense about it, she said.

> I was never frustrated about it because they didn't like me or something. That's not the way it was at all. I mean, I loved hanging out with them.

One day an "unattractive" but "smart" guy informed Ginger of a conversation about her he had taken part in.

> They were all going on like, you know, oh, you know, "Ginger's really pretty, Ginger's really nice, so why aren't we all crazy about Ginger? Why are we going for Anja and Noel and Celia, all of whom have like their little bitchies and things like that." And so, him and one of his friends came to the conclusion that I had no sex appeal.

Another girl would have died on the spot. Ginger let him have it.

> I just ripped it up and I'm like, "Out of my house. Get out! Get out!" He apologized. And I'm like, "I don't want an apology."

The experience gave her pause. In the fall, she invested her babysitting pay in a trendy new look and began to search for someone to catch and kiss. Instead of just setting her heart on a random object of desire, the way fast-track narrators like Elise did, Ginger looked for someone she thought might also be looking for her. Tom came to mind. She liked him and they had danced at parties, but he had never made a move. An "infinite possibility" narrator would have overridden his passivity, but Ginger knew she couldn't do it entirely on her own, and she told him so.

> I say how he drives me crazy because I don't know if he likes me and stuff like that. And he's just sitting there, and he goes, "Yeah, well, ditto." And I go, "Ditto!?"
>
> And he's like, "Yeah, you know, same thing," like he had a crush on me last year and blahblahblahblah.
>
> And I'm like, "You can't just say 'Ditto,' Tom. You have to tell me something back."
>
> And he's like, "No, I mean, I know what you're talking about. I get your drift." And I'm like, "Nonono, no no, you have to say it to me."
>
> And he won't tell me he likes me. He just can't say it. He said, "Ginger, you can say things like that to people. I can't say things like that to people. . . . I can't talk to girls like this. I can't. I'm not into it. That's why I don't ask girls out. I can't do this stuff." You know, so he keeps telling me, "I can't do it."
>
> And I'm like, "Tom, I can't do everything."

Finally, he spoke up.

The elements that are specific to these narratives are evident in Ginger's account. Like the fast-track friends, these narrators not only positioned themselves as active, able, and optimistic rather than passive and anxious, but also took themselves humorously, something true-love narrators never could do and others seldom did. Treating the self humorously can cut in a number of ways. Self-deprecation is a standard variety joke: It's funny, vents humiliation and anger, and is restorative; but in women's traditional humor, it also often totally undermines the teller's entitlement to pain or pleasure. The humorousness of these narrators derived, rather, from a well-developed sense of who they were and a solid sense of perspective, and it enabled them to stand up for their own interests without turning every tiny desire into a life-or-death issue. This relative detachment lightened the load of expectations they brought to bear on the self and the future, and that, in turn, lightened everything and helped them maintain a level gaze on the object of their affections.

Unlike all the girls who viewed their love object as a credential-to-be or means-to-an-end, equality narrators never gave a lover the power to affirm or destroy them. They didn't go in much for the kind of "understanding" practiced by many girls when confronted with lovers' fickleness, unreliability, or cruelty (as in, "That's when the man in him came out," or "He can't help it, he had such a hard childhood"). They had a sense of the bodies and characters they were dealing with. They included graphic physical descriptions; used epithets—Mr. Studlee, Mr. New Guy to Notice; referred to topics of conversation—sports, politics, school, professional hopes. And they replaced the romantic tunnel vision of their peers with a comparative sense:

He's a little bit more confident, and he's fooled around with so many girls.

Because they realized there was someone on the other side of their daydream, they were prone to notice early on when they were dealing with a louse or likely to be taken advantage of:

He says, "Um, I'm cleaning my house. You can come over and clean my house if you want."
I'm like, "Okay." I mean, I went all the way there. I mean, it was like ridiculous.

At the same time, they recognized that as subjects—equals—they too might risk exploiting a partner. A girl who'd just engaged in some exploratory fooling around told me, "I feel badly about experimenting at someone else's expense."

To those narrators who wanted to achieve true love in adolescence, youth—like innocence—represented one of the most valuable chips they would ever be able to stake on the future; to fast-track narrators, youth was the promise of achievement; to girls who went after men, it was at once an ethical obstacle and

a hot erotic position. To romantic strategists, youth and innocence were a pleasure, a *bonne chance* they were having the good
fortune to enjoy. Youth also offered perspective. They might
make a mistake today, go with the wrong guy, get dumped when
they weren't quite ready. But there was always tomorrow—another day, another chance. This further lightened the weight romance had to bear. At the same time, they treated youth as a
humorous situation that often generated funny—that is, awkward
or comical—trains of thought or experience. If they were bum-
bling, they were nonetheless sympathetic characters to themselves, the objects of affectionate delight rather than the butts of
self-loathing.

MANY TEENAGE GIRLS enter the lists of teen romance as best
friends, as Anja and Ginger did, but with the exception of popular girls, few continued to privilege that friendship once they
became involved with a lover, and popular narrators accomplished this mainly by steering clear of intimacy altogether.
Equality narrators, by contrast, both held on to their friends as
lovers came and went and cultivated intimacy. This both enabled
and unburdened their romances.

Stacey faltered at the beginning of our talk, searching for the
right starting point. She gave up on a sentence about Arthur,
went to Leroy, then stopped herself and started over one last
time.

Oh wow. I remember. Gigi was my friend.

She went on to tell the story of the affair Gigi helped her begin,
rather than her first affair or her current one. Gigi's friendship
was important to Stacey initially because Stacey's family had just
moved to a new city, and Gigi was indispensable in helping Stacey
understand and fit into the elite circle of African-American
middle-class students in her new school. As Stacey put it, Gigi
was "the first person I ever met"—that is, her first friend in that
group.

Other cliques, we have seen, concerned themselves with establishing and enforcing the acceptable behavior of their members.
The narrators of these romantic comedies, in contrast, talked a

lot about each other but little about their differences from other girls or the difference between the good kind of girl and the bad. They represented friends as partners in the game of love. Instead of warning each other off, these friends evidently egged each other on. Stacey on Gigi:

> She's a fun outgoing-type person. And so I was like "cool." And that day she asked me, Did I want to go to lunch? So I went to lunch with her. And Arthur—we met up with Arthur in the hall. I was like, "Oh, he's so cute," you know, and everything.

Gigi introduced Stacey to Arthur and asked him to come along with them to McDonald's.

> And I was like, "Oh god, why did you ask him that?" you know? And he was like, "Yeah, sure."

She and Gigi plotted bedding Arthur as conspiratorially as Anja and Ginger played Doubles Killer. They started with contraception.

> She told me, "You should always be safe" because—Gigi is just the most crazy person and she talks about everything and nothing is taboo for her, you know. She'll just pop right out of the clear blue sky, "So are you on the pill?"

Gigi accompanied Stacey to Planned Parenthood. Once on the pill and counting on her friend for moral support, Stacey was ready to make a sexual move. But she didn't just go after Arthur out of the clear blue; like Anja and Ginger, she understood the rule of back-and-forth. Romance was a game to be played, not a fate to simply submit to, nor a fantasy to act out in its entirety or not at all. Arthur had spent time at her house. She had spent time at his. She could fairly assume he'd return her interest if he knew about it. She went to his house one afternoon when his parents weren't home. He was "nervous." She was forthright. He asked if she wanted to watch TV.

> And I was like, "No, I want you to show me your bedroom." And he was like, "You want me to what?"
> And I said, "Well, you never gave me a tour of your whole house."

So he finally took me upstairs . . . and he was like, "Well, this is my room, you know, look at it."
  And I was like, "Well, aren't we gonna go in?"
  And he said, "Well, no, there's no reason, you know, to go in."
  And I was like, "Child, what's the matter with you? Don't you—?"
  And he's like, you know, "I guess" and everything.
  And then he was so shy.

Stacey clearly liked the feeling of knowing more than he did about sex. Her approach to equality was somewhat different from Anja's and Ginger's: she liked to be slightly more than equal. One way she kept a moderately upper hand was by maintaining a humorous point of view. She had something funny to say about almost everyone, and often framed one funny story within another, pleating in several comic perspectives—for example:

My mother used to think it was so funny, because it would be ten degrees below zero, the snow would be this high, and there she'd see Pierre coming over on his bicycle. . . . And my dad was always spying on us. One day Pierre and I saw him looking out the window, and we walked around to the back of the house. Well, my dad— there was like a little table in the window seat, and he was standing on it and he kept scooting over to keep his eyes on us, lost his balance, fell over, and pulled all the curtains down.

The year her city friends talked about nothing but how "perfect" sex was, Stacey resolved to keep her virginity a secret until school ended, then have sex with her summertime boyfriend who lived near her grandparents in the country. He was an engineering student several years older than she whom her grandparents and her mother idolized and assumed she would marry after college. She didn't want to marry him but she decided he'd be the best choice for first sex because she had known him for so long and he seemed safe.

He wouldn't make fun of me or anything, because he knew I was a vir . . . That was another thing for me. I didn't want anybody to say, "Ha, ha, ha. You don't know what you're doing."

Plus, he couldn't hurt her emotionally because she had already "gotten tired of him."

I had known him so long.

She knew he would introduce the idea and he did.

It was a week after I turned sixteen and it was on a Sunday night. There's a lake. . . . We drove down there. And after I did it I came home and, you know, I went to the bathroom and I was bleeding and I went in and I told my mom, "Oh my gosh, mom, I think I'm dying."
   And mom said, "What?"
   And I said, "I think I did something I wasn't supposed to do."
   And mom said, "What's the matter?"
   And so I told her and everything and then mom told me how that happens, you know, and then she was kind of upset because she didn't think I was ready but she said, you know, she didn't think there was anything she could do to stop me.

She went back to school experienced and knowledgeable— ready to teach Arthur to love.

He was so bumbly. I kind of liked that too, because I was like, Hey, this is cool. I know more than you know.

EVEN NARRATORS who represented themselves almost totally as passive victims revealed a strategic component to their romantic thinking. Tracy, for example, pondered long and hard about how to get her boyfriend "wrapped" before she agreed to have sex, but she relied on an unrealistic notion of love as a lasso that would give her control of him once she got it around his neck. Equality narrators had a very different sense of romantic power, consciously realizing that even the most tender or committed gender relations include power differentials. They knew that they were playing with that differential and they admitted a degree of cool calculation in romantic encounters that never appeared in the true-love narratives:

I was playing with him a little bit.

It was a little bit of a power play.

When they "played" with the masculine ego or entered the game of romance, they played to win. For them being a competitor rather than a victim was, if not eroticized, certainly exciting, and they described knowing exactly what they were doing:

That was my tactic and it happened to work.

Such strategies effectively prevented romantic falls in the early stages of a romance because love was never an opening bid. An-ja's lovability wasn't on the line when she bet she could go out with Sam. Fifty dollars was. Win or lose, she would have shown romantic mettle, and gained points for taking the kind of risk boys take all the time. Nor did these narrators talk about love, as they moved slowly to coitus, a development delayed not by an extended negotiation about sex and love, but by a gradual, ex-ploratory, sensuous erotic progress—a lot of kissing, a lot of mak-ing out. They knew that they walked a dangerous line between flirtation and falling for someone in the course of this experi-ence, and they paced themselves very carefully, as Ginger's ac-count of a spring fling with Jeff indicates:

So we were all at my house and we fell asleep on this mattress. And these kids took a long time to come back from their walk. So we were like just—I can't remember exactly the sequence of events. But we were lying down and talking and listening to music and we were throwing things at each other. The lights were off. So eventually we just like started fooling around. It was no big deal. It was just like kissing and, uh, you know, just kind of caressy kissy stuff. It was really childish. The whole situation. So these kids come back and they ring the doorbell. So like *djung*, we jump up, let them in, they come in, you know, they fall asleep or whatever. Jeffrey goes to sleep in one place. I go to sleep in another. . . . And I was really cool to him in the morning because I didn't want to act like I wanted to go out with him or anything. Because he's like Mr. Studlee. I didn't want to get him to think that something was like a problem.

She and Jeffrey went around as friends for a few weeks after that; then he started seeing someone else. She was "pretty jealous" for about three weeks.

And then it totally cooled off and I was not jealous anymore. I just got over him. It just ended.

At the time she thought this was unexpected and "very strange." But next time she would know that she could wait a crush out. Not get upset. Not lose anything from it. Gain the experience. Go on.

Anja had a much longer and more involved relationship. It began the night of a cast party after the last performance of a school play. Her account of the romance ran like thread from a spool, event after event connected with dozens of "and's" and "and so's."

Steven came over and sat down next to me and started talking to me. And so I was talking to him and we were just sort of sitting there, and he started holding my hand . . . and I was kind of like, What's going on? And then I kind of fell asleep on his shoulder. And that was it.

She told Ginger on the way home.

And she said, "Well, don't, don't think it's anything yet." And I said, "I know, I know." Because I thought, you know, he was sort of that kind of guy, you know, an older guy. Older guys might hold your hand, you know, but who knows what they mean, right? So, so I said, "No, no, I don't think anything."

That week at school they had a free period at the same time and he asked her to walk in the park with him.

Then we were walking back and he said something about wanting to go for a limo ride.
    And I said, "Oh, that's nice."
    And he said, "When I have enough money."
    And I said, "Well, don't forget your old friends, you know, when you do."
    And he said, "No, of course not."
    And I said, "When are you thinking of doing that?"
    And he said, "Friday."
    And I said, "Oh."

And he said something like, "And you can pay—I'll pay for the limo and you can pay for something."

And I was—I mean, I thought, you know—I wasn't sure if it was a joke or not. So I kind of said, "Oh, sure, that would be fine," and went to class, you know.

She told Ginger, who "kind of smiled." Then she told Ben, who said Steven had said he was going to ask her out on a date.

And I said, "Really? A date?"

Dates were even more unusual in their school than in 1980s teenage culture generally. Thrilled, she called all her friends.

And then Steven called me that night, and I was really glad that Ben had told me he was serious, or I would have been really surprised when he said, "So we're definitely going out?"

So I said, "Oh, yeah."

And he said, "Well, I don't know if I can afford a limo, but I'll take you out."

And I said, "Okay."

So I was really excited about that. And Celia and Noel both reacted kind of badly. And I felt bad but I was a little bit kind of gloating because they both liked him and I hadn't even done anything to go after him, and he liked me.

Dates used to be the way teenagers got to know each other. To Anja, it made more sense to get to know each other better *before* they went out, so the day before their date she sat with him on the bus.

I'd been sort of talking to him, and he'd kind of asked me if I wanted to go over to his house, and I kind of figured, Yeah, maybe I should do that before our date. Just like so—so our date isn't the first time I have to talk to him and I suddenly realize I can't, you know. So I decided to go over to his house.

And that's just what she did. The next day they went out for the dinner they planned together the afternoon before.

The thing about Steven was that he was definitely worth showing off, because he was good-looking and he was very popular. . . . It—it was good that way.

They followed the plan they had made—give or take a little improvisation.

We had dinner and then we went to a play and it was fun and we were just sort of sitting in the play and he was laughing a lot and he sort of started like rocking his knee kind of. So I started kind of like laughing. And to tease him I sort of like hit it, like that. So he sort of looked at me and then he took my hand. So we were holding hands.

Outside the theater, she continued to take her share of the sexual initiative:

We were just sort of walking, so I kind of just hooked my arm in his. And so then he kind of put his arm around me. So we were walking together like that. And then we passed a bunch of people from our school and so he had his arm around me, and that was kind of fun. And then we walked over to the park and . . . and there was this little cat that looked really hungry. So we went and bought food. And then we were standing there and sort of talking. And then he starts kissing me. So we just did that for a while. And then he walked me to the train and I went home.

They started spending their free time together at his house. "After school and things like that." All along the way, she kept checking to make sure that he was as interested in her as she was in him. She didn't want to be more involved than he was. She began to nudge him to formalize their relationship—to say publicly they were "going out"—because she thought that would prevent an unannounced, unexplained end to their relationship.

I was sort of teasing but I kind of wanted to know . . . because I just had this feeling that if we were going out, then he'd have to formally break up with me. To stop going out.

She was willing to give up the relationship like a sport when the time came but she didn't want the end to surprise her. He said it was silly. He wouldn't do it.

> And I went, "Come on, come on."
> He said, "No, no, I can't."

She kept after him, but ultimately she had to do it for him.

> So finally like that weekend I was at his house, and I said, "All right, Steven. Do you want me to ask you out?"
> And he said, "Yes, go ahead."
> And I said, "Do you want to go out with me?"
> And he said, "Yeah, yeah, I do."
> So I said, "Okay, great."
> So then we were going out, you know.

Anja claimed she still wasn't blown away by him. "I sort of liked him when he looked really nice, and then when he didn't that was kind of like mnnnnnhhh." Her friends remembered it differently. "She was over there every day," said Ginger. "Or she talked to him on the phone, and she was so obsessed with him." Other signs as well indicate that she was more serious about Steven—and more vulnerable—than she later acknowledged. She told much of the story in direct discourse, suggesting that the original exchanges had lost none of their power and intensity. Finally, while she was hardly passive with Steven, the ultimate power to make or break the relationship clearly rested with him not her.

But Anja was willing to give the relationship up if it endangered her, and that resolve both preserved her equilibrium and gave her power. No matter how much she loved Steven, for example, she wasn't about to have unprotected sex, and she drew the line at intercourse, not because she wasn't prepared to go all the way, but because she didn't like Steven's cavalier attitude toward contraception.

> He was just kind of talking about sleeping with me, and I was kind of like, "Remember birth control" . . . and he wasn't really thinking about that, so I just said, "Forget it."

They only went together from the end of May till the end of school, but that was long enough for "little arguments" to start.

> One time we were supposed to go to the movies together and he was late and I called his house and he said, "Oh, I was just leaving," and I said, "Okay," and I waited for him for the longest time. And then once he told me to wait for him in there. And then he called on the phone and said, "Oh, I realize I lost my wallet in the park," and so it took him like an hour to get there. And he finally showed up and meanwhile I had met his friend Lee and I'd been waiting with him and was just so mad at him. And then he said, "Well, it's so late. Now I have to go home because I have to take a test tomorrow."

In other narratives, behavior like this has been received with the high seriousness of tragedy. Anja didn't pretend to like it, but neither did she act like it was a mortal blow. Who was he, after all? Only the first in what would surely be a long line of boyfriends and lovers, some honorable, some louts, some who would love her too much, others who would love her too little. At the same time, she gave as good as she got.

That summer Anja and a friend went to Europe, where Anja met an "older man" of twenty-two or so, who helped the two travelers move their stuff from a hotel to an apartment. At the apartment, they smoked hash and "got kind of silly."

> And there was this like four-night special V on TV . . . and we'd been watching it and it was really bad but we really liked it and that was on that night. . . . He started kind of being very flirty and I was kind of playing with a string and swinging it around. And he said, "Stop that!" And I said, "No, no, I want to swing it." And so he grabbed me and jumped me and tackled me to get the string away from me and I was like, "Oh, forget it."

It was all a conscious effort on her part to galvanize his attention—the flirtation, the tease, the seeming irritation—and it worked.

> He started saying things to my friend like, "Well, why don't you go make us some tea?" And she was like looking at me like, "Should I or shouldn't I?" And I was like, "I don't care." So finally she said

okay and she went and she made some tea. So he like sort of pinned me down and tried to kiss me and . . . I wasn't really sure I wanted to but I was also a little bit high, so I kind of—did. And he was like, "Come on. Let's go in the other room."

It was "sort of like a switch" because she was in charge. She "didn't let him do anything" to her except touch her breasts "a little bit." As she described her reasoning:

In my mind, I sort of said, Well, you know, I'll never see this guy again. Might as well try all the things I've never tried. . . . We were kissing and then I—I gave him a blow job, as they say. And, uh, it wasn't too much fun. But I figured, Well, I've got to try it. Might as well try it on a guy who won't think anything. Who's completely stoned and I'll never see him again. So I did. And I said, Oh, that's no fun, you know.

Q: Well now, how did you know how to do that?

A: I didn't really know. That was why I was trying it. I had read some of those books like *Sex Tips for Girls*. And I thought, Well, I'll try it and see if it actually works. You know, that was my theory. And it didn't really. I just sort of said, "Well, I guess—I guess that's enough time."

Q: It didn't work?

A: Not—well, I wasn't concentrating very hard but it—it—no. I didn't really spend much time on it. I kind of said, "Forget it. I don't want to do this." And then it suddenly occurred to me that *V* was going to be on really soon, and I suddenly had this overwhelming desire to get away from him and go watch TV and he got sort of offended and said, "What are you talking about?" You know. He was like, "You're not going anywhere." And I was like, "No, look, I really have to go. My friend is in there all alone. This is so rude. I really have to go watch." And finally I just like ran away and went and sat down next to her and said, "Hi."

And she was like [suspicious sound], "Hi."

And I said "What did I miss?" you know.

So then he came into the room and he said, "Well, I'm going to go." So I walked him to the door, and I felt kind of pleased with myself because he was a lot older than me. He was twenty-two. I was fifteen. And I didn't care. I just walked out on him. I thought it was really funny, you know. I didn't think he was particularly interested in me, so I didn't have to feel like I was hurting his feelings. But it was still kind of fun, you know.

He tried to see her again. She wasn't interested.

When she went back home, she and Steven didn't see each other for months. She had other flirtations; seduced and disappointed a few boys, getting revenge where she could. One night at a party at her ex-boyfriend's apartment she found herself on a couch with a boy she knew liked her.

I think I felt a little bit crushed by Steven—you know, that he had kind of gotten the upper hand in the end. I didn't really make a move on Rodney, but we were lying so close together and so I sort of kissed him and we ended up kind of you know just really kissing.

In the morning when she woke up, she said, "Oh no. Why did I do that? That was so terrible." She "wasn't interested in him at all," but it took her a few days and three awkward meetings to break the news to Rodney, and even then it was only because he forced the issue. He called her over a weekend. She didn't call him back. The next school day:

We were all hanging around. And Rodney sort of said something to me like, "Anja, can I talk to you?" And I was like, "Okay." And I went over and I was like, "What?"
    And he was like, "What's going on with us?"
    And I was like, "Nothing's going on with us."
    And he said, "Oh."

That was enough to do the job, but she didn't stop. She went for "a little bit of a power play."

I said, "I just want you to know that I don't owe you anything."
    And he said, "I know, I know."
    And I said, "Well, I just get the feeling you think I do."
    And he said, "No, no, no. Forget it."

She took some satisfaction in these small vengeances, but they also made her wonder about herself. All in all, she still had a bad taste in her mouth from her romance with Steven. Then one night:

He called me up and said, "Oh, why don't you come over and I'll make you dinner." And I'm like, "Okay." And so he made me dinner and then he said, "Oh, let's get some wine." We got wine. He poured me a lot of wine and I started getting a little bit tipsy, and he said, "Oh, you shouldn't go home on the train alone. You should stay over here."

And I was like, "Okay."

And, um, so, I was just sitting on the couch and he started kissing me and I was like, Oh no. But then I said, Oh, what the hell. What do I care? I've done it before with him anyway. And so we—I spent the night at his house. And that was—and then we did, we did all up through 4b except we didn't sleep together. And that was the first time I had, you know, a really good time fooling around. Um, uh, you know, we spent the whole night there and it was—I mean I really didn't like Steven all that much, so it was sort of funny that way. But sexually it was, it was really good.

THE ROMANTIC strategies by which these girls cushioned or prevented romantic falls in the early stages of a romance also had an important role in first intercourse. The act that narrators like Tracy saw as their downfall, as a major rite of passage that left girls tender and vulnerable to romantic injury, was kept well in perspective by this group of narrators. They continued the practice of noting exactly what was happening moment by moment in the course of each romantic exchange as they approached intercourse itself, and this vigilance allowed them to stay on the realistic side of romantic planning. First, they integrated work and romance from the start, persisting with their studies and maintaining an active extracurricular life of music, dance, theater, debates, hanging out, and partying. Second, they kept sex and reproduction separate, a necessity the almost obsessional first-sex plans of the true-love narrators never included, largely because the narrators were too caught up in the problem of exchanging sex for love. Finally, romantic strategists didn't talk about love but about pleasure and experience, and they ranked contraception just below desire (which the true-love narratives never even mentioned) as a coital precondition. Because they weren't bargaining for love, they had plenty of leverage in structuring intercourse according to their desires. Anja, for example, had refused to sleep with Steven, the first boy who moved her sexually, because he seemed oblivious to the risk she would run. She surely could have gotten him to use contraception or she could have used it herself, but she figured that if he couldn't think of it himself, he wasn't worth it. She was more certain from the start that she would sleep with her next boyfriend. When he too seemed oblivious to the issue of birth control, she put him off without saying anything. Finally, he asked her straight out if she wanted to sleep with him. She shrugged. "Aren't you forgetting something?" He didn't ask what she meant and he didn't mention contraception the next time they got together. He just tried making moves. She turned him down flat again. By their next encounter, he had gotten the hint.

As successfully as the romantic strategists avoided unwanted pregnancies, they also escaped the kind of crushing despair that sank other girls for days, weeks, even years at a time following romantic disappointment. They did experience setbacks in their love lives. But they simply and consciously refused melodrama; that was a big part of what made them equal. Instead they assumed a comic stance toward their experiences characterized by realism, irony, and courage. They got a lot of help from the good friends who were there at the beginning and were still there at the end. They chose a perspective that salvaged their pride and kept them from generalizing their disappointment in one guy to all guys.

> At that point, it was a lot easier to decide that I hated him than that I hated most men, so I decided the guy was a real schmo. Well, interesting experience.

Having serial expectations helped, they said.

> I have this opinion that you can't get over somebody until there's something that gets it over.

And:

> If you have one guy who likes you, it gives you the confidence to like another guy and be successful at it.

Easy to summarize, hard to live. Of the narratives in this group, Anja's was the one that dealt most fully with romantic disappointment. Anja had a light case of romantic fever and a rare awareness of the potential breadth and tumult of physical desire. Yet she neither stopped herself from pursuing romantic adventure nor went wild. After her night of heavy petting with Steven, she felt ready for a relationship that would include intercourse, but she needed a lover with whom she had enough sexual and romantic power to keep the scales of gender even—one who mattered but not too much. Then Monty turned up. If Steven was day, Monty was night. Both Ginger and Anja talked about him. Less urbane than they, he came to their magnet school from a blue-collar suburb and pointedly went against the cosmopolitan grain—dressing sloppily, drinking beer, talking dirty. Once he put notes in both Ginger's and Anja's lockers, inviting them to have sex with him. Anja heard through the grapevine he had been making comments about her body.

> He'd say, "Oh, look at those big tits," and things like that, you know. And I'd go, "Oh, god." I started to think it was really kind of funny, you know. Because it was a joke really. He was just kidding around. You know, he wasn't really sleazy.

He didn't have "a very good name in school," particularly in her class. Anja represented his mediocre standing as a defect in her sexual and romantic assessment, but it may also have struck her as insurance that he would never be in a position to hurt or subsume her. She went on, weighing his physical assets and liabilities:

> He had a really nice body. He was really well built. But he wasn't really good-looking besides that.

She began her acceptance of him with that negative twister "but":

> But I started to really like him as a person. You know, he was a really nice guy. He was really funny. And, uh, I think I was a little bit attracted to him.

Ginger began going out some with Monty's best friend, Willy, adding convenience and sociability to the list of reasons Anja was accumulating for beginning a romantic association with Monty. They could go out as a foursome. She and Ginger would have

even more to talk about than they did already. Willy tried to tease
her into fooling around with Monty.

> We'd always make jokes about the way Monty dressed and he said,
> "Come on, come on, fool around with Monty."
> And I said, "No, no." I said, "I'll tell you what, Willy. You make
> sure he dresses nice for two weeks and then I'll fool around with
> him."
> And he was like, "I will. I'll really do it."
> And I was like, "Okay, you do that."
> And Monty started like dressing a little—like pushing his socks
> down instead of pulling them up to his knees and stuff like that, you
> know.

She found his efforts to transform himself according to her
guidelines "really funny," but at the same time she read them
as a sign that he really wanted her, and sexual power was what
interested Anja—both having it and coming under its sway.

> So, and then one day we were talking to Ginger and Willy. We all
> walked across the park to Ginger's house and we had pizza and then
> Willy left. And Ginger had her piano lesson and Ginger said, "Well,
> if you guys wait an hour, we can do something after my piano lesson.
> Like go out for ice cream."
> So I said, "Well, Monty come with me." So we just talked in the
> park, and we had a really good time talking. We still talked pretty
> sexually. Like we talked about what turns us on and stuff like that,
> you know. Ginger and I were always saying how watching guys play
> basketball turns us on. And he said things like how girls' necks turn
> him on. So then we went and we met Ginger and we had ice cream.
> And we talked about like who we liked to watch playing basketball,
> and he told us about how he thought we were both so pretty and
> everything.

Ginger had to go home. Anja and Monty started walking downtown to the train,

> And then we like stopped by the park, and we were just talking, and
> I was kind of leaning on the wall at Central Park West, and he was
> kind of talking to me. And I could kind of tell really. We were set
> up for it because it was dark and we were standing right by the park
> and then he kind of leaned over and kissed me.

She smiled as she recalled that he had changed his appearance for her.

> And he said, "Why are you smiling?"
> And he had sort of like pinned me to the railing.
> And I said, "I don't know."
> And he said, "Oh god." And he like unpinned me.
> And I thought, Oh-oh.

They both felt it then—sexual attraction.

> And then he sat up on the wall next to me and I was just sort of standing there. We weren't really talking. And then he started going like this to me, like to my neck. And that felt really nice and I was kind of like, Um, like, Oh. And then we started kissing some more, so we just like did that for a while. And then we just walked down. He was like holding my hand.

A few days later they were at a baseball game:

> And he kind of like leaned over to kiss me and I moved my head because I didn't want to kiss him in the middle of the schoolyard. It seemed so possessive, you know.

He couldn't own her or take her for granted. She had to make sure he knew that. That Friday night, she went to a party. When he wasn't there, she thought, Oh, I really want to fool around with Monty. Finally, he showed up and they went for a walk. She still wasn't "sure" she liked him but she was "really turned on by him." They started going out and "fooling around a lot." One night he asked if she wanted to sleep with him.

> I was like, "Aren't you forgetting something?" And so I just sort of said, "No, not really." I don't think he realized why I was saying no.

She didn't "want to say it" and once again, she didn't want to have sex with a boy so oblivious he didn't even think of contraception. The next time they were fooling around, he fell asleep.

> And the next day, I was like, "I can't believe you fell asleep." And he said, "Ohhhh, well, you know, if you'd been sleeping with me I

wouldn't have fallen asleep, you know, but you didn't keep me awake." And I was like, "Oh, fuck you," you know. . . . He was sort of kidding, but . . .

To hold his interest and maintain romantic power, she concluded, she was going to have to sleep with him, a formulation that was at once similar to and very different from that in the true-love narratives. Anja didn't want love. She wanted power within the context of a genuinely interesting sexual relationship. Mere power alone isn't that hard to come by; as long as the cords binding sex, love, permanence, and reproduction are cut, nerve and detachment will do it along with the willingness to drop anyone who doesn't act right—doesn't accept your power. An interesting relationship, by comparison, is much more difficult to achieve, because both parties have some power and some investment, making it harder just to walk away and easier to get hurt. If power had been all Anja wanted, she might have been happy with some of the guys she made out with along the way who were smitten with her. But she wanted to feel desire as well, and she wanted to be interested in the person she was involved with.

One weekend she and a few friends had access to an empty apartment. Monty, having gotten the picture, made a point of stopping at a drugstore for condoms. All the signs were right: while Ginger and Willy watched a movie in the living room, Anja and Monty had sex for the first time on the master-bedroom floor.

'Cause the bed was small. I mean, it was a huge floor and carpeted and so . . . And, uh, it hurt a little bit but it wasn't terrible. And I felt good because I liked Monty. I did like him a lot. And good also because I was very attracted to him and good because I was, like, it was another thing I could get out of the way, but also because it felt like the right time—I mean, because, you know, I'd always said to myself, I'm not going to do it if it's the wrong time, you know, I'm not going to do it when I don't want to. I'll just wait till I really want to. And I did want to and I was glad I wanted to and you know, the moment was right.

Her summation explained her equanimity, in part: "So. That was fun." Fun, not love, not a contract of the heart or body.

As if to emphasize the relative ordinariness of the event, she and Monty went out to get Chinese food afterward.

Coming back, we woke them up again and we ate some food and everything and they were like, "You guys are so weird," you know. And then we went to sleep.

Later they went out for a walk with Ginger and Willy.

And I wanted to tell her but I didn't know how to bring it up. You know. So I said something like, I said something about, like—oh, I remember, I remember. Because Monty like had bones that had hurt my thighs. So I said something about that, like "my thighs . . ."

And she was like, "What are you talking about? How could that have happened?"

And I was like, "Well, I don't know . . ."

And she was like, "Oh, you didn't."

And I was like, "Yeah, I did."

And she was like, "Oh my god, I can't believe it. Oh my god! What was it like?"

And they were like a couple feet behind us. I was like, "Keep it down, okay?"

So I just sort of told her it was pretty good and she was like "Oh, my god, I can't believe it! I can't believe it!" You know.

And she told me, she said, "Wait! Was that before or after you came waking us up saying you wanted to go get food?"

And I was like, "Before."

And she was like, "I don't believe it. You mean you came running in, waking us up, and ran out for food afterward?"

And I said, "Yeah."

So that was really funny.

For all Anja's offhandedness, she took glee and satisfaction in the event and in her sophisticated ability to act as if nothing about the experience was throwing her off balance. She felt it was a milestone, and she was pleased to know that she'd been more than up to the occasion. Later Monty referred cryptically to "last night."

And I said, "What are you talking about? Last night? I don't remember anything about last night."

And he was like, "Very funny."

>And I was like, "Really. I remember like we smoked a little bit and walked toward the master bedroom and then everything's a blur. I just can't remember anything else."
>And he said, "Very funny."
>And I said, "What did we do last night, Monty?"
>And he said, "We had incredible sex last night."
>And I said, "Oh, really?" I said, "I remember sex, now that you mention it. I don't remember anything incredible. But I remember sex."

The next week they went to the prom and then out for a horse-and-buggy ride and then back to her house, where they slept together on a single bed.

>The first time, you know, it hurt a little bit, so it was hard to really enjoy it. But that time I—I really did enjoy it a lot.

They slept together a few more times and then started to argue. Anja didn't describe this as Tracy had, as all "his" doing. Rather, she said, it was their doing. They just didn't get along that well.

>And I suddenly felt like he was going to say, "Let's break up."

Her reaction was one of the most extraordinary aspects of her account. Instead of fighting off a breakup and descending into melodrama, she thought it over:

>And I sort of felt like, Oh no, because I really did like him. But then I said, He's right, he's right, he's right.

She steeled herself but he didn't say it. He wanted to "keep trying." She didn't think he really did try, though. The next weekend, she called him to beat him to the punch. He said he was about to call her.

>And I said, "What about?" And I figured—I was so ready to pass it over to him, you know, because I didn't want to have to say it. And he said, "Well, you called me, tell me what you were going to tell about."

And I said, "Well, I think we were probably calling each other about the same thing."

And he said, "Well, yeah, I mean I hate to do this over the phone but I guess we should break up."

And I said, "Yeah, I guess so."

And we were kind of really cool about it at first. And then we started like really getting into things. And then we started yelling at each other over the phone. I mean, like really nasty, all these little things.

And he kind of—he just took all the blame, which kind of made me mad because I felt like, um, he kind of said to himself, Oh no. I know I've been terrible. You've been wonderful.

She hated him for this, because it implied that their relationship was ending merely because of the arbitrary nature of his desire. That was frightening and so was his power.

And I was like, Great! You know, here, I've been wonderful. That leaves me like with nothing. It leaves me feeling like I just tried and tried and I just couldn't get, you know, it made me feel like no matter how hard I tried, I wasn't good enough, and sort of like he had all the power.

She didn't let on that she felt that way. She didn't complain or implore him to see her. She took it like an equal. That was it, then. The end. They didn't talk for the rest of the summer. The relationship had failed; he had gotten sick of her; she had not maintained the balance of power; but she was able to save her sense of self.

In the aftermath of a breakup, true-love narrators blamed their lovers for everything. Denied what they most wanted—love—they insisted on innocence, goodness, and victimhood. Anja, in contrast, looked for a point of view that fit her image of herself and made acceptable sense of the experience. She concluded it was "an experience, you know, and it was important to have." Time helped. When school started, it had all "sort of faded" and her feelings toward Monty resolved into a vague friendliness.

Like Cindi's, Anja's account was remarkable for its balance. In the heat of desire, she thought about protection. (Cindi had intercourse once without protection; Anja never did.) In the midst of romantic negotiations, she crammed for tests and fulfilled all her academic responsibilities. At the nadir of romantic loss, she maintained a sense of herself. And Anja had to work harder than Cindi to maintain her romantic and erotic balance. She came upon no dream lover. (Maybe she wouldn't have desired one if she had.) Rather, by choice or by fate, she, like most girls, had to struggle and strategize to remain equal. But she didn't accomplish this by just staying still and safe; she stepped forward continually, made herself vulnerable to love, and took sexual risks. In the process, she achieved two out of three of Katharine Hepburn's objectives in *Adam's Rib*—balance and equality. As for "mutual everything," the once highly touted ideal of companionate marriage, while love was a goal of Anja's and the other narrators in this group, that was not. Perhaps it is incompatible with a power struggle, separate identities, and continued growth, a false ideal, a remnant of the time before we realize, as small, small infants, that we have left the sweet velvet warmth of the womb. But there is a fine ideal underneath all these narratives all the same: a model in which affection, recognition, and equality—not blind neediness and desperation—generate the force of love.

CONCLUSION

Going All the Way

The instincts of love are hard to educate; education
of them achieves now too much, now too little.

—Sigmund Freud

If sex seemed safer than ever before for teenage girls when
I began gathering these accounts, it seems more dangerous
than ever now, and many adults conclude that teenagers
shouldn't have sex at all. As a result, abstinence education, in a
variety of forms, is the order of the day. When will you be ready
for sex? the most extreme lesson plans ask rhetorically. The answer: When you're ready to die.[1] Opponents of abstinence education frequently reply that teenagers have always had sex: it's
natural; there's no stopping it. But although birth tables indicate
that some teenagers have probably always had sex, a far lower
percentage of teenagers did so in the 1890s than in the 1990s,
and it is conceivable that teenagers might be even more abstinent
by the year 2000 than they were in 1954. Adolescence is, after
all, a socially constructed hiatus between puberty and adulthood:
it's taken different forms before and it can again.

Whether fear tactics can put an end to teenage sex is another question. Sexual fear paralyzes many girls, their accounts show, and increasing that fear is less likely to stop teenage sex than to lead to more and more sex that "just happens," with all its tragic sequels—from pregnancy to sexually transmitted infections, including AIDS.

The Southern Baptist Convention's True Love Waits campaign takes a different tack. If you don't have sex until you're married, you won't have to worry about disease or pregnancy and your marital love will last forever, this campaign claims.[2] Informed by the traditions of teenage romance, this is a very shrewd approach. It exploits girls' desire to secure love and offers boys a strong reason to endure intimacy. But how much of a protection, finally, is marriage?

A marriage license *is* more of a guarantee than a mere promise. At the very least, it's a contract that provides some measure of protection with regard to property and parenting. But teenage marriage is an even less viable idea today than it was in the early 1960s. A couple that can't make a living can't support a baby, and a marriage license can't force two parties of any age to always love each other, never have sex with anyone else, use only bleached needles, and never contract any virus that might subsequently be sexually transmitted.

In the end, it's much easier to protect against AIDS than against a broken heart. Properly using a latex condom will do the job, but girls' accounts suggest that some approaches to sex and romance increase the likelihood of both physically and emotionally surviving teenage romance.[3] In general, the more a teenage girl viewed the elements of sex, reproduction, and love as fused and expected them to generate the central meaning of her life, the less likely she was to use protection or contraception and the greater the likelihood of, if not melodrama or tragedy, at least a loss of strength, possibility, and confidence. The more a narrator took the romantic equation apart, in contrast, anticipated and understood pleasure, balanced the desire for love with an array of other concerns and relationships or accepted love as ephemeral, the more likely she was to be realistic, even humorous, about romance. With realism and humor came recognition of the necessity of protection and contraception as well as a host of other benefits whose importance the fear of AIDS must not be allowed to overshadow. Realism is as essential to learning and development, for example, as it is to prudence. In romantic experience, it increases the likelihood that sex and love will produce social and erotic insight, and, along with humor, it is a critical factor in maintaining the sense of proportion that is finally the best protection against being ruined by love.

The greatest danger girls narrated was love. Once in love or set on trying to get love, even cautious girls said they closed their eyes to sexual and psychological danger. Nevertheless, most still wanted love, a reminder, if one is needed, that love is actually worth almost all the risks girls take to get it. When love goes badly, true, it adds to the anxiety of separation and makes it harder to leave childhood behind. But when it goes well, when romantic wishes and prospects are in relative accord and consent emerges from desire, sex and love not only ease the process of separation but transform adolescence into an enormous pleasure. And even when love goes badly, those brave enough to learn from romantic experience will find they've been well served.

But if love can contribute as much to development as it does to life as a whole, it's never secure. While there is such a thing as safe sex and there are ways to moderate the damage love can do, "there's an irreducible risk in loving," as feminist essayist Ellen Willis once wrote.[4] Short of living without love, the best girls can do, their own accounts suggest, is to act with realism and courage: condition consent on desire and protection; continue interests and associations other than romance no matter how much in love or in need of love they are; and refuse to accept love as a reason to endanger themselves or foreclose the future. The more girls follow this—finally, their own—advice, and the more they act in concert, the farther they will travel away from heartbreak, subordination, and danger toward pleasure, safety, equality, and true love.

NOTES

INTRODUCTION

1. In *Metaphors of Self: The Meaning of Autobiography* (Princeton, NJ: Princeton University Press, 1972), James Olney speaks of arias of declaration and assertion. On the rhetorical aim of socializing boys, see Judith L. Fischer, "Transitions in Relationship Style from Adolescence to Adulthood," *Journal of Youth and Adolescence* 10, no. 1 (1981): 15–22.

2. Maris A. Vinovskis, "An 'Epidemic' of Adolescent Pregnancy? Some Historical Considerations," *Journal of Family History* 6, no. 2 (Summer 1981): 208.

3. Ellen Ross and Rayna Rapp, "Sex and Society: A Research Note from Social History and Anthropology," in Ann Snitow, Christine Stansell, and Sharon Thompson, eds., *Powers of Desire: The Politics of Sexuality* (New York: New Feminist Library, Monthly Review Press, 1983), pp.

51–73. H. R. Styles, *Bundling: Its Origins, Progress and Decline in America* (Albany: Joel Munsell, 1869). Jacqueline Jones, *Labor of Love, Labor of Sorrow* (New York: Basic Books, 1985), pp. 27, 33–35. Daniel Scott Smith and Michael S. Hindus, "Premarital Pregnancy in America 1640–1971: An Overview and Interpretation," *Journal of Interdisciplinary History* 5, no. 4 (Spring 1975): 537–70. Christine Stansell, *City of Women: Sex and Class in New York 1789–1860* (New York: Alfred A. Knopf, 1986), pp. 87–88, 176. Susan E. Harari and Maris A. Vinovskis, "Adolescent Sexuality, Pregnancy and Childbearing in the Past," in Annette Lawson and Deborah L. Rhode, eds., *The Politics of Pregnancy: Adolescent Sexuality and Public Policy* (New Haven: Yale University Press, 1993), p. 27. F. Philip Rice, *The Adolescent: Development, Relationships, and Culture* (Boston: Allyn and Bacon, 1975), pp. 431, 436. Maurine LaBarre and Weston LaBarre, "The Triple Crisis: Adolescence, Early Marriage and Parenthood," p. 35 in *The Double Jeopardy, the Triple Crisis—Illegitimacy Today* (New York: National Council on Illegitimacy, 1969). Vinovskis, "An 'Epidemic,' " pp. 210–12.

4. Generally, ideas about gender equality as well as adolescent rights and responsibilities countered and modified the doctrines of *parens patriae* and differential treatment in the 1960s and 1970s. *In re Gault*, 387 U.S. 1 (1967) determined that respondents in delinquency proceedings had the right to some due process rights, *In re Winship*, 397 U.S. 358 (1970), the right to proof beyond a reasonable doubt. *Reed* v. *Reed* (1971) made gender discrimination a constitutional problem. *Eisenstadt* v. *Baird*, 405 U.S. 438, 453 (1972) affirmed that single as well as married people had a right to contraception. Title IX of the 1972 Educational Amendment Act entitled pregnant or married students as well as mothers to remain in school. *Roe* v. *Wade*, 410 U.S. 113 (1973) established abortion as a matter of privacy between a woman and her doctor. *Planned Parenthood of Central Missouri* v. *Danforth*, 428 U.S. 52 (1976) ruled out a parental veto on first-trimester abortions. *Carey* v. *Population Services International* (1977) established the right of a minor to purchase over-the-counter contraception. Title VI of the Adolescent Health Services and Pregnancy Prevention Act (1978) directly addressed sex and pregnancy among young unmarried teenagers, a legislative first. *Bellotti* v. *Baird*, 443 U.S. 662, 821 (1979) found consent statutes without judicial bypass and confidentiality provisions unconstitutional. Charles Silberman's *Criminal Violence, Criminal Justice* (New York: Random House, 1978) treats the history of *parens patriae* (pp. 429 and 431).

5. *Michael M.* v. *Superior Court of Sonoma County* (California) (1981). Justice Rehnquist, writing for the majority, concluded that the state had a sufficiently compelling interest in preventing teenage pregnancies to justify age-of-consent laws. On the same day, the Court upheld a Utah statute requiring parental notification before abortion in part on the grounds of the "State's interest in full-term pregnancies." The irony apparently escaped the Court. *H.L.* v. *Matheson,* 450 U.S. 398 (1981).

6. Sandra L. Hofferth, Joan R. Kahn, and Wendy Baldwin, "Premarital Sexual Activity Among U.S. Teenage Women over the Past Three Decades," *Family Planning Perspectives* 19, no. 2 (March/April 1987): 49. Precise figures fluctuate from cohort to cohort (and study to study), but the overall picture remains the same.

7. August Hollingshead, *Elmtown's Youth: The Impact of Social Classes on Adolescents* (New York: John Wiley & Sons, 1949), p. 315. Alfred C. Kinsey et al., *Sexual Behavior in the Human Female* (Philadelphia and London: W. B. Saunders Company, 1953), p. 285. David J. Kallen and Judith J. Stephenson, "Talking about Sex Revisited," *Journal of Youth and Adolescence* 11, no. 1 (1982): 15. Joan Jacobs Brumberg, " 'Ruined' Girls: Changing Community Responses to Illegitimacy in Upstate New York, 1890–1920," *Journal of Social History*, Winter 1984, p. 251. Rickie Solinger, *Wake Up Little Susie: Single Pregnancy and Race Before* Roe *v.* Wade. (New York: Routledge, Chapman and Hall, 1992), pp. 6, 105, 120–21, 140–41. The silence wasn't total, Solinger's work indicates. As psychology gained authority, some maternity homes urged girls to talk through their experiences with counselors. Moreover, rules or no rules, girls talked among themselves while in confinement. Since they typically used pseudonyms, however, it was probably rare for a friendship forged inside a maternity home to continue later.

8. Ladner, *Tomorrow's Tomorrow* (Garden City, NY: Anchor Books, Doubleday & Company, 1971), p. 113. Similarly illuminating studies include Molly Dougherty, *Becoming a Woman in Rural Black Culture* (New York: Holt, Rinehart and Winston, 1978) and Joyce Aschenbrenner, *Lifelines: Black Families in Chicago* (New York: Holt, Rinehart and Winston, 1975). Unfortunately, Kinsey's *Sexual Behavior in the Human Female* included only white women in its tabulations (p. 22). There's still time to fill in some of the missing history through interviewing but witnesses are becoming scarcer as time passes. Relevant works of fiction include Zora

Neale Hurston, *Their Eyes Were Watching God*, as well as the work of Harriet A. Jacobs, Nella Larsen, Gwendolyn Brooks, Toni Morrison, and Alice Walker. Two films begin to fill in the past as well: Camille Billops's *Finding Christa* and Marco Williams's *In Search of Our Fathers.*

9. "11 Million Teenagers: What Can Be Done About the Epidemic of Adolescent Pregnancies in the United States," published in 1976 by the Alan Guttmacher Institute, was the source for the figure 11,000,000. Sharp critical analyses of the statistics include Rosalind Pollack Petchesky, *Abortion and Woman's Choice: The State, Sexuality and Reproductive Freedom* (New York: Longman, 1984), pp. 205–38, and Kristin Luker, "Dubious Conceptions: The Controversy over Teen Pregnancy," *The American Prospect* no. 5 (Spring 1991): 73–83. Kristin Moore and Martha Burt note that the number of fourteen- to seventeen-year-olds in the U.S. population increased significantly in the 1970s—from 11.2 million in 1960 to 16.3 million in 1979. *Private Crisis, Public Cost* (Washington, DC: The Urban Institute Press, 1982), p. 35. Cheryl D. Hayes, ed., *Risking the Future: Adolescent Sexuality, Pregnancy, and Childbearing*, vol. 1 (Washington, DC: National Academy Press, 1987), p. 52. Laurie Schwab Zabin and Sarah C. Hayward, *Adolescent Sexual Behavior and Childbearing* (Newbury Park, CA: Sage Publications, 1993), p. 15. Vinovskis, "An 'Epidemic,' " pp. 208, 226.

10. Petchesky, *Abortion and Woman's Choice*, p. 209; "Teenage Births Decline by 18 Percent in Decade but Number of Children Born Out of Wedlock Rises," *Family Planning Perspectives* 18, no. 2 (March/April 1986): 87. Kristin A. Moore, Margaret C. Simms, and Charles L. Betsey, *Choice and Circumstance: Racial Differences in Adolescent Sexuality and Fertility* (New Brunswick, NJ: Transaction Publishers, 1986), p. 10. Petchesky's chapter, "Abortion and Heterosexual Culture: The Teenage Question," is essential reading.

11. Sandra L. Hofferth, "Contraceptive Decision-Making Among Adolescents," in Cheryl D. Hayes and Sandra L. Hofferth, eds., *Risking the Future*, vol. 2, pp. 63–68, summarizes many studies on contraception. Just one set of examples to illustrate the contradictions: H. B. Kaplan et al. found that teenage mothers devalue themselves; Faigel that they have a low sense of self-worth; Barth et al. that comparison groups not teenage mothers display low self-esteem and high anxiety. H. B. Kaplan, P. B. Smith, and A. D. Pokorny, "Psychosocial Antecedents of Unwed

Motherhood Among Indigent Adolescents," *Journal of Youth and Adolescence* 8: 181–207. Harris C. Faigel, "Unwed Pregnant Adolescents—a Synthesis of Current Viewpoints," *Clinical Pediatrics* 6: 281–85. Richard P. Barth, Steven Paul Schinke, and Josie Solseng Maxwell, "Psychological Correlates of Teenage Motherhood," *Journal of Youth and Adolescence* 12, no. 6 (1983): 471–87. The quote is from Melvin Zelnik, John F. Kantner, and Kathleen Ford, *Sex and Pregnancy in Adolescence* (Beverly Hills: Sage Publications, 1981), p. 173.

12. Laurie S. Zabin et al., "Adolescent Sexual Attitudes and Behavior: Are They Consistent?" *Family Planning Perspectives* 16, no. 4 (July/August 1984): 181. Zabin also scrutinized institutional practices, asking what was wrong with clinics as opposed to noncontraceptors. Laurie Schwab Zabin and Samuel D. Clark, Jr., "Institutional Factors Affecting Teenagers' Choice and Reasons for Delay in Attending a Family Planning Clinic," *Family Planning Perspectives* 15, no. 1 (January/February 1983): 25–29.

13. For a popular treatment of being swept away, see Carol Cassell, *Swept Away: Why Women Confuse Love and Sex* (New York: Fireside, Simon & Schuster, 1984). Kristin A. Moore, Christine Nord Winquist, and James L. Peterson, "Nonvoluntary Sexual Activity Among Adolescents," *Family Planning Perspectives* 21, no. 3 (May/June 1989): 111. Debra Boyer and David Fine, "Sexual Abuse as a Factor in Adolescent Pregnancy and Child Maltreatment," *Family Planning Perspectives* 24, no. 1 (January/February 1992): 7.

14. This line of thought derives from the work of Russian scholar Mikhail Bakhtin, but there's a feminist route to the same conclusion. If, as literary critic Rachel DuPlessis has argued, for example, romance is a "trope" for the "sex-gender system," then there's a direct relation between genre and experience. (The term "sex/gender system" was coined by anthropologist Gayle Rubin to describe the interrelationship between sexuality—erotic acts, desires, and pleasure—and gender—biological difference between male and female.) Rachel Blau DuPlessis, *Writing Beyond the Ending: Narrative Strategies of Twentieth-Century Women Writers* (Bloomington: Indiana University Press, 1985), p. ix. Gayle Rubin, "The Traffic in Women," in Rayna Reiter, ed., *Toward an Anthropology of Women* (New York, Monthly Review Press, 1975), pp. 157–210, and "Thinking Sex: Notes for a Radical Theory of the Politics of

Sexuality" in Carole S. Vance's anthology *Pleasure and Danger: Exploring Female Sexuality* (Boston: Routledge & Kegan Paul, 1984), pp. 267–319.

15. I have worked most closely with a representative subsample of one hundred narratives gathered from the three hundred sexually initiated girls. Narrators in the subsample all went well beyond answering direct questions to give extensive life histories about sex, romance, or pregnancy. Young women who grew up on or were currently living on AFDC are referred to as poor; girls who said their parents held factory or nonmanagerial service jobs and gave no indication that either parent had a college degree are treated as working-class.

Only one adult, a grandmother, stood her ground. Canceling an appointment her granddaughter had made the previous afternoon in a shopping mall, she apologetically observed that I might be in the white-slave trade.

16. The very few cross-class or cross-clique referrals had unique histories: a former popular girl who had joined the fast track referred an old friend from the popular clique; a working-class girl brought along her "best friend"—a professor's daughter who went wild when her parents divorced and became downwardly mobile for a while.

17. Carol Gilligan's work on upper-middle-class girls is often treated as if it applies to all girls, while John Modell's historical study reads the demographics of dating, sex, and marriage from 1920 to 1975 as "a national story" of female "patterns" steadily converging on male. It's a fair, well-buttressed point and Modell develops an African-American variant, but he had to rely on broad demographics that didn't cast light on other important divisions in U.S. society or offer clues to the residual effects of historical differences. Carol Stack made a similar case for the importance of difference in "Different Voices, Different Visions: Gender, Culture, and Moral Reasoning," in Faye Ginsburg and Anna Lowenhaupt Tsing, eds., *Uncertain Terms: Negotiating Gender in American Culture* (Boston: Beacon Press, 1990), pp. 19–27. Modell, *Into One's Own: From Youth to Adulthood in the United States 1920–1975* (Berkeley: University of California Press, 1989), pp. 35, 317.

African-American and white coital rates moved closer in the 1970s and so did boys' and girls', but it was white rates and girls' rates that changed dramatically and this implies a different experience. Hofferth et al., "Premarital," pp. 47–48. William F. Pratt and Gerry E. Hendershot, "The Use of Family Planning Services by Sexually Active Teenage Women," National Survey of Family Growth, National Center for Health Statistics, Hyattsville, MD 20782, 1984.

18. I am particularly indebted to historians Linda Gordon and Christine Stansell, anthropologists Gayle Rubin and Carole S. Vance, social critics Ann Snitow and Ellen Willis, and literary critics Rachel DuPlessis and Peter Brooks. Finally, I see this work as a contribution to a line of work on girls and adolescence, especially Margaret Mead's *Coming of Age in Samoa*, Gisela Konopka's *The Adolescent Girl in Conflict*, Joyce Ladner's *Tomorrow's Tomorrow*, and Angela McRobbie's *Feminism and Youth Culture*.

1. VICTIMS OF LOVE

1. Sandra L. Hofferth, Joan R. Kahn, and Wendy Baldwin, "Premarital Sexual Activity Among U.S. Teenage Women over the Past Three Decades," *Family Planning Perspectives* 19, no. 2 (March/April 1987): 47. Melvin Zelnik and Farida K. Shah, "First Intercourse Among Young Americans," *Family Planning Perspectives* 15, no. 2 (March/April 1983): 64.

2. Christine Stansell, *City of Women: Sex and Class in New York 1789–1860* (New York: Alfred A. Knopf, 1986), pp. 87–88, 176. Cheryl D. Hayes, ed., *Risking the Future: Adolescent Sexuality, Pregnancy, and Childbearing*, vol. 1 (Washington, DC: National Academy Press, 1987), pp. 35–36, 60–61. Maris A. Vinovskis, "An 'Epidemic' of Adolescent Pregnancy? Some Historical Considerations," *Journal of Family History* 6, no. 2 (Summer 1981): 205–39. Susan E. Harari and Maris A. Vinovskis, "Adolescent Sexuality, Pregnancy and Childbearing in the Past," in Annette Lawson and Deborah L. Rhode, eds., *The Politics of Pregnancy: Adolescent Sexuality and Public Policy* (New Haven: Yale University Press, 1993), p. 27. F. Philip Rice, *The Adolescent: Development, Relationships, and Culture* (Boston: Allyn and Bacon, 1975), p. 431. Maurine LaBarre and Weston LaBarre, "The Triple Crisis: Adolescence, Early Marriage and Parenthood," in *The Double Jeopardy, the Triple Crisis—Illegitimacy Today* (New York: National Council on Illegitimacy, 1969), p. 35. Seymour M. Farber, M.D., and Roger H. L. Wilson, M.D., *Teenage Marriage and Divorce* (Berkeley, CA: Diablo Press, 1967).

3. Phyllis Blanchard and Carolyn Manasses, *New Girls for Old* (New York, 1930), p. 71, as quoted in Paula Fass, *The Damned and the Beautiful* (New York: Oxford University Press, 1977), p. 273. Beth L. Bailey disputes the notion that dating, going steady, and sexual expression were as persistently related to love and marriage as most such commentators assume in *From Front Porch to Back Seat: Courtship in Twentieth-Century America* (Baltimore and London: The Johns Hopkins University Press, 1988, 1989), pp. 26, 49–51.

4. Winston Ehrmann's *Premarital Dating Behavior* (New York: Henry Holt and Company, 1959), pp. 169 and 181. Ehrmann investigated the connection between going steady, love, and intercourse in staggering empirical detail—see especially pp. 132–143. See also Carlfred Broderick, "Going Steady: The Beginning of the End," in Farber and Wilson, eds., *Teenage Marriage and Divorce*, pp. 21–24; August B. Hollingshead, *Elmtown's Youth: The Impact of Social Classes on Adolescents* (New York: John Wiley & Sons, 1949), pp. 237–39; C. Wayne Gordon, *The Social System of the High School: A Study in the Sociology of Adolescence* (Glencoe, IL: Free Press, 1957), pp. 122–24; Patricia Y. Miller and William Simon, "Adolescent Sexual Behavior: Context and Change," *Social Problems* 22 (1974); and Ira L. Reiss, especially *The Social Context of Premarital Sexual Permissiveness* (New York: Holt, Rinehart and Winston, 1967), pp. 76–91. Gisela Konopka's early 1970s study of 1,000 girls between twelve and eighteen indicated that sex within a steady relationship was seen as a kind of test run for marriages that were quite likely to occur. *Young Girls: A Portrait of Adolescence* (Englewood Cliffs, NJ: Prentice-Hall, 1976), p. 33. Curiously, Modell argues that boys devised going steady to protect *their* reputations: "The fear of being told no . . . was a specter many dreaded, since girl gossip might record the concurrent loss of face for all to see." *Into One's Own: From Youth to Adulthood in the United States 1920–1975* (Berkeley: University of California Press, 1989), p. 237. Bailey's *From Front Porch to Back Seat* tartly recounts the history of going steady (pp. 49–56).

5. Sol Gordon's *How Can I Tell I'm Really in Love?* (1980) and *Ten Heavy Facts About Sex* (1980, revised 1983), both published in Fayetteville, NY, by Ed-U Press, are influential, widely distributed examples.

6. Sales figures: $20 million in 1980s (*BP Report*, 1983). The 1992 figure is a "guesstimate" of Jim Million, editor of *BP Report*, in a private tele-

phone conversation, September 24, 1992. Linda Christian, "Becoming a Woman Through Romance: Adolescent Novels and the Ideology of Femininity," Ph.D. dissertation, University of Wisconsin–Madison, 1984, pp. 15–17. Linda Christian-Smith, "Romancing the Girl: Adolescent Romance Novels and the Construction of Femininity," pp. 76–101 in Leslie G. Roman et al., eds., *Becoming Feminine: The Politics of Popular Culture* (London, New York, and Philadelphia: Falmer Press, 1988), p. 87.

7. Anthropologist Ruth Horowitz observed that love gave male domination priority over virginity among Chicana girls. *Honor and the American Dream: Culture and Identity in a Chicano Community* (New Brunswick, NJ: Rutgers University Press, 1983), p. 123.

8. Mark's desire was common. When intercourse became an integral part of teenage romance, couples no longer fit as easily into cliques and crowds. At the same time, drugs came to rival sex as an object of desire and this generated competition between the ethos of friendship and the group and that of romance. Historian John Modell sees teenage culture split from that point on between that built from peer relations—the subculture of the party—and that built from the couple—the subculture of romance. In Modell's reading of this split, only those likely to marry right after high school stuck with romance. The rest went with the party. It's a great observation, and Chapter 5 introduces teenage girls who put party and group above romance, but while some girls partied in the 1980s without a thought of finding a true love among the scammers and guzzlers, for many the party was simply a place to look for boys. Modell, *Into One's Own*, pp. 304–5.

9. Marian Wright Edelman, *The Measure of Our Success: A Letter to My Children and Yours* (Boston: Beacon Press, 1992), p. 82. Donna Gaines's *Teenage Wasteland* (New York: Pantheon Books, 1990) poignantly describes young men's economic depression (pp. 54, 150–51, 155–56). LaBarre and LaBarre, "The Triple Crisis," p. 35.

10. Barbara Tomko talks about the grieving that occurs when an individual surrenders a cherished expectation or fantasy. "Mourning the Dissolution of the Dream," *Social Work* 28, no. 5 (September/October 1983): 391–92. On recognition and its relationship to infancy, see Jes-

sica Benjamin, *The Bonds of Love: Psychoanalysis, Feminism and the Problem of Domination* (New York: Pantheon Books, 1988), p. 31.

11. Nancy L. Wade's "Suicide as a Resolution," *Adolescence* 22, no. 85 (Spring 1987): 169–77, discusses suicide as an effort to assuage separation anxiety by reconstructing a safe "symbiotic state." A 1987 study by Dr. Michael Brodsky reported that it's actually possible to die of a broken heart since stress causes palpitations, rapid heartbeat, and even heart failure. "Heartsore," *New York Times* editorial, April 23, 1987, p. A26.

12. The exent of some of the memory difficulties demonstrated by some of these narrators suggests very profound damage—previous abuse, for example.

13. On the whole, historians have been less sympathetic than literary critics, largely because melodrama seems implicated in some egregious political mystifications of the past. In the nineteenth century, for example, social purity melodramas about the supposed capture and enslavement of white girls, featured in the tabloid press, led to the passage of highly repressive legislation. Deborah Gorham, *The Victorian Girl and the Feminine Ideal* (Bloomington: Indiana University Press, 1982); Judith R. Walkowitz, *Prostitution and Victorian Society: Women, Class, and the State* (Cambridge, Eng.: Cambridge University Press, 1980).

14. Peter Brooks, *The Melodramatic Imagination: Balzac, Henry James, Melodrama, and the Mode of Excess* (New York: Columbia University Press, 1985), pp. xii, 28–29, 32, 41. On the uses women make of soap operas, see Tania Modleski, *Loving with a Vengeance: Mass Produced Fantasies for Women* (New York: Methuen, 1982), pp. 85–109.

15. Carol Gilligan, *In a Different Voice: Psychological Theory and Women's Development* (Cambridge, MA: Harvard University Press, 1982). The Gilligan school is much more critical of separation than I am, often using the term as a synonym for isolation or alienation. "Separation" does not refer to cutting all ties, however, but to a psychological and social shift from being a dependent—a child—to being largely responsible for oneself—an adult. This strikes me as at least a critical development that builds strengths that girls could well use. In addition, the more girls feel able to stand on their own, the more able they will be to leave

abusive relationships. On the implications of the mother-daughter relationship for separation, see Nancy Chodorow, *The Reproduction of Mothering: Psychoanalysis and the Sociology of Gender* (Berkeley: University of California Press, 1978), and Dorothy Dinnerstein, *The Mermaid and the Minotaur: Sexual Arrangements and Human Malaise* (New York: Harper & Row, 1977). Dinnerstein is brilliant as well on the erotic resonance of infancy.

16. In April 1993, the New York City Board of Education's HIV/AIDS Advisory Council decided to add "secondary virginity" to the AIDS curriculum. "It's a nice way of saying that even if you have been sleeping around for years, you can be clean again," said board member Dr. Liliana Trivelli. *Newsday*, May 17, 1994, p. A5. The "Sex Respect" curriculum funded by the Office of Adolescent Pregnancy Programs during the Reagan administration promoted the idea of secondary virginity.

17. On censorship and sexual education, see James Anthony Whitson, "Sexuality and Censorship in the Curriculum," pp. 59–77; Mariamne H. Whatley, "Whose Sexuality Is It Anyway?" p. 78; Bonnie K. Trudell, "Inside a Ninth-Grade Sexuality Classroom," pp. 203–25; and Lynn Phillips and Michelle Fine, "What's 'Left' in Sexuality Education?" pp. 242–49, all in James T. Sears, ed., *Sexuality and the Curriculum: The Politics and Practices of Sexuality Education* (New York: Teachers College, Columbia University, 1992). Linda Christian-Smith covers the boom in teen romances in "Romancing the Girl," pp. 76–101, and "Young Women and Their Dream Lovers: Sexuality in Adolescent Fiction," pp. 206–27, in Janice Irvine, ed., *Sexual Cultures and the Construction of Adolescent Identities* (Philadelphia: Temple University Press, 1994). See also Brett Harvey, "How Far Can You Go in a Teen Romance?" *Village Voice*, February 10–16, 1982, pp. 48–49.

18. Christian-Smith, "Young Women and Their Dream Lovers," p. 219.

19. Ann Snitow, "Mass Market Romance: Pornography for Women Is Different," in Ann Snitow, Christine Stansell, and Sharon Thompson, eds., *Powers of Desire: The Politics of Sexuality* (New York: New Feminist Library, Monthly Review Press, 1983), p. 252.

20. Snitow, "Mass Market," p. 252.

21. Obviously, this isn't just a teenage pleasure. Romance novels sell to women of all ages. A wonderful essay by Valerie Walkerdine begins with a friend's childhood memory of her grandmother seated at the piano longingly singing "Some Day My Prince Will Come." "Some Day My Prince Will Come," in Angela McRobbie and Mica Nava, eds., *Gender and Generation* (London: Macmillan, 1984), p. 162.

22. Modleski, *Loving with a Vengeance*, p. 45.

23. This is particularly dangerous, because, as Valerie Walkerdine has pointed out, it is in school that the relationship between femininity and intellectuality is established. "No Laughing Matter: Girls' Comics and the Preparation for Adolescent Sexuality," in J. Broughton, ed., *Critical Theories of Psychological Development* (New York: Plenum, 1987), p. 117. On other inequities, see Peggy Orenstein in association with the American Association of University Women, *Schoolgirls: Young Women, Self-Esteem, and the Confidence Gap* (New York: Doubleday, 1994).

24. Another study exploring the implications of conditioning sexual consent on romantic expectations for protection against HIV/AIDS is Janet Holland, Caroline Ramazanoglu, Sue Scott, Sue Sharpe, and Rachel Thomson, "Sex, Gender and Power: Young Women's Sexuality in the Shadow of AIDS," *Sociology of Health & Illness* 12, no. 3 (1990): 336–50, which Marysol W. Ascensio called to my attention when she generously shared her files on AIDS and adolescence with me.

25. On the invention of adolescence, the all-time best reference is that primary source, G. Stanley Hall's *Adolescence: Its Psychology and Its Relations to Anthropology, Sex, Crime, Religion, and Education*, 2 vols., 2nd ed. (1905; reprint ed., New York: Arno Press and New York Times, 1969). Joseph F. Kett's *Rites of Passage: Adolescence in America 1790 to the Present* (New York: Basic Books, 1977) is a useful secondary source although it focuses, like so much work on adolescence, on boys.

2. PLAYING THE FIELD

1. Elizabeth Douvan and Joseph Adelson, *The Adolescent Experience* (New York: John Wiley & Sons, 1966), pp. 100–1, 320–21. Beth L. Bailey offers a provocative reading of the history of dating and popularity in *From*

Front Porch to Back Seat: Courtship in Twentieth-Century America (Baltimore and London: The Johns Hopkins University Press, 1988, 1989), pp. 25–34.

2. As Barbara Ehrenreich has observed, for decades America was the only country in the world in which the middle class "customarily employed its own women as domestic servants." *Fear of Falling: The Inner Life of the Middle Class* (New York: Pantheon Books, 1989), p. 40. Ninety-six percent of Douvan and Adelson's sample indicated that marriage was their primary vocation and the psychologists saw a direct connection between the culture of popularity and the marriage market. *The Adolescent*, p. 42.

3. John Modell sees dating as substantially different from the older courtship form of "keeping company" in that it took place away from home and wasn't chaperoned. "Dating Becomes the Way of American Youth," in David Levine et al., eds., *Essays on the Family and Historical Change* (Arlington: Texas A & M University Press, 1983), pp. 93, 99. Eighty-one percent of girls dated by the 1940s. August Hollingshead, *Elmtown's Youth: The Impact of Social Classes on Adolescents* (New York: John Wiley & Sons, 1949), pp. 392, 424. Patricia J. Campbell's wonderful *Sex Education Books for Young Adults, 1892–1979* (New York and London: R. R. Bowker Company, 1979), p. 96, includes examples of advice books' pronouncements on going steady and sex. Ira Reiss's *The Social Context of Premarital Sexual Permissiveness* (New York: Holt, Rinehart and Winston, 1967), pp. 76–91, reported that girls were more likely to desire or agree to sex in a steady relationship but boys were less likely to demand sex from a steady.

4. Hilda Taba, *School Culture: Studies of Participation and Leadership* (Washington, DC: American Council on Education, 1955), p. 24. This splendid ethnography merits rediscovery. Wini Breines has commented, "Just hearing the word 'popularity' is enough to generate a cold sweat." *Young, White, and Miserable: Growing Up Female in the Fifties* (Boston: Beacon Press, 1992), p. 111.

5. Thomas Doherty, *Teenagers & Teenpics: The Juvenilization of American Movies in the 1950s* (Boston: Unwin Hyman, 1988), pp. 42–61.

6. Helen Merrell Lynd and Robert S. Lynd, *Middletown: A Study in Modern American Culture* (New York: Harcourt, Brace & World, 1929, 1956), p. 216.

7. Working-class and poor teens reported feeling uncomfortable at school dances. Hollingshead, *Elmtown's Youth*, pp. 302–12, especially p. 306. Dorothy Neubauer and Robert Havighurst, "Community Factors in Relation to Character Formation," in Robert James Havighurst and Hilda Taba, eds., *Adolescent Character and Personality* (New York: John Wiley & Sons, 1949), pp. 27–46, reported, rather more firmly than the evidence seemed to support, that imitating the majority—and middle-class mores and style—was enough to turn lower-class girls into candidates for popularity.

8. James Coleman, *The Adolescent Society: The Social Life of the Teenager and Its Impact on Education* (New York: Free Press of Glencoe, 1961), pp. 102, 106–7. John R. Seeley, R. Alexander Sim, and Elizabeth W. Loosley, *Crestwood Heights: A Study of the Culture of Suburban Life* (New York: John Wiley & Sons, 1963), pp. 326–39.

9. John Modell, *Into One's Own: From Youth to Adulthood in the United States 1920–1975* (Berkeley: University of California Press, 1989), p. 304. Catherine S. Chilman, *Adolescent Sexuality in a Changing American Society*, 2nd ed. (New York: John Wiley & Son, 1983), p. 47.

10. Carnegie statistics are from Ernest L. Boyer, *High School: A Report on Secondary Education in America* (New York: Harper & Row, 1983). Ralph W. Larkin describes the dissolution of high school extracurricular life as "The Great Refusal." *Suburban Youth in Cultural Crisis* (New York: Oxford University Press, 1979), p. 145.

11. In her analysis of a British teenage magazine, Angela McRobbie concludes that readers recognize that they can't measure up to the "ideal standard" and resolve to do something "through the use of commodities," striving not to make "this obvious since to do this would be to defeat the whole point." "Jackie: An Ideology of Adolescent Femininity," Women's Series: SP No. 53, Stencilled Occasional Paper, Centre for Contemporary Cultural Studies (Birmingham, Eng.: University of Birmingham, April 1978). Reprinted in McRobbie, *Feminism and Youth Culture: From* Jackie *to* Just Seventeen (Boston: Unwin Hyman,

1991). In the United States teenage girls spent over $22 billion a year on wardrobes, beauty aids, and jewelry in the 1980s, according to Lawrence Graham and Lawrence Hamdan, *Youth Trends: Capturing the $200 Billion Youth Market* (New York: St. Martin's Press, 1987), p. 198. A fascinating guide to popularity appears in Ellen Peck's cold-bloodedly strategic *How to Get a Teenage Boy* (New York: Bernard Geis Associates, 1969; New York: Avon, 1974). Organizer Fran Sugarman told me she and her friends lived by it.

12. Louise Bernikow, "Confessions of an Ex-Cheerleader," *Ms.*, October 1973, p. 65.

13. Histories of girls of color who shared popular perspectives but did not define themselves as popular and weren't defined that way by others appear in Chapter 8, "The Game of Love." Larkin found that the "rah-rah" crowd of popular teens at "Utopia High" came from upper-middle-class Protestant families. *Suburban Youth*, p. 70.

14. James Coleman adds the reasonable observation that they represent local mainstreams. *The Adolescent Society*, p. 102. C. Wayne Gordon, *The Social System of the High School: A Study in the Sociology of Adolescence* (Glencoe, IL: Free Press, 1957), generally. Prospective cheerleaders had to learn how to charm women because cheerleaders picked their own replacements. The key, Bernikow said, was imitating them ("Confessions," pp. 64–67, 98). Jules Henry talks about the drive to have fun while waiting for the end of the world. The popular girls I talked with seemed to have all their attention on the social microcosm. *Culture Against Man* (New York: Vintage Books, 1963), pp. 168–69, 271.

15. Alix Kates Shulman, *Memoirs of an Ex-Prom Queen* (New York: Bantam Books, 1973; orig. pub. Alfred A. Knopf, 1972), p. 53.

16. More technically, popular girls rely on "a restricted code" to communicate among themselves. Restricted codes emerge when members of a group know each other or a situation very well. They sustain social forms and facilitate the kind of exclusion that seems natural because it is never discussed. Basil Bernstein, "A Sociolinguistic Approach to Socialization; with Some Reference to Educability," in John J. Gumperz and Dell Hymes, eds., *Directions in Socio-Linguistics* (New York: Holt, Rinehart and Winston, 1972), pp. 465–97; Mary Douglas, *Natural Sym-*

bols: Explorations in Cosmology (New York: Pantheon Books, 1970, 1973, 1982), pp. 22, 55. Or as Ellen Peck put it: "Much communication in a crowd is unspoken. The fact that you are in is unspoken" (*How to Get*, p. 31).

Popular teenagers frequently mislead adults, Gary Schwartz noted, not so much by lying (since lying can compound trouble) as by not revealing much. *Beyond Conformity or Rebellion: Youth and Authority in America* (Chicago: University of Chicago Press, 1987), pp. 97, 262. In the 1940s, Hollingshead observed similar clandestine tendencies with regard to sex. Hollingshead, *Elmtown's Youth*, e.g., pp. 289, 315.

17. Initiation emphasized cheerleading standards by forcing initiates to transgress them. For her initiation, Gail had to dress as one of the polar opposites of a popular girl, a hippie.

18. Fast-track girls make a similar case against popular girls. Chris also distinguished between nice popular girls and mean ones, whom she considered insecure.

19. Anthropologist Gary Schwartz, *Beyond Conformity*, pp. 97, 262.

20. Gary Alan Fine's essay, "One of the Boys: Women in Male-Dominated Settings," in Michael Kimmel, ed., *Changing Men: New Directions in Research on Men and Masculinity* (Newbury Park, CA: Sage Publications, 1987), pp. 131–47, suggests that women have to be team players and slough off sexual teasing and joking to get by in masculine settings. These girls were team players but I'd be surprised to learn they countenanced sexual harassment.

21. Hollingshead noted that class formatted clique as well as dating relations and that cliques paired up for dating. To cross more than one class line took social genius and the nerve to stare down public opinion (*Elmtown's Youth*, pp. 223–27).

22. If her fear of his possessiveness seems overemphatic, it may be because in the Chicana community where she grew up, boys frequently controlled their girlfriends' associations completely.

23. On being a Deadhead, see Anthony Pearson's "The Grateful Dead Phenomenon: An Ethnomethodological Approach," *Youth and Society* 18, no. 4 (June 1987), as well as Chapter 5.

24. Henry, *Culture,* p. 271.

25. Most of the girls who narrated this chapter probably recouped some of their high school losses—learned to study in the first years of college; found a market niche in which their abilities and interests were productive. After all, as parents of the 1920s and '30s knew, a gift for popularity is a gift for striking bargains, and that's helpful in making a living.

26. On boys talking girls into having their babies to prove their love, see Chapter 4. On AIDS and the traditions of love, see Janet Holland, Caroline Ramazanoglu, Sue Scott, Sue Sharpe, and Rachel Thomson, "Sex, Gender and Power: Young Women's Sexuality in the Shadow of AIDS," *Sociology of Health & Illness* 12, no. 3 (1990): 336–50, and Anke Ehrhardt, Sandra Yingling, and Patricia A. Warne, "Sexual Behavior in the Era of AIDS: What Has Changed in the United States," *Annual Review of Sex Research* 2 (1991): 25–47. Anke A. Ehrhardt and Judith N. Wasserheit, "Age, Gender, and Sexual Risk Behaviors for Sexually Transmitted Diseases in the United States," in Judith N. Wasserheit et al., eds., *Research Issues in Human Behavior and Sexually Transmitted Diseases in the AIDS Era* (Washington, DC: American Society for Microbiology, 1991), pp. 97–121.

27. Winston Ehrmann, *Premarital Dating Behavior* (New York: Henry Holt and Company, 1959), p. 162.

3. INFINITE POSSIBILITIES OF DOING

1. In *The Female Imagination,* Patricia Spacks observed that Doris Lessing's Martha and Sylvia Plath's Esther Greenwood, like the narrators of this chapter, shared "two burdens inconceivable" to earlier heroines, "the weight of a new kind of self-consciousness and that of the infinite possibilities of doing." New York: Alfred A. Knopf, 1972, p. 191.

2. Coleman reasonably used grades as his index, but it's possible that in an atmosphere in which intellectuality constituted a variety of resistance, the best grades might not have gone to the most critical thinkers. *The Adolescent Society: The Social Life of the Teenager and Its Impact on Education* (New York: Free Press of Glencoe, 1961), pp. 68–76, 143–72, and 244. Sociologist Ralph Larkin was amazed to come across an elite intellectual crowd at "Utopia High" because he'd never read about one's existence. *Suburban Youth in Cultural Crisis* (New York: Oxford University Press, 1979), p. 72.

3. Two good sources on being female in the 1950s are Wini Breines, *Young, White, and Miserable: Growing Up Female in the Fifties* (Boston: Beacon Press, 1992), and Brett Harvey, *The Fifties: A Women's Oral History* (New York: HarperCollins, 1993). Elizabeth Douvan and Joseph Adelson, *The Adolescent Experience* (New York: John Wiley & Sons, 1966), pp. 216–17.

4. Most dreams of success, these students believed, would be dashed by institutionalized racism. The few who would succeed would abandon or betray their race and their sexuality in the process. Signithia Fordham and John U. Ogbu, "Black Students' School Success: Coping with the Burden of 'Acting White,' " *Urban Review* 18, no. 3 (1986): 176–205.

5. Elise and I spoke for two years before an opportunity arose to meet her three closest friends. A year after that, on a cross-country interviewing trip, I visited the western suburb where all four had grown up and spent two weeks interviewing more than a dozen other members of the fast track as well as a group of teenage mothers in a nearby central city. Occasional quotes come from interviews with similarly successful students from other parts of the country.

6. The homogeneity of the group was striking and troubling. Terry Kershaw argues that tracking has replaced segregation as an impediment to African-American mobility. Kershaw, "The Effects of Educational Tracking," *Journal of Black Studies* 23, no. 1 (September 1992): 152–69. See also J. E. Rosenbaum, *Making Inequality: The Hidden Curriculum of High School Tracking* (New York: John Wiley & Sons, 1976).

7. Both ideas can actually be traced to Sigmund Freud. See "Civilized Sexuality and Modern Nervous Illness," in James Strachey, ed. and trans., *The Standard Edition of the Complete Psychological Works of Sigmund Freud* (London: Hogarth Press, 1961), vol. 9, p. 199, and *Civilization and Its Discontents, The Standard Edition,* vol. 21.

8. Many girls fail to make it through this passage. They step into their mothers' lives before they know it.

9. She alone among the narrators shared Freud's view that sexual suppression inhibits the ability to think. "Civilized Sexuality," p. 199.

10. An excellent source on the story of development is Elizabeth Abel, Marianne Hirsch, and Elizabeth Langland, eds., *The Voyage In: Fictions of Female Development* (Hanover, NH, and London: Published for Dartmouth College by University Press of New England, 1983), especially Catherine R. Stimpson, "Doris Lessing and the Parables of Growth," pp. 186–205.

11. In fact, although all their romantic associations were with successful top-track boys, they never talked about boys as intellectual equals or even cited their ideas. Boys were for emotional support, the soft side of life; girls were colleagues.

12. Miller, *The Drama of the Gifted Child: The Search for the True Self,* trans. Ruth Ward (New York: Basic Books, 1981), p. xvi.

13. At the time these interviews took place, the primary concern was pregnancy, not sexually transmitted infection.

14. "The Mind, the Body and Gertrude Stein," *Critical Inquiry* 3, no. 3 (Spring 1977): 490. Stimpson is discussing late-nineteenth and early-twentieth-century women.

15. On the continued relevance of gender, see Peggy Orenstein in association with the American Association of University Women, *Schoolgirls: Young Women, Self-Esteem, and the Confidence Gap* (New York: Doubleday, 1984). "S.A.T.'s Are Biased Against Girls, Report by Advocacy Group Says," *New York Times,* April 17, 1987, p. B2, vs. "Numbers Don't Lie: Men Do Better Than Women," *New York Times,* July 5, 1989,

p. A21. High school honors students' slowdown in adulthood is reported in *Psychology Today*, April 1989, p. 20. *Mother Daughter Revolution* also brings home the continued relevance of gender to female adolescence very powerfully. See, in particular, the vignette about a daughter who didn't believe the AAUW report, tested her own class, and got the same results. Elizabeth Debold, Marie Wilson, and Idelisse Malave, *Mother Daughter Revolution: From Betrayal to Power* (Reading, MA: Addison-Wesley, 1993), p. 11. Myra and David Sadker, *Failing at Fairness: How America's Schools Cheat Girls* (New York: Charles Scribner's Sons, 1994), pp. 161–96.

4. HAVING MY BABY

1. Cheryl D. Hayes, ed., *Risking the Future: Adolescent Sexuality, Pregnancy, and Childbearing*, vol. 1 (Washington, DC: National Academy Press, 1987), p. 53. Laurie Schwab Zabin and Sarah C. Hayward, *Adolescent Sexual Behavior and Childbearing* (Newbury Park, CA: Sage Publications, 1993), p. 15. Even the number of adolescent pregnancies began to decline in the early 1980s in spite of the rise in the number of sexually active girls. African-American girls began to lower their pregnancy rate even before the late 1970s, arguably in response to the gains of the civil rights movement as well as the possibility of abortion. Melvin Zelnik and John F. Kantner, "Sexual Activity, Contraceptive Use and Pregnancy Among Metropolitan-Area Teenagers: 1971–1979," *Family Planning Perspectives* 12, no. 5 (September/October 1980): 233, notes that the African-American premarital pregnancy rates declined between 1971 and 1976 but attributes the decline, in part, to the underreporting of abortion. Rosemary L. Bray eloquently reveals how the hopes of the civil rights movement resonated for a young black student whose family was on welfare, in "So How Did I Get Here," *New York Times Magazine* (November 8, 1992), p. 39.

2. Diane Gersoni-Edelman, *Sexism and Youth* (New York and London: R. R. Bowker Company, 1974), pp. 101–2.

3. Rickie Solinger, *Wake Up Little Susie: Single Pregnancy and Race Before Roe v. Wade* (New York: Routledge, Chapman and Hall, 1992), pp. 95, 104–5, 109–10, 120–21, 141. Solinger offers an extremely complex and layered depiction of the vectors influencing adoption, marriage, and

single motherhood before 1973. Maris A. Vinovskis, "An 'Epidemic' of Adolescent Pregnancy? Some Historical Considerations," *Journal of Family History* 6, no. 2 (Summer 1981): 211–12. Robert J. Havighurst, Paul Hoover Bowman, Gordon P. Liddle, Charles V. Matthews, and James V. Pierce, *Growing Up in River City* (New York: John Wiley & Sons, 1962), p. 120. F. Philip Rice, *The Adolescent: Development, Relationships, and Culture* (Boston: Allyn and Bacon, 1975), pp. 431–432, 441. Maurine LaBarre and Weston LaBarre, "The Triple Crisis: Adolescence, Early Marriage and Parenthood," in *The Double Jeopardy, the Triple Crisis—Illegitimacy Today* (New York: National Council on Illegitimacy, 1969), pp. 9–10, 25. Harold T. Christensen and Hanna H. Meissner, "Studies in Child Spacing III—Premarital Pregnancy as a Factor in Divorce," *American Sociological Review* 18 (December 1953): 641–44. Harold T. Christensen and Bette B. Rubinstein, "Premarital Pregnancy and Divorce: A Follow-up Study by the Interview Method," *Marriage and Family Living* 18 (May 1956): 114–23. Robert E. Furlong, "Easy Marriage, Easy Divorce," and Paul Bohannan, "The Natural History of the Divorced Teen-Ager," in Seymour M. Farber, M.D., and Roger H. L. Wilson, M.D., eds., *Teenage Marriage and Divorce* (Berkeley, CA: Diablo Press, 1967), pp. 105–19, 120–29, as well as the introduction. In the late 1980s a debate regarding teenage marriage arose, with some arguing it would be a good idea to bring it back: P. Lindsay Chase-Lansdale and Maris A. Vinovskis, "Should We Discourage Teenage Marriage?" *The Public Interest* (Spring 1987), pp. 23–28. Frank F. Furstenberg, Jr., provides an excellent history of the debate in "Bringing Back the Shotgun Wedding," *The Public Interest* (Winter 1988), pp. 121–27.

4. Rice, *The Adolescent*, pp. 444–45. Vinovskis, "An 'Epidemic,' " p. 221. Dawn M. Upchurch and James McCarthy, "Adolescent Childbearing and High School Completion in the 1980s: Have Things Changed?" *Family Planning Perspectives* 21, no. 5 (September/October 1989): 199–202.

5. Ros Petchesky with Rayna Rapp, "Women Under Attack: Abortion, Sterilization Abuse, and Reproductive Freedom" (New York: Committee for Abortion Rights and Against Sterilization Abuse, 1979). Stanley K. Henshaw and Lynn S. Wallisch, "The Medicaid Cutoff and Abortion Services for the Poor," *Family Planning Perspectives* 16, no. 4 (July/August 1984): 170–72, 177–80. Linda Greenhouse, "Battle on Abortion

Turns to Rights of Teen-Agers," *New York Times,* July 16, 1989, pp. 1, 23; Tamar Lewin, "Hurdles Increase for Many Women Seeking Abortions," *New York Times,* March 15, 1992, pp. 1, 18. Sue Halpern's "The Fight over Teen-age Abortion" is a succinct, pointed legal history up to 1990. *New York Review of Books,* March 29, 1990, pp. 30–32. Her account of Becky Bell's death starkly underscores the necessity for unimpeded confidential abortion. "Telling the Truth," in *Migrations to Solitude* (New York: Pantheon Books, 1992), pp. 99–116. Also see *No Way Out* (New York: Reproductive Freedom Project of the American Civil Liberties Union Foundation, 1991). Patricia Donovan, "Judging Teenagers: How Minors Fare When They Seek Court-Authorized Abortions," *Family Planning Perspectives* 15, no. 6 (November/December 1983): 259–67. *Parental Notice Laws* (New York: Reproductive Freedom Project of the American Civil Liberties Union Foundation, 1986). Aida Torres, Jacqueline Darroch Forrest, and Susan Eisman, "Telling Parents: Clinic Policies and Adolescents' Use of Family Planning and Abortion Services," *Family Planning Perspectives* 12, no. 6 (November/December 1980): 284–92. The narrators of this chapter also lived through the Squeal Rule, the Gag Rule . . .

6. Rosalind Pollack Petchesky, "The Power of Visual Culture in the Politics of Reproduction," *Feminist Studies* 13, no. 2 (Summer 1987): 263–92. Rebecca Stone and Cynthia Waszak, "Adolescent Knowledge and Attitudes About Abortion," *Family Planning Perspectives* 24, no. 2 (March/April 1992): 52–57.

7. "Justices Say They Will Rule on Teen-Ager Chastity Law," *New York Times,* November 11, 1987, p. A24. Patricia Donovan, "The Adolescent Family Life Act and the Promotion of Religious Doctrine," *Family Planning Perspectives* 16, no. 5 (September/October 1984): 222–28.

8. On proms, honors, and cheerleading: "When the Cheering Had to Stop," *New York Times,* October 5, 1993, p. A26. "The Case for and Against Arlene," *Seventeen,* June 1984, p. 80. "Officials Deny Pregnant Girl School Crown," *New York Times,* October 14, 1992, p. A17.

9. Just 9,965 teenage girls under fifteen had babies in 1984, over 2,000 fewer than gave birth in 1972. Hayes, ed., *Risking the Future,* vol. 1, p. 54. Zabin and Hayward, *Adolescent Sexual Behavior,* p. 6. But that was not the way it sounded in the press. Consider just a few titles: David R.

Gergen, "Childhood Lost," *U.S. News & World Report,* October 28, 1985, p. 78; "Young, Innocent and Pregnant," by Elizabeth Stark, *Psychology Today,* October 1986, pp. 28–35; Ken Auletta, "Children of Children," *Parade,* June 17, 1984; Claudia Wallis, "Children Having Children: Teenage Pregnancies Are Rending the Country's Social Fabric," *Time,* December 9, 1985, pp. 78–82, 84, 87, 89–90; Leon Dash, *When Children Want Children: The Urban Crisis of Teenage Childbearing* (New York: William Morrow and Company, 1989); Ann Hulbert, "Children as Parents," *New Republic,* September 10, 1984, pp. 15–23.

This chapter is based on the life histories of a hundred teenage mothers from the Northeast, Midwest, and Southwest who had babies and stayed in or soon returned to school. Participants came from model programs for teenage mothers generated by the 1978 Adolescent Health Services and Pregnancy Prevention Act and the 1981 Adolescent Family Life Act, as well as high school equivalency programs for teenage mothers—two programs in the Northeast, one in the Southwest, and one in the Midwest. The interviews typically took place in the buildings where the programs were located and in restaurants. I was rarely invited to the homes of teenage mothers whom I did not already know. With a few white exceptions, about half the teenage mothers were African-American and about half were Hispanic—more Chicana than Puerto Rican.

10. As Debra Boyer and David Fine have suggested, sexual coercion is one cause of sex that just happens, but girls point as well to sheer ignorance and fear. "Sexual Abuse as a Factor in Adolescent Pregnancy and Child Maltreatment," *Family Planning Perspectives* 24, no. 1 (January/February 1992): 4–11, 19.

11. Lee Rainwater discussed the relationship of fatalism and contraception in *And the Poor Get Children: Sex, Contraception, and Family Planning in the Working Class* (Chicago: Quadrangle Books, 1960), pp. 29, 52–54. He understood its sources very well but perhaps not its usefulness. On the many psychological issues that may be involved in an adolescent pregnancy, see Sara Ruddick, "Educating for Procreative Choice: The 'Case' of Adolescent Women," *Women's Studies Quarterly* 19, nos. 1/2 (Spring/Summer 1991): 102–104; Nancy E. Adler and Jeanne M. Tschann, "Conscious and Preconscious Motivation for Pregnancy Among Female Adolescents," in Annette Lawson and Deborah L. Rhode, eds., *The Politics of Pregnancy: Adolescent Sexuality and Public*

Policy (New Haven: Yale University Press, 1993), pp. 144–58, as well as Michelle Fine and Nancie Zaine, "Bein' Wrapped Too Tight: When Low-Income Women Drop Out of High School," *Women's Studies Quarterly* 19, nos. 1/2 (Spring/Summer 1991): 77–99.

12. Constance Lindemann refers to the point when girls finally consult physicians as "the expert stage." Lindemann, *Birth Control and Unmarried Young Women* (New York: Springer Publishing Co., 1974), pp. 9–10, 47–75. Nathanson found that teenagers granted experts—typically, nurses—more credibility than peers. *Dangerous Passage: The Social Control of Sexuality in Women's Adolescence* (Philadelphia: Temple University Press, 1991). Even so, girls keep right on listening to each other throughout the contraceptive process.

Girls became increasingly diligent contraceptors. By 1982 less than 15 percent of sexually active girls reported they had never contracepted. Almost half of all girls said they didn't contracept every time they had intercourse, however. One explanation for the inconsistency is the typically sporadic nature of adolescent coitus. In one study, about a quarter of girls reported having had intercourse only once or twice in the previous month while 40 percent said they hadn't had intercourse at all within the month. Hayes, ed., *Risking the Future*, vol. 1, pp. 42, 46–47.

13. About a third of Frank Furstenberg's sample of sexually active girls in their late teens said they would be pleased to have a child. *Unplanned Parenthood: The Social Consequences of Teenage Childbearing* (New York: Free Press, 1976), p. 57. See also Dash, *When Children Want Children*.

14. The Children's Defense Fund report, "Preventing Adolescent Pregnancy: What Schools Can Do" (Adolescent Pregnancy Prevention Clearinghouse, 1986) demonstrated a relationship between income level, basic skills, and the probability of pregnancy. Barbara Devaney and Katherine Hubley report that educational aspirations affected the probability of pregnancy among both blacks and whites even after controlling for family background, age at first intercourse, and consistent contraception. "The Determinants of Adolescent Pregnancy and Childbearing," Final Report to the Center for Population Research, National Institute of Child Health and Human Development (Washington, DC: Mathematica Policy Research, 1981). See also Helen Rauch-Elnekave, "Teenage Motherhood: Its Relationship to Undetected Learning Prob-

lems," *Adolescence* 29, no. 113 (Spring 1994): 91–104. But although girls who do better in school are more likely to finish before they have babies, they do not necessarily do a great deal better in the longer run than those who have babies before they finish school. In fact, there's some evidence that early childbearers are more likely to be in the workforce and have a higher per capita income at mid-life, because their children have already left home. Frank F. Furstenberg, Jr., Jeanne Brooks-Gunn, and S. Philip Morgan, *Adolescent Mothers in Later Life* (New York: Cambridge University Press, 1987). Sandra L. Hofferth, "Social and Economic Consequences of Teenage Childbearing," in Cheryl D. Hayes and Sandra L. Hofferth, eds., *Risking the Future*, vol. 2, pp. 132–35. Arline Geronimus and Sandford Korenman, "The Socioeconomic Consequences of Teen Childbearing Reconsidered," Research Report 90-190 (Ann Arbor: University of Michigan Population Studies Center, 1990). Geronimus, "Teenage Childbearing and Social and Reproductive Disadvantage: The Evolution of Complex Questions and the Demise of Simple Answers," *Family Relations*, October 1991, pp. 463–71. Ann Phoenix, "The Social Construction of Teenage Motherhood: A Black and White Issue?" in Lawson and Rhode, eds., *The Politics of Pregnancy*, pp. 82–86.

15. Mercer Sullivan, *"Getting Paid": Youth Crime and Work in the Inner City* (Ithaca, NY: Cornell University Press, 1989). Benjamin P. Bowser, "African-American Male Sexuality Through the Early Life Course," in Alice S. Rossi, ed., *Sexuality Across the Life Course* (Chicago: University of Chicago Press, 1994), p. 141.

16. On the complicated feelings that daughters of poor single mothers may have for their mothers, see Gloria I. Joseph and Jill Lewis, *Common Differences: Conflicts in Black & White Feminist Perspectives* (Boston: South End Press, 1981). Michelle Fine, *Framing Dropouts: Notes on the Politics of an Urban High School* (Albany, NY: State University of New York, 1991), p. 172. Ruth Horowitz discusses maternity and fortuity in *Teen Mothers: Citizens or Dependents* (Chicago and London: University of Chicago Press, 1995), pp. 151–53.

17. Fordham and Ogbu report that ghetto peer groups discourage members from "putting forth the time and effort required to do well in school" by labeling, excluding, and assaulting students who work hard. Seduction and impregnation can conceivably be read as

another—gendered—aspect of the same process, and not just in communities of color. Signithia Fordham and John U. Ogbu, "Black Students' School Success: Coping with the Burden of 'Acting White,' " *Urban Review* 18, no. 3 (1986): 183.

18. Joyce Ladner, *Tomorrow's Tomorrow* (Garden City, NY: Anchor Books, Doubleday & Company, 1971), p. 160.

19. Peter W. Cookson, Jr., and Caroline Hodges Persell, *Preparing for Power: America's Elite Boarding Schools* (New York: Basic Books, 1985), pp. 156, 150. Richard L. Zweigenhaft and G. William Domhoff add that white students may erect extremely subtle obstacles between themselves and African-American students in elite boarding schools. *Blacks in the White Establishment: A Study of Race and Class in America* (New Haven and London: Yale University Press, 1991), pp. 36–37, 58.

20. Elijah Anderson, *Street Wise: Race, Class, and Change in an Urban Community* (Chicago: University of Chicago Press, 1990). Bowser, "African-American Male Sexuality," p. 141. Mercer L. Sullivan notes that young men's responses to paternity were "powerfully influenced" by kin. "Ethnographic Research on Young Fathers and Parenting: Implications for Public Policy," paper prepared for the Conference on Young Unwed Fathers, October 1–3, 1986, at Catholic University, Washington, DC, p. 9. Finally, Eliot Liebow's classic *Tally's Corner* depicts boys' and men's frustrated responses to their inability to support their families. Boston: Little, Brown & Company, 1967.

21. Jeff Grogger and Stephen Bronars found that teen mothers who had twins were significantly less likely to graduate from high school than those who had a single infant. "The Socioeconomic Consequences of Teenage Childbearing: Findings from a Natural Experiment," *Family Planning Perspectives* 25, no. 4 (July/August 1993): 156–61, 174.

22. Steven D. McLaughlin, William R. Grady, John O. G. Billy, Nancy S. Landale, and Linda D. Winges, "The Effects of the Sequencing of Marriage and First Birth During Adolescence," *Family Planning Perspectives* 18, no. 1 (January/February 1986): 12–19.

23. Emily Martin, *The Woman in the Body: A Cultural Analysis of Reproduction* (Boston: Beacon Press, 1987), pp. 77–79.

24. Teenage mothers are often discussed as if they have no work ethic, but the work ethic is heavily at play in this set of narratives. When these narrators err, it's often by trying too hard to do too much.

25. McLaughlin et al., "The Effects of the Sequencing," p. 12. Melvin Zelnik, "Second Pregnancies to Premaritally Pregnant Teenagers, 1976 and 1971," *Family Planning Perspectives* 12, no. 2 (March/April 1980): 69, 72–76. Frank F. Furstenberg, Jr., Jeanne Brooks-Gunn, S. Philip Morgan, "Adolescent Mothers and Their Children in Later Life," *Family Planning Perspectives* 19, no. 4 (July/August 1987): 142.

26. Teenage mothers' rate of high school completion tripled between 1958 and 1986. Upchurch and McCarthy, "Adolescent Childbearing and High School Completion." Zelnik, "Second Pregnancies," pp. 69, 72–76. A variety of other factors affect school completion as well, as Namkee Ahn's "Teenage Childbearing and High School Completion: Accounting for Individual Heterogeneity" explains. *Family Planning Perspectives* 26, no. 1 (January/February 1994): 17–21.

27. Lancaster suggests that the seemingly altruistic willingness of some men to parent children from a woman's previous relationship may be a mating strategy correlated with fathering a subsequent child. Jane B. Lancaster, "Human Sexuality, Life Histories, and Evolutionary Ecology," in Rossi, ed., *Sexuality*, pp. 39–62.

28. For a fuller treatment of these narrators, see Sharon Thompson, "Drastic Entertainments: Teenage Mothers' Signifying Narratives," in Faye Ginsburg and Anna Lowenhaupt Tsing, eds., *Uncertain Terms: Negotiating Gender in American Culture* (Boston: Beacon Press, 1990), pp. 269–81.

29. Harriet B. Presser, "Sally's Corner: Coping with Unmarried Motherhood," *Journal of Social Issues* 36, no. 1 (1980): 107–29. Ramona T. Mercer, Kathryn C. Hackley, and Alan Bostrom, "Adolescent Motherhood: Comparison of Outcome with Older Mothers," *Journal of Adolescent Health Care* 5, no. 1 (January 1984): 7–13. Mark W. Roosa, "A Comparative Study of Pregnant Teenagers' Parenting Attitudes and

Knowledge of Sexuality and Child Development," *Journal of Youth and Adolescence* 12, no. 1 (1983): 213–23. Mark W. Roosa and Linda Vaughan, "A Comparison of Teenage and Older Mothers with Preschool Age Children," *Family Relations*, April 1984, pp. 259–65. Mark W. Roosa, Hiram E. Fitzgerald, and Nancy A. Carlson, "Teenage and Older Mothers and Their Infants: A Descriptive Comparison," *Adolescence* 17, no. 65 (Spring 1982): 1–17. Furstenberg et al., "Adolescent Mothers and Their Children in Later Life."

30. Susan Gustavus Philliber, "Socialization for Childbearing," *Journal of Social Issues*, 36, no. 1 (1980): 30–44. Katherine F. Darabi, "The Education of Non-High School Graduates After the Birth of a Child," Research Report, National Institute of Education, Department of Health, Education, and Welfare, September 30, 1979. Mark W. Roosa, Hiram E. Fitzgerald, and Nancy A. Carlson, "Emotional Support, Cognitive Stimulation at Home Improve Outlook for Children of Teenage Mothers," *Family Planning Perspectives* 23, no. 1 (January/February 1991): 42–43. Horowitz discusses obstacles to teaching parenting effectively in *Teen Mothers*, pp. 156–57, 160–62, 164–78.

31. Fine, *Framing Dropouts*, pp. 84–86. Alternative programs and schools are treated in Louise Warrick, Jon B. Christianson, Judy Walruff, and Paul C. Cook, "Educational Outcomes in Teenage Pregnancy and Parenting Programs: Results from a Demonstration," *Family Planning Perspectives* 25, no. 4 (July/August 1993): 148–55. Sharon Thompson, "Pregnant on Purpose: Choosing Teen Motherhood," *Village Voice*, December 23, 1986, pp. 1, 31–34, 36–37. Catherine Chilman discusses the sexism in many programs for teenage parents in "Feminist Issues in Teenage Parenting," *Child Welfare* 64, no. 3 (May/June 1985): 225–34. Mara Taub called my attention to the problem of separate, unequal programs.

32. John Bowlby, *Attachment and Loss* (New York: Basic Books, 1969). Shelly Lundberg and Robert D. Plotnick, "Effects of State Welfare, Abortion and Family Planning Policies on Premarital Childbearing Among White Adolescents," *Family Planning Perspectives* 22, no. 6 (November/December 1990): 249. Rochelle Sharpe, "States of Confusion," *Ms.*, July/August 1992, pp. 83–88. "Abortion Ratio Fell to Lowest Since '77," *New York Times*, December 24, 1994, p. 7.

5. YEARS OF HELL AND FREEDOM

1. Barbara Hudson, "Femininity and Adolescence," in Angela Mc-Robbie and Mica Nava, eds., *Gender and Generation* (London: Macmillan, 1984), p. 35.

2. Arthur L. Stinchcombe, *Rebellion in a High School* (Chicago: Quadrangle Books, 1964), pp. 8–9, 50–51. He described their condition as "passive" rather than "expressive" alienation.

3. Joanna Russ, *The Female Man* (Boston: Beacon Press, 1986), p. 151.

4. Gisela Konopka, *The Adolescent Girl in Conflict* (Englewood Cliffs, NJ: Prentice-Hall, 1966), pp. 18–19, 131–33. Vera Institute of Justice, "Family Court Disposition Study" (Vera Institute of Justice, 1981), pp. 424–95. Charles E. Silberman, *Criminal Violence, Criminal Justice* (New York: Random House, 1978), pp. 432–501.

5. Konopka, *The Adolescent Girl*, p. 40.

6. *In re Gault*, 387 U.S. 1 (1967). *In re Winship*, 397 U.S. 358 (1970). *Reed* v. *Reed* (1971).

7. Sohnya Sayres, Anders Stephanson, Stanley Aronowitz, Fredric Jameson, *The Sixties Without Apology* (Minneapolis: University of Minnesota Press in cooperation with *Social Text*, 1984).

8. Ralph Larkin, *Suburban Youth in Cultural Crisis* (New York: Oxford University Press, 1979), pp. 151, 153. Curiously, Larkin's findings are very close to those of Kenneth Keniston, although the samples are very different. *The Uncommitted: Alienated Youth in American Society* (1960; reprint ed., New York: Dell Publishing Co., 1967), especially pp. 180–200.

9. Donna Gaines, *Teenage Wasteland* (New York: Pantheon Books, 1990), p. 206.

10. Gaines, *Teenage Wasteland*, p. 63.

11. Leslie G. Roman calls equal opportunity one of middle-class punk young women's "codes." "Intimacy, Labor, and Class: Ideologies of

Feminine Sexuality in the Punk Slam Dance," in Leslie G. Roman, Linda K. Christian-Smith, with Elizabeth Ellsworth, *Becoming Feminine: The Politics of Popular Culture* (London, New York, and Philadelphia: Falmer Press, 1988), p. 156.

12. See, for example, Freda Adler, *Sisters in Crime: The Rise of the New Female Criminal* (New York: McGraw-Hill, 1975).

6. PASSIONATE FRIENDS

1. Elizabeth Wilson's essay "Forbidden Love" describes meetings in which lesbianism was discussed as a *"solution* to heterosexuality." *Feminist Studies* 10, no. 2 (Summer 1983): 216–17. See also Ann Heron, ed., *One Teenager in Ten* (Boston: Alyson Publications, 1983); Alice Echols, *Daring to Be Bad: Radical Feminism in America 1967–1975* (Minneapolis: University of Minnesota Press, 1989), pp. 210–41; and Susie Bright, "The More Things Change . . ." in *Susie Sexpert's Lesbian Sex World* (Pittsburgh and San Francisco: Cleis Press, 1990), pp. 123–27. Rachel Blau DuPlessis includes lesbianism as a counter-romantic narrative strategy in *Writing Beyond the Ending: Narrative Strategies of Twentieth-Century Women Writers* (Bloomington: Indiana University Press, 1985), p. xi. Sol Gordon's *The Sexual Adolescent: Communicating with Teenagers About Sex* (Belmont, CA: Wadsworth Publishing Company, 1973) exemplifies the "stage" theory of adolescent homosexuality, as do many psychoanalytic texts.

2. 1988 New York Study sponsored by the Governor's Task Force on Bias-Related Violence as reported by Daniel Goleman, "Homophobia: Scientists Find Clues to Its Roots," *New York Times*, July 10, 1990, pp. C1, C11.

3. Two methodological differences involved in the lesbian interviews bear mentioning. First, only lesbian narrators asked about my own sexual experience before agreeing to participate in the study, and thus only they knew that I had lesbian experience. Second, on average, the narrators from lesbian and gay discussion groups are two or three years older than most of those represented in this book—seventeen to nineteen.

Most lesbians come out after high school, several studies indicate. E. Coleman, "Developmental Stages of the Coming Out Process," *Jour-*

nal of Homosexuality 7, nos. 2/3 (1981/82): 31–43, reported age twenty for females coming out. Pat Califia, "Lesbian Sexuality," *Journal of Homosexuality* 4, no. 3 (Spring 1979): 259. Beata E. Chapman and JoAnn C. Brannock's 1987 survey of 197 women, 96 percent of whom were lesbian, found that the mean age at which the respondents thought they *might* be lesbian was seventeen, while the mean age reported for resolving the question of sexual identity was twenty-one and a half years. "Proposed Model of Lesbian Identity Development," *Journal of Homosexuality* 14, nos. 3/4 (1987): 73. Alfred Kinsey et al. found that the number of females conscious of erotic responses to other females and the number who had made sexual contacts with other females rose gradually until about age thirty, where they leveled off, respectively, at 25 and 17 percent. *Sexual Behavior in the Human Female* (Philadelphia: W. B. Saunders Company, 1953), pp. 452–53. Robert T. Michael, John H. Gagnon, Edward O. Laumann, and Gina Kolata reported a lower percentage in *Sex in America: A Definitive Survey* (Boston: Little, Brown & Company, 1994), p. 175—just over 4 percent said they had had sex with another woman at some point in their lives. Sex may have meant something quite different to women in 1992 than it meant in 1953. Bonnie Zimmerman, "Exiting from Patriarchy: The Lesbian Novel of Development," in Elizabeth Abel et al., *The Voyage In: Fictions of Female Development* (Hanover, NH, and London: Published for Dartmouth College by University Press of New England, 1983), pp. 244–57, notes that the autobiographical literature of feminism is replete with stories about coming out or having lesbian thoughts in high school, whereas the lesbian novel of development typically centers "on the heroine's adolescence, much like the traditional *Bildungsroman*" (p. 247). Some of these are acts of narrative reconstruction, of course. Now that these speakers and writers believe that they are lesbians, they search their childhood for lesbian clues and find them everywhere.

4. Gagnon and Simon observed that lesbian respondents reported a "romantic drift into sexual behavior." John H. Gagnon and William Simon, *Sexual Conduct: The Social Sources of Human Sexuality* (Chicago: Aldine Publishing Company, 1973), p. 184, and their "On Becoming a Lesbian," in Jack D. Douglas, ed., *Observations of Deviance* (New York: Random House, 1970), p. 107.

5. In "Secrecy in the Lesbian World," in Carol Garren, ed., *Sexuality: Encounters, Identities, and Relationships* (Beverly Hills and London: Sage

Publications, 1977), Barbara Ponse explains the term "coming out" as disclosing the gay self to an expanding series of audiences (p. 55).

6. On nineteenth-century female friendships, see Carroll Smith-Rosenberg, *Disorderly Conduct: Visions of Gender in Victorian America* (New York: Alfred A. Knopf, 1985), pp. 53–76, and Lillian Faderman, *Surpassing the Love of Men: Love Between Women from the Renaissance to the Present* (New York: William Morrow and Company, 1981). Patricia J. Campbell, *Sex Education Books for Young Adults, 1892–1979* (New York and London: R. R. Bowker Company, 1979). William Lee Howard, *Confidential Chats with Girls* (New York: E. J. Clode, 1911), p. 41. Irving David Steinhardt, *Ten Sex Talks to Girls* (Philadelphia: J. B. Lippincott, 1914), p. 43. Lois Lloyd Pemberton, *The Stork Didn't Bring You!* (New York: Hermitage Press, 1948; New York: Nelson, rev. ed., 1961), p. 101. Evelyn Duvall's influential *Facts of Life and Love for Teenagers* (New York: Association Press, 1950, rev. ed. 1956) included same-sex crushes as one of several varieties of "love under a cloud."

7. A few lucked into Simone de Beauvoir, whose mixed review of lesbian life at least included a vision of autonomy, desire, and variability. Joanna Russ, "Not for Years but for Decades," in Julia Penelope Stanley and Susan J. Wolfe, eds., *The Coming Out Stories* (Watertown, MA: Persephone Press, 1980), p. 106. Simone de Beauvoir, *The Second Sex*, trans. H. M. Parshley (New York: Bantam Books, 1961; orig. U.S. pub. Alfred A. Knopf, 1953; orig. French pub. Librairie Gallimard, 1949), p. 394. See also Blanche Wiesen Cook, " 'Women Alone Stir My Imagination': Lesbianism and the Cultural Tradition," *Signs* 4, no. 4 (1979): 718–39.

8. "More Than Friends: Conversations with Lesbian and Gay Youth," by Donald Suggs, *Village Voice*, March 24, 1987, pp. 18 ff.

9. Deborah Goleman Wolf, *The Lesbian Community* (Berkeley: University of California Press, 1979), p. 89.

10. Perhaps only lesbian teenagers who had positive feelings about their sexual experience came out in the interview process or agreed to be interviewed. Lesbians have undergone the same sexual socialization as other women and do have at least some sexual problems. See, for example, Califia, "Lesbian Sexuality."

11. Then, too, sex with a girl may seem more "natural" because it is a mother-and-child reunion, while heterosexual sex resonates with the oedipal period—with gender polarity and the triangle of the family, a time of loss, jealousy, sadness, and compromise. Jessica Benjamin surveys and expands the psychoanalytic understanding of pre-oedipal and oedipal stages in *The Bonds of Love: Psychoanalysis, Feminism and the Problem of Domination* (New York: Pantheon Books, 1988).

12. Catherine R. Stimpson, "Zero Degree Deviancy: The Lesbian Novel in English," *Critical Inquiry*, Winter 1981, pp. 363–79. See also Bertha Harris, "What We Mean to Say: Notes Toward Defining the Nature of Lesbian Literature," *Heresies*, Fall 1977, pp. 5–8. Some readers will wonder why I haven't organized this chapter according to the categories most at play in contemporary lesbian discourse—particularly butch and fem. The answer is: they weren't narrated.

13. Although Jean was African-American, she never talked about being African-American or distinguished one friend from another by color. Racism came up in her history, but when she made distinctions between friends, they had to do with who was lesbian and who wasn't.

14. Women fear lesbianism generally, psychologist Charlotte Wolff has suggested, because of a "propensity." But even friends who do not feel implicated themselves may experience a sense of loss when a friend comes out. Charlotte Wolff, *Love Between Women* (New York: St. Martin's Press, 1981), p. 165. See also Suggs, "More Than Friends," p. 39.

15. Recent theory posits a final stage in which lesbian identity is integrated with the many other aspects of the self. These narrators didn't place that stage last. Throughout coming out, they held on to the other aspects of themselves. Vivienne Cass, "Homosexual Identity Formation: A Theoretical Model," *Journal of Homosexuality* 4, no. 3 (Spring 1979): 219–35. Historian Marilyn Young suggested that the financial contribution made by a lesbian partner may be very persuasive. Private conversation, 1987.

16. Susan Krieger, "Lesbian Identity and Community: Recent Social Science Literature," *Signs* 18, no. 1 (Autumn 1982): 91–108. Chela Sandoval, "Comment on Krieger's 'Lesbian Identity and Community,' " *Signs* 9, no. 4 (Summer 1984): 725–29. Ann R. Bristow and Pam Lang-

ford Pearn, "Comment on Krieger's 'Lesbian Identity and Community,'" *Signs* 9, no. 4 (Summer 1984): 729–32. Krieger's *The Mirror Dance: Identity in a Women's Community* (Philadelphia: Temple University Press, 1983). The fusion debate has also been reframed in terms of codependency. See Sondra Smalley, "Dependency Issues in Lesbian Relationships," *Journal of Homosexuality* 14, nos. 1/2 (1987): 125–35. Other research has suggested that feminism tempered dyadism and increased autonomy in lesbian relationships. Letitia Anne Peplau et al., "Loving Women: Attachment and Autonomy in Lesbian Relationships," *Journal of Social Issues* 34, no. 3 (Summer 1978): 7–27.

17. To my knowledge, no one I talked with committed suicide, but young lesbians and gays are thought to do so approximately three times as often as other teenagers. This may overstate the problem, but that doesn't mean there is none. "Report of the Secretary's Task Force on Youth Suicide," 1989, U.S. Department of Health and Human Services. Ronald F. C. Kourany, M.D., "Suicide Among Homosexual Adolescents," *Journal of Homosexuality* 13, no. 4 (Summer 1987): 111–17; Scott A. Hunt, "An Unspoken Tragedy: Suicide Among Gay and Lesbian Youth," *Christopher Street*, no. 169 (1992): 28–30.

18. A. Damien Martin and Emery S. Hetrick, "The Stigmatization of the Gay and Lesbian Adolescent," *Journal of Homosexuality* 15, nos. 1/2 (1988): 163–83, and Ritch C. Savin-Williams, "Coming Out to Parents and Self-Esteem Among Gay and Lesbian Youths," *Journal of Homosexuality* 18, no. 1/2 (1989): 1–35. Lucy R. Mercier and Raymond M. Berger observe that those who come out go through a grieving process as the "dissonance between social and self concepts emerges." "Social Service Needs of Lesbian and Gay Adolescents: Telling It Their Way," *Journal of Social Work and Human Sexuality* 8, no. 1 (1989): 75–95.

19. Torie Osborn, "The Fountain of Youth," *The Advocate*, November 29, 1994, p. 80. The Hetrick-Martin Institute in New York City has a drop-in program that offers lesbian and gay teens a place in which to hang out and talk as well as take part in an assortment educational activities that should be replicated all over the country. *HMI Report Card*, Summer 1993. In 1993, Massachusetts Governor William F. Weld announced a statewide training program to help lesbian and gay high school students. "Gov. Weld Asks Schools to Aid Gay Students," *New York Times*, July 4, 1993, p. 15. Important in-school and out-of-school

programs are described in Virginia Uribe's "Project 10: A School-Based Outreach to Gay and Lesbian Youth" and Hugh Singerline's "Out-Right: Reflections on an Out-of-School Gay Youth Program," both in *The High School Journal* 77, nos. 1/2 (October/November 1993): 108–112 and 133–137, respectively.

7. PRECARIOUS TIME AND FUGITIVE PASSAGE

1. Mary Odem, "Statutory Rape Prosecutions in Alameda County California," in "Delinquent Daughters: The Sexual Regulation of Female Minors in the U.S." (Ph.D. diss., University of California, 1989). Christine Stansell, *City of Women: Sex and Class in New York 1789–1860* (New York: Alfred A. Knopf, 1986). Elizabeth Lunbeck, " 'A New Generation of Women': Progressive Psychiatrists and the Hypersexual Female," *Feminist Studies* 13, no. 3 (Fall 1987): 513–43. Gisela Konopka, *The Adolescent Girl in Conflict* (Englewood Cliffs, NJ: Prentice-Hall, 1966).

2. *Michael M.* v. *Superior Court of Sonoma County* (California), Real Party in Interest No. 79-1344 (1981).

3. Gayle Rubin, "Sexual Politics, the New Right, and the Sexual Fringe" in Daniel Tsang, ed., *The Age Taboo: Gay Male Sexuality, Power and Consent* (Boston: Alyson Publications, 1981), p. 112. For a spectrum of opinion on consent, see the interview with Kate Millett, "Sexual Revolution and the Liberation of Children," by Mark Blasius, in Tsang, ed., *The Age Taboo*, pp. 80–83; Florence Rush, *The Best Kept Secret: Sexual Abuse of Children*, Introduction by Susan Brownmiller (Englewood Cliffs, NJ: Prentice-Hall, 1980); and Carole Pateman, "Women and Consent," *Political Theory* 8, no. 3 (May 1980): 149–68.

4. Ann Snitow, "Mass Market Romance: Pornography for Women Is Different," in Ann Snitow, Christine Stansell, and Sharon Thompson, eds., *Powers of Desire: The Politics of Sexuality* (New York: New Feminist Library, Monthly Review Press, 1983), pp. 245–63; orig. pub. *Radical History Review* 20 (Spring/Summer 1979): 250–51. Tania Modleski, *Loving with a Vengeance* (New York: Methuen, 1982), pp. 15–19, 35–58. Marguerite Duras, *The Lover*, trans. Barbara Bray (New York: Pantheon Books, 1985).

5. Michael Schofield, *The Sexual Behaviour of Young People* (Boston: Little, Brown & Company, 1965), pp. 59–61. Sorenson found that 60 percent of all nonvirgins had first sexual intercourse with older partners and that girls had older lovers more often than boys. Robert C. Sorensen, *Adolescent Sexuality in Contemporary America: Personal Values and Sexual Behavior, Ages 13–19.* (New York: World Publishing Company, 1973). Melvin Zelnik and Farida K. Shah, "First Intercourse Among Young Americans," *Family Planning Perspectives* 15, no. 2 (March/April 1983): 65, reported young women's mean age at first intercourse as 16.2 and the average age of partners as 19. Curiously, men also reported first partners older than they although considerably less older than girls reported. Black and white reports matched. Twenty-eight percent of African-American teenagers and 45 percent of white teenagers who give birth have partners twenty years of age or older, but some of these narrators came from almost every group. Janet B. Hardy et al., "Fathers of Children Born to Young Urban Mothers," *Family Planning Perspectives* 21, no. 4 (July/August 1989): 159.

One of the narrators in this chapter was over eighteen.

6. On the importance of recognition, see Jessica Benjamin, *The Bonds of Love: Psychoanalysis, Feminism and the Problem of Domination* (New York: Pantheon Books, 1988), especially pp. 11–50.

7. Juliet Mitchell, *Psycho-Analysis and Feminism: Freud, Reich, Laing and Women* (New York: Vintage Books, 1975), p. 117.

8. Rachel Blau DuPlessis describes "reparenting" as the "return by the female hero to parental figures in order to forge an alternative fictional resolution to the oedipal crisis that these parent figures evoke. *Writing Beyond the Ending: Narrative Strategies of Twentieth-Century Women Writers* (Bloomington: Indiana University Press, 1985), p. 83.

9. The women in the lesbian narratives were extremely atypical. A woman who becomes involved with a girl is, after all, breaking one of the strongest taboos in Western culture.

10. This evidence contrasts with studies indicating that men father many teenage pregnancies and this sample could be anomalous, but those studies didn't include control groups of girls who didn't become mothers. Janet B. Hardy et al., "Fathers of Children Born to Young

Urban Mothers," *Family Planning Perspectives* 21, no. 4 (July/August 1989): 159–63.

11. Michel Foucault, *The Use of Pleasure: The History of Sexuality*, vol. 2, trans. Robert Hurley (New York: Vintage Books, 1980), p. 199.

12. Pateman, "Women and Consent," p. 162. Janet Holland, Caroline Ramazanoglu, Sue Scott, Sue Sharpe, and Rachel Thomson, "Sex, Gender and Power: Young Women's Sexuality in the Shadow of AIDS," *Sociology of Health & Illness* 12, no. 3 (1990): 336–50. Anke Ehrhardt, Sandra Yingling, and Patricia A. Warne, "Sexual Behavior in the Era of AIDS: What Has Changed in the United States," *Annual Review of Sex Research* 2 (1991): 25–47. Anke A. Ehrhardt and Judith N. Wasserheit, "Age, Gender, and Sexual Risk Behaviors for Sexually Transmitted Diseases in the United States," in Judith N. Wasserheit et al., eds., *Research Issues in Human Behavior and Sexually Transmitted Diseases in the Aids Era* (Washington, DC: American Society for Microbiology, 1991), pp. 97–121.

13. Jeffrey Weeks has suggested the criteria of relationship, context, and meaning. *Sexuality and Its Discontents: Meaning, Myths and Modern Sexualities* (London: Routledge & Kegan Paul, 1985), p. 21.

8. THE GAME OF LOVE

1. On the opposition of pleasure and danger in women's lives, see, preeminently, "Pleasure and Danger: Toward a Politics of Sexuality," in Carole S. Vance, ed., *Pleasure and Danger: Exploring Female Sexuality* (Boston: Routledge & Kegan Paul, 1984), pp. 1–24.

2. Stanley Cavell, *Pursuits of Happiness: The Hollywood Comedy of Remarriage* (Cambridge, MA: Harvard University Press, 1981), p. 16. For feminist reflections on mothering daughters, see Elizabeth Debold, Marie Wilson, and Idelisse Malave, *Mother Daughter Revolution: From Betrayal to Power* (Reading, MA: Addison-Wesley, 1993).

3. DuPlessis posits reparenting, woman-to-woman and brother-to-sister bonds as the primary tactics of dissent suggested by women's literature. Rachel Blau DuPlessis, *Writing Beyond the Ending: Narrative Strategies of*

Twentieth-Century Women Writers (Bloomington: Indiana University Press, 1985), pp. 5–6.

4. Teenage mothers who talked about being nasty and cold, for example, proclaimed total dissociation (except for maternal love), and popular girls committed themselves only to groups larger than the twosome.

5. Andrea Dworkin, *Ice and Fire* (New York: Weidenfeld & Nicolson, 1987), pp. 9–10. Barrie Thorne, *Gender Play: Girls and Boys in School* (New Brunswick, NJ: Rutgers University Press, 1993), p. 68. See also Barrie Thorne and Zella Luria, "Sexuality and Gender in Children's Daily Worlds," *Social Problems* 33, no. 3 (February 1986): 176–90.

6. RCK has many different names. Janet Lever observed that girls typically don't have boys' team spirit and/or ability to resolve disputes. These girls did, but then these girls were unusual and these interviews were carried out enough years after Lever's study for feminism to have had an effect. Janet Lever, "Sex Differences in the Games Children Play," *Social Problems* 23 (1976): 478–83. Gary Alan Fine found that women who do well in mainly male situations have to be team players. "One of the Boys: Women in Male-Dominated Settings," in Michael Kimmel, ed., *Changing Men: New Directions in Research on Men and Masculinity* (Newbury Park, CA: Sage Publications, 1987), pp. 131–47.

7. Carol Gilligan, *Making Connections: The Relational Worlds of Adolescent Girls at the Emma Willard School* (Cambridge, MA: Harvard University Press, 1990), for example p. 10; Lynn Mikel Brown and Carol Gilligan, *The Girls We Were; The Women We Learn to Be* (Cambridge, MA: Harvard University Press, 1990). Debold, Wilson, and Malave, *Mother Daughter Revolution*, pp. 44–45.

8. J. Richard Udry and Benjamin C. Campbell, "Getting Started on Sexual Behavior," discussion paper for the MacArthur Conference on Sexuality, May 1, 1992, in Alice Rossi, *Sexuality Across the Life Course* (Chicago: University of Chicago Press, 1994). The idea that, unless the strongest possible measures are taken, biology will drive adolescence has a long tradition. It's powerfully expressed in Stanley Hall's *Adolescence* and the work of John Harvey Kellogg. For a wonderful critique of the nineteenth-century literature on puberty and femininity, see Carroll

Smith-Rosenberg's *Disorderly Conduct: Visions of Gender in Victorian America* (New York: Alfred A. Knopf, 1985), pp. 182–96. On one danger of such a course, see Paula M. Howat et al., "The Influence of Diet, Body Fat, Menstrual Cycling, and Activity upon the Bone Density of Females," *Journal of the American Dietetic Association*, September 1989, p. 1305.

9. It's important that Anja places herself and her friends as active subjects in RCK and casts the game as a peer tradition at her school. Her sense of "we" is very strong. While most girls stress the role they and their best friend play in games—and play mainly in units of two or three—Anja emphasizes the larger group. In this emphasis on team, she is talking the way boys traditionally have talked about group endeavors. But boys also tend to emphasize their individual contribution. Anja doesn't locate herself as a significant individual except as one who thinks and remembers.

10. Participation in Doubles Killer highlighted the connection between game and experience for these narrators—a connection analogous to that between romantic ideology and experience for the victims of love.

CONCLUSION. GOING ALL THE WAY

1. For a good dose of fear-based sexual education, see *No Second Chance*, Jeremiah Films. The Ionnis Mookas and Tom Beers video, *Peer Education, Not Fear Education*, includes many startling clips from that and other films.

2. The concept "True Love Waits" began as a campaign sponsored by the Southern Baptist Convention. "New Strategies for Abstinence-Only Proponents," *Siecus Advocates Report* 1, Issue 4 (July 1994): 3. " 'True Love Waits' for Some Teen-Agers," *New York Times*, June 21, 1993, p. A12.

3. The key is using condoms correctly—that is, using a new condom for every act of penetration, putting it on properly, lubricating with a water-based lubricant, and withdrawing right after ejaculation, holding the condom in place. To put a condom on right, hold the tip and unroll the condom onto the erect penis, so that there's no air trapped

in the condom but there is a space at the tip. CDC National AIDS Clearinghouse, "Facts about Condoms and Their Use in Preventing HIV Infection and Other STDs," *Journal of School Health* 64, no. 5 (May 1994): 215–16.

4. Ellen Willis, *Beginning to See the Light* (New York: Random House, 1981), p. 145.

ACKNOWLEDGMENTS

In addition to the four hundred teenage girls who talked this book into existence, many, many scholars, activists, and friends lent a hand in the form of a book, a file, an argument, a reading, a citation, a critique, a commentary, or a cup of coffee. One hot summer Ann Snitow and Edna Haber even financed an air conditioner for my office, and I put hundreds of miles on Rhonda Copelon's jalopy after my own gave out. The splendid Anne Hart came up with the initial assignment that developed into this project. Faye Ginsburg, Don Guttenplan, Janice Irvine, M. Mark, Carol A. Pollis, Alice S. Rossi, Sohnya Sayres, and that wizard of the Socratic method Carole S. Vance sharpened my thinking as they edited articles published along the way and other readers furthered particular chapters—especially, Jonathan Ned Katz, Gil Zicklin, David Schwartz, B. Ruby Rich, and Marilyn Young. Aviva Goode referred a record number of narrators to me. Christine Stansell, Janice Irvine, Edna Haber, and Carole S. Vance read a manuscript a third again as long as this and they were always there when I needed advice.

Ann Snitow taught me to push way beyond the boundaries of genre. As for Sara Bershtel, they say her kind of editor doesn't exist in publishing anymore, but there she is—brilliant, dedicated, loyal, and uncompromising. I am in debt as well to her exacting associate Ariel Kaminer, one of the great apologists of love and meaning and a superb editor in her own right. Linda MacColl shepherded the manuscript through production with tact and finesse.

Although confidentiality has required changing all the names that appear in the stories that make up this book, some narrators gave me permission to include them in this list of people who made intellectual and personal contributions to this project, and I'm extremely glad of the chance to thank them by name, since so much of this book is their creation: Vicki Alexander, Marysol W. Ascencio, Carol Ascher, Alice Baggett, Joanette Barber, Janet Benshoof, Kyre Boles, Meryl Braunstein, Gwen Braxton, Camille Bristow, Barbara Cameron, Tammy Cheeks, Katy Chevigny, Cathy Cockrell, Harriet Cohen, Muriel Dimen, David Dollar, Martin Duberman, Lisa Duggan, Barbara Ehrenreich, Rosa Ehrenreich, Leslie Fingerman, Janet Gallagher, Felicita Garcia, Shannon Gates, Florence Georges, Joan Gibbs, Daniel Goode, Desiree Angelica Hayes, Connie Hernandez, Iris Hernandez, Maria Hernandez, Joyce Hunter, Ta-Shira Jones, Tracy Jones, Rose Kaplin, Emily Kuenstler, Judy Levin, Heather Lewis, Robin Liebgott, Joelle Lipscomb, Kathy Lobato, Carla Lopez, Nava Lubelski, Mildred MacDonald, Donna Mandel, Carmen Martin, Charlene Martinez, Robert Master, Elizabeth McGee, Toni McGuffie, Ken Mum, Lee Natazly, Mary Odem, Jessica Otero, E. Palmer, Sydney Palmer, Lynn Paltrow, Rosalind Pollack Petchesky, Megan Posey, Tracy Powell, Janet Price, Bernadette L. Quintana, Alice Radosh, Barbara Rainwater, Katie Randolph, Rayna Rapp, Lisa Ross, Gabrielle Safran, Connie Samaras, Ann Shonle, Catherine R. Stimpson, Marcia Storch M.D., Fran Sugarman, Andrea Swanson, Dana Symons, Mara Taub, Nadine Taub, Meredith Tax, Ronald Thompson, Dorothea Tilly, Sheila Turner, Elizabeth Van Couvering, Michelle Visser, Rebecca Walkowitz, Sturgis Warner, Sandy Weinbaum, Shawn Whitaker, Elizabeth Wood, Michelle Wood, Sarah Wood, Judith Wyse, and Mary Zachary.

And, finally, thanks to my fellow participants in the New York University Institute of Humanities Seminar on Consumerism, Sex, and Gender, chaired by Ann Snitow, and to the few courageous institutions that allowed the young people they serve to participate: the Center for Open Education; "Expanding Options for Teen Mothers"; FIRE;

Hetrick-Martin Institute; John Dewey High School; Kearney High School; Lincoln-Sudbury High School; the Young Women's Resource Center–Des Moines, Iowa; New Youth Connection; Sierra Vista High School; the Santa Fe Healthy Birth Project; Santa Fe High School; B. F. Young Alternative High School; TAP-AWARE; and Youth NOW.

INDEX